COLLEGE FAITH 3

COLLEGE FAITH 3

150 Christian Leaders and Educators Share Faith Stories from Their Student Days

Edited by

Ronald Alan Knott

ANDREWS UNIVERSITY PRESS

BERRIEN SPRINGS, MICHIGAN

Andrews University Press
Sutherland House
Berrien Springs, MI 49104–1700
Telephone: 269-471-6134; Fax: 269-471-6224
aupo@andrews.edu
http://universitypress.andrews.edu

Printed in the United States of America
10 09 08 07 06 5 4 3 2 1

ISBN 978-1-883925-53-6
Library of Congress Card Number: 2006927855

Project Director and General Editor	Ronald Alan Knott
Assistant Project Director	Thomas Toews
Line Editors	Ronald Alan Knott, Kevin Wiley
Copy Editor	Denise McAllister
Proofreader	Deborah L. Everhart
Distribution Coordinator	Ernõ Gyéresi
Cover Designers	Robert N. Mason, Christopher Peteranecz
Typesetter	Thomas Toews

Typeset: 10.2/12.5 ITC Berkeley Old Style

TABLE OF CONTENTS

PUBLISHERS' PREFACE

Come and hear, all ye that fear God, and I will declare what he hath done for my soul. Psalm 66:16

The psalmist has set a good example, an example that has been followed admirably by the 150 contributors to this third volume in the *College Faith* series of personal testimonies. Each of the writers tells a simple story, the essence of which is, "This is what the Lord did for me."

It's not always fashionable these days to be so transparent, so vulnerable, so full of conviction, so *plain*–unless, of course, we are ranting about a sporting event, a political candidate, a favorite restaurant, or a cheap entertainment–anything or anyone but Jesus. All too often, this irony is especially and depressingly true in the academy–even the Christian academy. Cultural individualism, hoary convention, a yearning for sophistication, or a presumption of impersonal objective analysis all whisper winsomely that everything would be so much more socially *comfortable* if the messy details of God's work in our lives remained a private affair.

The history of the Christian faith, of course, teaches the opposite. The church is strongest when personal, experiential faith–not just doctrinal faith–is proclaimed in the clearest terms. The blind man hauled before the Pharisees didn't have the benefit of a complete Christology. But he did have a vivid experience with Jesus. So he said: "One thing I know, that, whereas I was blind, now I see."

Many great revivals of primitive godliness began on college campuses, fueled by personal testimonies to the moving of the Holy Spirit. Testimony meetings in other times and in various traditions also helped shape the faith as we know it today.

It is our loss that those valuable spiritual exercises have fallen out of fashion in much of institutional Christendom. In response, we feel called to host some testimony meetings in book form. Thus, we have been pleased, since 2002, to publish the *College Faith* series. *College Faith 3* continues our practice of presenting, in one volume, fifteen "meetings" (chapters) of ten testimonies each.

These are simple "meetings" and simple testimonies. They modestly recount the work of God in the lives of the writers while they were students somewhere in the stream of higher education, from freshman to doctoral candidate. Few of the testimonies are of the dramatic, Damascus-Road variety. All of them do what the psalmist and the Spirit call us to do.

In organizing these meetings we have resisted the powerful temptation to group testimonies for narrative or thematic effect. Life, and testimony meetings, don't necessarily order their events into tidy packages that exude literary charm or desk-reference logic. The Spirit works in ways that to us may sometimes seem random or disconnected. Thus one will not find the stories about financial struggles neatly strung together. A story about the heartbreak of breaking up is not followed, inevitably, by one about the joy of finding a spouse. Rather, each meeting has been organized to provide a meaningful variety of testimonies covering a wide range of issues faced by any Christian student in any age: academic struggles, financial crises, satisfying or frustrating personal relationships, opportunities to witness, and, ultimately, the call to follow Jesus.

We praise our Lord for calling us to this good work. And we thank the writers who have opened their hearts for the benefit of the family of God. What rich benefits await that family when every reader fulfills our God-given obligation to do the same.

The Publishers
Andrews University Press

Andrews University Press is the academic publishing authority operating under the auspices of Andrews University. The Press publishes books, journals, and papers that make a scholarly and/or professional contribution to their respective fields and are in harmony with the mission of Andrews University. Publication emphases include such areas as biblical archaeology, biblical studies, religion, education, faith and learning, and selected areas of science. The Press also occasionally publishes non-academic materials that relate in more general ways to the mission of Christian higher education.

Andrews University is a Christian institution operated by the Seventh-day Adventist Church. Originally established in 1874 in Battle Creek, Michigan, the school was relocated and reestablished in Berrien Springs, Michigan, in 1901. A doctoral-degree-granting institution, the university comprises the College of Arts and Sciences, the College of Technology, the Division of Architecture, the School of Business, the School of Education, and the Seventh-day Adventist Theological Seminary. The University encourages its students to study, practice, and develop an active Christian faith experience. Through corporate worship, community service, and a common concern for all, Andrews University students are led to develop a philosophy that makes them Christian not just in name, but in deed.

THE FIRST MEETING

"Come and hear, all ye that fear God, and I will declare what he hath done for my soul."

Psalm 66:16

Ed Robinson
President, MidAmerica Nazarene University

Marsha Daigle-Williamson
Professor of English, Spring Arbor University

David Brooks
Vice President for Student Services, East Texas Baptist University

James Halteman
Carl R. Hendrickson Professor of Business and Economics, Wheaton College

Linda Hutcherson
Associate Professor of Education, Wayland Baptist University

Stephen Kaufmann
Professor of Education, Covenant College

Brian Jackson
Professor of Mathematics and Economics, Oklahoma Wesleyan University

Holly Hill-Stanford
Associate Professor of English, Southwest Baptist University

Janis Flint-Ferguson
Chair, Department of English, Gordon College

Glenn Settle
Chair, English Department, Northwest University

REPROGRAMMED FOR JOY

Ed Robinson
President
MidAmerica Nazarene University
Olathe, Kansas

MY DREAM was to become a first-rate computer programmer. That doesn't seem terribly ambitious in 2006, but in the spring of 1970, the idea of manipulating the connections within the electronic behemoth known as the "main frame" bordered on science fiction.

Then came the day when my dream for the future was on the line. I walked into the classroom for the final exam in differential equations with a bad case of test anxiety. This was the first math course in my life that I wouldn't ace. I had been in a sea of confusion for the last half of the semester, understanding nothing the professor presented in class. His explanations seemed as foreign as if he'd come from another planet. There were days when I was sure he had.

I wrote my name at the top of the test paper, looked over each problem, recopied each mathematical symbol with my sharpened No. 2 pencil, and then proceeded to stare blankly at the paper for two hours. I couldn't make another jot, mark, or smudge. I was frozen in ignorance. With each passing minute my confidence dropped and my dreams faded.

For the first time in my life I had flunked an exam. Worse than that, for the first time in my life I had to face the sting of my own academic failure and the reality that what I hoped to achieve was beyond my reach. My fountain of confidence was bone dry. I wondered if I had any chance at a professional future. I worried about succeeding again at anything. It was going to be a long summer break.

I moved back home and went through the motions of summer employment without much purpose or joy. At night I tried to read the Scriptures and pray, but my spiritual life was as dry as my confidence.

One Sunday evening I attended a camp meeting service held in an old wooden tabernacle on the outskirts of my town. I went without much purpose, merely following a habit of my heritage and culture. I don't remember the preacher's message, but I do remember his invitation to yield my goals and dreams to God's gracious care. I walked to the front of that crude sanctuary that night and placed my failure on the altar of God's grace. As I stood there, I regained a sense of my purpose in God's purpose for me. I felt a renewed confidence as I felt God's divine confidence in me. He gave me a new sense of direction, meaning, and calling.

That evening was more than thirty-six years ago. The journey from that tabernacle to my present assignment at a Christian university has been one of incredible adventure. God used my failure (which, at the time, seemed devastating) to open a door of opportunity for the journey of a lifetime of fulfillment and joy. I have not regretted a moment of the journey. I wouldn't trade my various jobs along the way for anything, particularly anything in computer science or math.

For surely I know the plans I have for you . . . to give you a future with hope. Jeremiah 29:11 NRSV

ONE-SECOND CONVERSION

Marsha Daigle-Williamson
Professor of English
Spring Arbor University
Spring Arbor, Michigan

WHILE WORKING on my master's degree at the University of Wisconsin, I had concluded that the world's problems were social and their solution was political. By the time I reached the University of Michigan for a Ph.D. program in 1967, I had left religion completely behind as useless hypocrisy. But in the first part of 1968, the assassinations of both Martin Luther King, Jr., and Robert F. Kennedy put me in a real quandary. Suddenly it was clear to me that politics was a fragile, undependable means to cure the ills of the world.

Needing to rethink my approach to life and having no school or work commitments in the summer of 1968, I decided to stay in my apartment until I knew "the truth" about how to live my life. I was starting with only one fact that I was sure of: Christianity was not true. That left many options open, of course, which should have been exciting; instead, it was terrifying because I was keenly aware somehow that the truth was not in me, and I had no idea how to proceed.

As a language and literature major, my shelves were lined with books, so I began to open books at random to see if anything I read would stand out as true. To my dismay, I found that I was able to refute everything I read.

I had a Bible, of course, that I used for reference in my literary studies. My "book roulette" experiment had failed for two days, but as I pulled the Bible off a shelf, I expected that it was at least good for centuries-old folk wisdom. It fell open to Matthew 13:13: "They seeing see not; and hearing they hear not, neither do they understand."

As I read the words, the best way I can describe what happened is that a trumpet spoke the words, and in one second flat I was engulfed in a spiritual realm that I did not know existed. I was instantly aware that God, a holy God, existed; that Jesus Christ really was His Son; and that the Bible was the true Word of God and deserved obedience and reverence. I simultaneously realized that I had served Satan all my life because my whole focus had been myself. Even when I had been nice to other people, it was so that they would like me.

I was shocked that the one thing that I "knew" was false turned out to be the Truth. I experienced becoming a new, different person on the inside. Two years later when I heard the expression "born again," I knew this was the articulation of my experience.

I now teach in a Christian university and although my discipline is literature, I know that the most important thing I can convey to my students is that life on earth is the clash of two kingdoms over the souls of human beings. Everything else is secondary to that fundamental reality.

He brought me up also out of an horrible pit, out of the miry clay, and set my feet upon a rock, and established my goings. Psalm 40:2

LEARNING AS FOR THE LORD

David Brooks
Vice President for Student Services
East Texas Baptist University
Marshall, Texas

I STUDIED BIOLOGY at a small Christian liberal arts college, East Texas Baptist College (now University). As with most liberal arts colleges, ETBU was not known for its science education. However, this was where I felt the Lord wanted me to go. Although the course work was more challenging than in high school, I was a quick learner. I was able to make "A's" and still have plenty of time to be involved in Christian ministries and have a social life.

I received my degree in biology and scored high enough on the Graduate Record Exam to attend graduate school at Texas A&M University. When I entered Texas A&M, I began my graduate work in a neuroscience lab. My first day at the lab, I was directed to the large-animal surgical ward. I found the professor in the middle of a surgery in which he was inserting a probe into a cow's brain. As he operated, he described the various regions of the brain as the probe passed through them. I soon discovered that I was totally ignorant of any of the anatomy he described. Embarrassed by my lack of knowledge, I quickly decided to blame the poor instruction I had received in my undergraduate anatomy class. I figured that the instructor had skipped those portions of the textbook because he did not know the material. After all, what should one expect from a small college where the science professors were probably second-rate or last-chance employees?

Some time later, I was moving boxes of my old textbooks when a lab manual fell to the ground. It was my human anatomy lab manual from ETBU. Remembering that first experience in the surgical ward, I took this opportunity to revisit the disgust I had been feeling about my former anatomy professor.

I turned to the nervous system section and found the picture of the brain. Instead of it being skipped over, I found every blank filled in with proper terminology–in my own handwriting!

Not only had the professor gone over this material, he had covered it completely. Apparently, my "quick learning" was not learning after all, but just short-term memorizing. I had crammed for tests and made the grade, but I had not learned the material.

I did finish my graduate work at Texas A&M. However, it took a couple of years longer than it should have because I had to spend time relearning the things that I had not thoroughly learned during my undergraduate years. Like I heard a wise older professor say once, "You'll need to learn this material sometime; you might as well learn it now."

Ironically, I became a science professor at a small Christian liberal arts college, where I encouraged my students to learn it right the first time. And this job was not my last choice. It was my calling.

Whatever you do, work at it with all your heart, as working for the Lord, not for men. Colossians 3:23 NIV

REAL CHRISTIANITY AND REAL LIFE

James Halteman
Carl R. Hendrickson Professor of Business and Economics
Wheaton College
Wheaton, Illinois

THE DAY I ARRIVED on the university campus to begin my graduate program, I was greeted by someone from the university who was also a member of a church from my denomination. My wife and I were drawn to the congregation, and it soon became a part of our journey.

Every week, members of the congregation who were also part of the university would meet for lunch. As we shared from our experience over those lunches, I was schooled in theological thinking and practical discipleship in ways that were totally foreign to the secular university environment.

The meaning of the community of faith came to life for me. I joined a small group that helped me to connect the purpose of my graduate education with my life purpose as a Christian. I was challenged to tithe, even though my wife and I were trying hard to make ends meet. I learned that spiritual disciplines are habits that are intentionally developed.

As I was drawn into the life of the congregation, I began to see the difference between being a Christian who happened to be an economist and being a Christian economist. That difference was not easy to sort out in the secular academic world, but my fellow believers in the church challenged me to think in new ways about philosophy of science and how it applied to my graduate work. My research and teaching to this day reflect the values I was challenged to consider by my church in those graduate years.

As I approached the end of my graduate training and began to pursue employment opportunities, the church played perhaps its most significant role in my life. I had an attractive job offer in Washington D.C. I also had an offer from a Christian college that could offer hardly more than half the salary and benefits of the job in Washington.

The Washington offer made logical sense to me. I was leaning in that direction when my small group challenged me to review why I had come to graduate school in the first place. They encouraged me to follow my calling instead of the material benefits that seemed more attractive. In the end, there really was no choice; I took the position at the Christian college.

It would have been very easy for me to "take a break from church" during my graduate studies, choosing to concentrate my energy on preparing for the real world. But through a church that took its faith seriously, God led me to a greater preparation, a preparation to live a real Christian life in the real world.

My prayer is not that you take them out of this world but that you protect them from the evil one. John 17:15 NIV

FIRST LOVE

Linda Hutcherson
Associate Professor of Education
Wayland Baptist University
Plainview, Texas

IN SEPTEMBER OF 1961, my family and I were traveling the long two-lane highway from the panhandle of Texas to central Oklahoma in our 1955 Studebaker coupe. Our destination was Oklahoma Baptist University, where I was about to start college. Because my parents had met and married while attending OBU, there was never any discussion needed about *whether* or *where* my little sister and I were going to college.

Since the age of two, I had lived in the same country home where my family had settled when my father returned from WWII in 1945. It was twenty-five miles from the nearest town. I spent the first six years of my school life in a one-room schoolhouse. The first year I sat in the first row, the second year in the second row, and so on. There were five students in my grade who went through school together from first through twelfth grade.

Beginning in the seventh grade, we rode the bus fifty miles a day to and from town.

Now I was off to college, seventeen years old, in love, and engaged to a wonderful young man. My parents had allowed me to date him steadily for the past year, though they did not approve of the impending marriage because of denominational differences.

And now, the separation from my family, my friends, and my fiancé created some very intense and mixed emotions. Making my own decisions was not something I had had much practice doing, and the newfound freedom to do so brought both anxiety and exhilaration in the semi-sheltered environment of OBU.

I had been raised in a Christian home, and our family had faithfully attended the small country church a mile from our home place. I had come to know Christ as my Lord and Savior at the age of eleven, and had never been challenged to doubt my decision or my experience.

That all changed during my first year at college. I felt lost again. There were many choices to make everywhere I turned. At the breakfast table, there was the choice of cereal, eggs, or fruit. Because I had never had choices of what to eat for breakfast, I ate them all!

I began to gain weight. My fiancé broke our engagement. My life was spinning out of control and continued to do so throughout my four years at OBU. I made many bad decisions in rebellion against my first love and my upbringing, both from anger and from lack of practice in making decisions. As I reflect, I am amazed by the grace of God. But for His grace and the grace of the university administration, I deservedly could have been suspended from school the very night before graduation.

The year 2005 marked the fortieth anniversary of that graduation. Two of my sorority suitemates persuaded me to come to the reunion. During the reunion luncheon, I was able to share my experience about the grace of God throughout the past forty years. I told my classmates how, because of that grace, God was, and is, and always will be my first love.

But you walked away from your first love–why? What's going on with you, anyway? Revelation 2:4 *The Message*

THE PHILOSOPHERS NEXT DOOR

Stephen Kaufmann
Professor of Education
Covenant College
Lookout Mountain, Georgia

I HAD JUST FINISHED DINNER and was returning to Carter Hall, the dormitory where I lived on the campus of Covenant College in northwestern Georgia. It was early in the fall of my freshman year. My aimless plan for the evening was to hang out and wait for the snack bar to open. As I approached my room, the fellow who lived next door to me came out in the hall. "Kaufmann, what are you doing?" he asked.

"Going to my room to listen to the Beatles for a while," I told him.

"That's dumb, Kaufmann. You should get your books and come in here and study with us." I think he knew that I needed to study for my Western civilization class.

This fellow was someone I looked up to, literally and figuratively. He was 6'4" and on the basketball team. He was also a junior, and I figured he knew lots of things I didn't know. So I got my books.

I spent that evening, and virtually every other evening during my freshman year, studying in the room of those two junior philosophy majors. One was from Illinois and was a starter on the basketball team. The other, from China, was a starter on the soccer team. We did much more than study. We drank tea and talked philosophy. We ate Chinese noodles and read the Bible. We discussed the future of the church, the state of politics, and our prospects for marriage, among other topics.

The philosopher Arthur Holmes, in his book *The Idea of a Christian College*, says that the peer group is the greatest single factor in shaping students of college age. Whatever students are, says Holmes, they are through their relationships with others. Looking back on my college experience, I have to agree with Holmes. Somehow, both the systematic presentation of the classroom and the rough and tumble of the bull session in the dorm are necessary for intellectual and spiritual growth.

Dorm life is a companion-rich and experience-rich life. It shapes us, for good or ill. Many do make bad choices of friends in college, and that surely could have happened to me. After all, I came to college wanting only two things: to play basketball and to have a good time. Had I connected early with a different peer group, I might have gotten nothing out of college beyond some basketball practice. It's only by the grace of God that I wasn't led to ruin.

Night after night, issue by issue, those friendly study sessions inducted me into a new world of Christian reflection. I thank God for the two junior philosophers next door who befriended this aimless freshman, and insisted that, morally, intellectually, and spiritually, I not settle for second best.

A man of many companions may come to ruin, but there is a friend who sticks closer than a brother. Proverbs 18:24 NIV

GOD SAVES A DREAM

Brian Jackson
Professor of Mathematics
and Economics
Oklahoma Wesleyan University
Bartlesville, Oklahoma

RETURNING TO SCHOOL full time to pursue a doctoral degree in economics at the age of forty-one was no doubt the gutsiest career move I would ever make. For the eleven years previous to this leap of faith, I had enjoyed a respectable position as a mathematics instructor for a state-supported junior college. My wife Kathy taught mathematics at the nearby high school. We were enjoying the American dream, raising our two children, Katie and Jonathan, in a quiet middle-class neighborhood.

Now, motivated by a sense that my biological clock was beginning to limit my future career possibilities, we finally made the decision I had personally contemplated for years. Kathy and I would resign our teaching positions, sell our home, and relocate one hundred miles away to the city where I could work on my Ph.D. degree.

This immediately led to numerous challenges for the family. We worked hard to establish the sense of the normalcy we had long enjoyed together, but now we had to find it in an unfamiliar setting. Gone was the steady income from my job, and though Kathy found another teaching position, it was only after a considerable time of anxious searching. Gone too were the children's everyday playmates; they were forced to build new relationships at school, at church, and with other youngsters in the apartment complex where we took up residence.

I am sure that many of our friends and relatives questioned our collective judgment for doing this. Even I sometimes wondered if selfishness on my part might have been behind our severing the ties of security we had been depending on for daily bread.

One week during the third semester of my program I experienced a suffocating sense of depression. I repeatedly turned over the question, "What have I done?" As I contemplated the odds against my little family ever regaining the comfortable situation we had left, I was suddenly overwhelmed with despair. Yet, I had to keep studying and moving forward through the program, regardless of that depression. There was simply no opportunity to turn back. The bridges behind were burned for good; we would have to make the best of it.

Now, just a few years later, I'm looking back on that experience as a new Ph.D. professor on the faculty of a wonderful midwestern Christian college. As I see my wife and children enjoying the best of work and school situations in our new hometown, I marvel at how God planned from the beginning to reward our trust in His care. He's given us blessings too great to be measured. In this journey, I have learned that God superintends the life events of His trusting servants toward the best of all outcomes.

And we know that all things work together for good to them that love God, to them who are the called according to his purpose. Romans 8:28

CANNED BEANS, THE TELEPHONE COMPANY, AND TITHE

Holly Hill-Stanford
Associate Professor of English
Southwest Baptist University
Bolivar, Missouri

I PICKED UP MY PAYCHECK from the cashier's window with mixed emotions. I was glad to be paid; yet I felt a twinge of sadness because this was my last paycheck as a teaching assistant at Iowa State University. Mostly, however, I felt fear.

Although I would be starting a new assistantship at the University of Kansas when I began work on my doctorate, three months would pass before I would be paid again. My limited wages as a teaching assistant had not allowed me to save even a few dollars, so I was facing the bleak prospect of existing for three months on one month's wages. Not only that, I had to complete my master's thesis during the next four weeks, and, since those were the days before everyone had a personal computer, I had to pay a typist.

On the following Sunday, I prepared to write the check for my tithe. I had always tithed, but for the first time, I hesitated before writing my check. If I gave my tithe, I did not know how I would survive financially. As I pondered my dilemma, I began to pray. "Lord, You know I have always given You a tenth of my income, and I want to do so now. But I don't know how I will survive without this money. Help me trust in You."

Immediately, I felt tremendously relieved. Though I would be totally dependent on God to sustain me, with great peace I wrote my check for the full amount of my tithe. I still didn't know how I would survive, but I was trusting God to provide for my needs.

Those three months were lean months. I knew my parents would help me financially if I asked, but they had already helped so much with my college education. I couldn't bear to ask them again. Instead, I cut every corner I could, especially in my food budget. Fortunately, I had always loved canned pork and beans; they now became the main staple of my diet.

Just when I wearied of eating beans, interesting things began to happen. Knowing that I would be graduating and moving away that summer, several families in my church decided to have me over for going-away dinners. I was thrilled to replace my bean diet several times with wonderful home-cooked meals.

Despite the improvement in my diet, financial burdens still loomed ahead, but God wasn't through providing for me. In June, my parents surprised me with a check instead of gifts for my birthday. While this significantly alleviated my financial obligations, one still remained to be paid.

Then the most remarkable blessing of all happened. When I needed it most, I received a refund check from the telephone company that was large enough to cover all my remaining expenses. Refunds from the telephone company were unheard of in those days. The accompanying letter stated that the refund was due to overpayments I had made, but I knew that God was the real source.

Cast all your anxiety on him because he cares for you. 1 Peter 5:7 NIV

WHEN RESPONSIBILITY BEGAN WITH AN "F"

Janis Flint-Ferguson
Chair, Department of English
Gordon College
Wenham, Massachusetts

"F." I LOOKED at it again. "F." In that moment my whole life flashed before my eyes and seemed summed up by that one big red "F."

As a first year student, I was taking an upper division French "literature in translation" course. Although doing well in college, I had come to the conclusion that there was no way I was going to be able to do the higher math required in biology. So as much as I had thought about being a high school biology teacher, I set that aside and took a good hard look at English language and literature. Why not? I loved literature. I loved language. I even loved grammar. Having already fulfilled the general education requirements for English, I was ready for the challenge of this upper division course. However, I was not ready for this assignment.

It was spring term and my days were full. In this upper division course there would be one major paper and one final exam for the grade. I had enjoyed reading the literature–Robbe-Grillet, Malraux, Butor, stuff that was so different from the traditional canon of Western literature I had studied in high school. But the professor was tough, aloof, French; and yet, I didn't want to work that hard. I was too busy being a college student to do new research and write a new essay—so I recycled. In high school I had written a French literature paper that had earned an "A." With a tweak here, a tuck there, and a whole day of retyping, I had no qualms about turning it in.

But when I saw the grade, I was second-guessing that decision. How could an "A" paper have been tweaked into an "F"? Ignoring my own responsibility, I decided that the professor must have missed the obvious quality of the essay. I stewed about it, lamented over it, and then turned against the whole college enterprise. Why should I even bother? I imagined flunking out at the end of the term and returning to the dry cleaners where I worked before college. From literature major to dry cleaner with one little essay. Instead I went to talk to the professor.

"This is just too flowery. It is impossible to determine what you really mean." He suggested that I rewrite the essay and then, if I did well on the final, the "F" would not stand as a final course grade. It was up to me to follow through.

The professor never knew the impact of that meeting. He was intimidating, but also fair. There was something of grace in our arrangement, something of redemption for me as long as I made a commitment to the work and to my responsibility as a student. I did. I rewrote and studied and completed the term with a "B." But more importantly, I recommitted myself to college and the gift God had given me. That passing grade was not the gift; the gift was a lesson in discipline.

Our fathers disciplined us for a little while as they thought best; but God disciplines us for our good, that we may share in his holiness. No discipline seems pleasant at the time, but painful. Later on, however, it produces a harvest of righteousness and peace for those who have been trained by it. Hebrews 12:10, 11 NIV

FEAR, WITNESS, AND FOUR FLIGHTS OF STAIRS

Glenn Settle
Chair, English Department
Northwest University
Kirkland, Washington

I WAS A SHY, first-year graduate student in English. A farm boy who had graduated from a small Christian college, I found the wide-swept lawns, the ivy-covered buildings, and the overall aura of the University of Oregon both attractive and intimidating. I didn't speak up during lectures or approach my professors outside of class.

But there came a time when I felt I had to talk to one of my professors about something. As I climbed the four long flights of concrete stairs in the English building, my legs trembled like two barn mice cornered by a cat. I had heard the rumors–a student getting a "C," just for getting on the wrong side of a professor, could be dismissed from graduate school!

Pausing outside his door, I wondered how this respected American literature scholar would respond to what I had to say. I knocked quietly. The door opened, and a man taller than he appeared in the classroom said, "Yes?"

"Dr. Nolte, I'm Glenn Settle," I blurted out. "I'm a student in your Emerson class. Do you have a minute?"

When he graciously asked me to sit, I nearly fell into a chair, my spongy knees relieved to get a rest.

"So, what's up?" he asked, sitting down across from me.

"Dr. Nolte," I began, "I wanted to come in and talk to you about something."

"Yes?" He smiled.

I looked out the window. "Well, sir, I just wanted to say, first, that I've learned a lot in your class about Whitman, about Emerson, about transcendentalism, and about a number of other things too. And I really enjoy the class."

He smiled again. "Okay, you've gotten my curiosity up. So what are we talking about here?"

I summoned what little courage I had left. "Well, sir, I wanted to come in today because I'd like to talk to you about . . . the Bible."

His arm moved a little. "What do you mean?"

"Well, sir, what I mean is that when you refer to the Bible in class, you sometimes misquote it and at other times quote it out of context."

"I do?"

"Yes," I said, my words running out faster. "And I haven't talked to anyone else about this, but I decided I wanted to talk to you about it."

"Well, I appreciate that," he said.

"And I'm not saying you have to believe the Bible or even venerate it or something. But even if it's just good literature, doesn't it deserve to be treated like other good literature? I mean, you wouldn't appreciate it if someone misquoted or quoted out of context, say, Emerson or Hawthorne."

"No, I probably wouldn't," he said. "So, what are some examples of what you're referring to?"

I began to bring up particular Bible passages. Dr. Nolte pulled a Bible off a shelf, and together we looked at verses and contexts.

Half an hour later he stood up, smiled broadly, and extended his hand. "I want to genuinely thank you for coming in here today, Mr. Settle. And I truly mean that. This has been a really profitable time. Thank you very much for coming in."

And that was it. The interview was ended. I had fulfilled my duty. I had borne an effective witness. God had gone with me, just as He promises.

I nearly floated down those four flights of stairs.

"Be strong and of good courage, do not fear nor be afraid of them; for the Lord your God, He is the One who goes with you. He will not leave you nor forsake you." Deuteronomy 31:6 NKJV

THE SECOND MEETING

"Come and hear, all ye that fear God, and I will declare what he hath done for my soul."

Psalm 66:16

Randy Pruitt
Professor of Human Communication, Colorado Christian University

Michael W. Firmin
Chair, Department of Psychology, Cedarville University

Edwin T. Childs
Professor of Sacred Music, Moody Bible Institute

Nelvia M. Brady
Professor of Business and Director of Ethnic Diversity, Trinity Christian College

Jane Hoyt-Oliver
Chair, Social Work Program, Malone College

James W. Thomas
Professor of English, Pepperdine University

Ronda O. Credille
Associate Professor of Business Administration, Southwest Baptist University

Crystal Downing
Professor of English and Film Studies, Messiah College

Lee Royce
President, Mississippi College

Mark A. Tatlock
Vice President for Student Life, The Master's College

DRY BROWN AND THE QUESTION MARK KID

Randy Pruitt
Professor of Human Communication
Colorado Christian University
Lakewood, Colorado

AS I RAMBLED down I-94 in my '64 Buick Skylark, I sang along with Crosby, Stills, Nash, & Young: "Tin soldiers and Nixon comin', we're finally on our own." At last my life was on the upswing. Traveling across the state to attend a midwestern college two hundred miles from home seemed like the best thing that could happen to this seventeen-year-old. No more arguments with my father. No more house rules. I had busted out. I was free. Free to do and say and be whatever I wanted.

University life turned out to be the perfect existence. Days were filled with new experiences and classes, and nights were jammed with meeting new friends. There was only one fly in the ointment, and he bugged me every afternoon at four. His name was Chris Brown, and he played first-chair baritone in the university's marching band.

Dry Brown, as he was sometimes called for his droll sense of humor, was tall, blond, and obnoxious. He lived and breathed only three things: music, dry wit, and Jesus Christ. I could handle the first two, but the third I could not. So I avoided this guy like the plague.

No matter how hard I tried to steer clear of this personal "hound of heaven," he would invariably corner me in the band room or on the field before practice. His first three words were always the same: "Praise the Lord!" Dry Brown believed there were only two kinds of people who needed to hear about Jesus–the willing, and the unwilling. The guy made me crazy inside.

After two months of playing hide-and-seek across campus, I determined that Chris Brown could not be avoided. So I changed my strategy. I decided to pester him to death. Starting sometimes early in the morning, I would call him up and ask him questions. "Hey, Dry. How many cows were there on the ark?"

"I don't know, but I'll get back to you," he would respond.

Late at night, after a few games of ping-pong, I would call him again. "It says in the Bible that 'no man knows the hour.' How about the month?"

I worked hard to make sure the questions were the pickiest, most inane questions he had ever heard. I was determined to see him lose his composure and ruin his "Praise the Lord!" image.

He never did. Chris Brown was one of the most genuine nice guys I had ever met. He handled every single one of my questions with a patience I had never seen in any other human being. This guy was for real.

Four months later, on January 8, 1973, I knelt by my bed and asked

Dry Brown's friend Jesus to come into my life. Whatever this guy had, I wanted it.

I have learned much since that afternoon driving down I-94 in my '64 Skylark. For one, I have learned what true freedom is. It is not *who* you are that makes you free; rather, it is *Whose* you are that makes all the difference.

You, my brothers, were called to be free. But do not use your freedom to indulge the sinful nature; rather, serve one another in love. Galatians 5:13 NIV

WORKING GOD'S WAY THROUGH COLLEGE

Michael W. Firmin
Chair, Department of Psychology
Cedarville University
Cedarville, Ohio

DURING MY TIME in Bible college, I sometimes found myself envious of fellow students who never needed to work to pay their school bills. They had wealthy parents, large savings accounts, or some other means of financial support. I knew other students who could share remarkable testimonies of opening their mailboxes and finding envelopes with money in them to cover tuition. Of course, they attributed their financial good fortune to their exercise of faith.

Was my faith too small? These miracles never happened to me. I tried to live a godly and spiritual life. Were their devotions bringing them closer to the Lord than mine? Had they somehow tapped into God's secret of financial success to which I was not privy? I wrestled with these questions, and tried to make sense of the spiritual dynamics around me.

Years later, the ways of God are more clear to me in this matter than they were during college. Throughout my undergraduate education and first master's degree, I worked full-time and attended school full-time. It's a hard thing to do, and I do not generally recommend it for students trying to make it through college. However, it worked for me, and God shaped my life through it.

So I would listen to my fellow students give chapel testimonies of God's miraculous provision and wrestle with the apparent implications–and then I'd go to work. Now I see that the same love that God showed to those who found money in the mailbox He also showed to me. The love simply was demonstrated through different means. And at the end of each semester, I had a school bill that was paid in full.

Despite all the work, I still maintained a productive college life filled with extra-curricular activities. These included being president of the Scripture Memory Club and director of the Hopeline Counseling Ministry, working as a resident assistant, participating in weekly evangelism ministry, teaching Sunday school, and preaching occasionally. The Lord sustained me in all this while I was taking a full college load–including Greek and Hebrew–and getting engaged. I had a full life, and through it all, I carried a 4.0 GPA most semesters.

God broadened and deepened my faith through my college years. I had to trust Him to help me use my time wisely, to help me stay healthy, to give me intellectual ability to compensate for less study time. He helped me practice good stewardship of my hard-earned income, to be diligent and responsible on the job, to learn how to say no to good things so I could focus on the better things. He taught me how to make a ministry out of daily life itself, rather than merely participating in ministries.

My college life, and all the work it involved, prepared me well for many of the same challenges that I face today in ministry. God grew my faith during those important years, but not often in the ways that grab attention in a chapel testimony. Today I have three master's degrees and two Ph.D. degrees without ever having any school debt. God's good hand, through the work He graciously provided, has been evident all along the way.

But my God shall supply all your need according to his riches in glory by Christ Jesus. Philippians 4:19

A HYMN FOR THE GREAT COMPOSER

Edwin T. Childs
Professor of Sacred Music
Moody Bible Institute
Chicago, Illinois

WHEN I WENT TO COLLEGE, I knew I would study music, but how to choose and settle on a specific major remained an enigma. Why couldn't I just play and enjoy music as I had done at home and throughout high school? I had learned to sing parts in church, taught myself to play the organ, accompanied my school choir, and played different instruments in both the band and orchestra.

At college I actually had to take courses in things like music history and theory, and I wasn't very engaged. I attended classes, but still contented myself with learning things my own home-grown way. Finally, in kindness, and perhaps desperation, my music theory professor, Miss Thompson, suggested I take composition lessons. Western art music was the school standard, but the red marks from her grading pen showed me that I had been following a different course.

Throughout this time of decision, my mother faithfully wrote a weekly letter that always included Proverbs 3:5, 6 with her signature. She knew the kind of encouragement I needed, and it helped me remember that the Lord really was directing my path.

During my senior year I entered a composition contest with an uncomplicated, hymn-like setting of "O Master, Let Me Walk with Thee." To my surprise it won first prize. The anonymous judge from another institution wrote gracious comments describing how my piece had been chosen from among others that were larger and more complex. The judge said he was impressed not by the "quantity" of notes, but by the "quality" of them.

That same year I applied to graduate school at one of the most prestigious schools in the nation. The week after my audition and interview, I was thrilled to receive a letter stating that not only had I been accepted, but that I had been awarded an all-expenses-paid scholarship to earn my doctorate. I excitedly shared the news with Miss Thompson, who had gotten me started in composition. God not only was directing my path, he was providing more than I could ask or think.

During that first year of doctoral study, I met a man who asked me to consider taking a position on his faculty at a Christian college. He told me he would wait to fill that position until I finished the degree. Again, in God's providence, my life's work began to unfold immediately.

During my years of teaching, I have sponsored annual contests for my composition students. I have always sent the entries to an impartial, off-campus judge. One year one of these judges shared with me his philosophy of evaluation. He told how he had judged a similar competition at my alma mater several years earlier. As he described the winning piece of that particular contest, I knew he was speaking of the one I had written when I was a student. It was a remarkable coincidence, since his philosophy of "quality" versus "quantity" had become the foundation for my composing and teaching. Twenty years later, when that man retired from his institution, I providentially ended up filling the position he left.

Today, Miss Thompson, who first saw and nurtured the spark of creativity in this struggling student, has become a close colleague and friend through fellowship at home and church. And professionally, I am standing in the same place as the person who gave me invaluable guidance with his perceptive analysis, enabling that spark to become a strong flame.

Neither my Christian parents nor I could have planned this incredible journey for me. This can only be the work of an omniscient God, the Great Composer.

"I know the plans that I have for you . . . to give you a future and a hope." Jeremiah 29:11 NASB

MEET THE COUNSELOR

Nelvia M. Brady
Professor of Business
and Director of Ethnic Diversity
Trinity Christian College
Palos Heights, Illinois

CHAMPAIGN-URBANA was a strange place for a young African-American woman who grew up in Rockwell Gardens, a public housing project on Chicago's West Side. The University of Illinois was huge, and I was afraid. I had never seen so many trees and so many white people.

I made my way from my Lincoln Avenue Residence Hall toward the admissions office to meet with a counselor who was supposed to help me plan my first semester schedule. On the way there, I kept looking around to see if there were others who looked like me. But there were very few brown faces. This was 1966, and though the University of Illinois in Urbana had a total enrollment of more than 30,000 students, only 225 of them were African American. Still, I deserved to be there, though there was little about the university that made me feel like I belonged.

The very sterile reception I got from the counselor did not improve matters. Not that he had to try hard to alienate me. In 1966, the mere atmosphere of the University of Illinois did that before I laid eyes on him.

Him. To this day, I can't recall his name, but I remember vividly the authoritative-looking white man who never proffered the customary handshake to greet me nor moved from behind his desk to dissolve the wall between us. Instead, he sat there with official-looking documents and charts, which I noticed had my name on them. While I sat there like a deer in the headlights, he fanned casually through details about me—that I graduated valedictorian with an "A+" average, that I scored a 29 on the ACT, that I was a National Merit Achievement Finalist, and a Mayor Richard J. Daley Youth Foundation Scholar, and an Illinois State Scholar. These were the records of a high achiever. I was proud of these records. Why, then, was this man acting as if I was a bitter pill he had to swallow?

I watched him gather my papers in his hands. He looked me seriously in the eyes and said, "If you work hard and stay away from Kams (a popular local bar), you *might* be able to make 'C's.'" Still the deer in the headlights, I said nothing. Shaken, I walked out of his office with my chin to my chest, my spirits bouncing off the toes of my shoes.

But I quickly regrouped. What did he mean "C's"? In my house, "C's" were synonymous with failing. I left that building determined to continue the high level of performance that my parents and my GOD required of me—and that I required of myself.

Apparently the counselor didn't know the prayers and sacrifice that it had taken for me to get to where I was. Apparently he didn't know my faith. Apparently he didn't know my GOD. But I did. I graduated in four years. I made the Dean's List. And I never once went to Kams.

Trust in the LORD with all thine heart; and lean not unto thine own understanding. In all thy ways acknowledge him, and he shall direct thy paths. Proverbs 3:5, 6

BEING NICE OR BEING HIS

Jane Hoyt-Oliver
Chair, Social Work Program
Malone College
Canton, Ohio

I WAS A NICE PERSON when I was a teenager. I was polite, worked hard, went to church, and volunteered in the community. But I didn't know much about Jesus. I didn't know how to live a distinctly Christian life. I was such a nice kid, though, that it never occurred to me that there was anything wrong with the way I was living my life.

One evening during my senior year in high school, I was invited to a Bible study. I met a group of people, my teenage peers, who were willing to be honest about what was real in their lives. The study leaders pointed to Jesus, the Son of God, and asked us to reorder our futures based on His call for our lives.

In the meeting that night, I came to understand that I was selfish, greedy, boastful, conceited, unkind, reckless, and swollen with pride, just as St. Paul described in 2 Timothy 3. "How could that be me? Nice, polite me?" I wondered. But because I didn't know Jesus, I had set my goals by the world's standards. I planned to get a good job, work hard at it, and establish a name for myself in my hometown. If I met those goals, I would "win." My job. My goals. My achievement.

But by the time I left the Bible study that night, I was beginning to learn that being a "nice person" was not what God wanted for me. He wanted me to be willing to make Jesus' priorities my first priority. God had opened my eyes to His world so I could see His set of values.

My plan had been to go to college and study ancient history. However, now I felt God asking me to engage with the present world rather than focus on the past. So I switched my major to social work.

During my college years, I met people from all walks of life, many of whom I never would have allowed in my former "nice person" life. As I interacted with these people, God showed me the richness and joy that come from embracing those whom the world ignores. I realized that, in God's eyes, I had not been so nice after all.

Though I had planned to make a name for myself in my hometown, I moved 250 miles away shortly after I became a Christian. I have never again lived any closer than that. So much for my plan, that is, the plan of the "nice" old me. Instead, because I have allowed God to work out His plans in my life, He is using me to proclaim His name, and not mine, in the place that He has put me.

When I was born again, God gave me new eyes. With those eyes, I was able to see beyond my own "niceness" and discern what God really wanted to do with my life. Now, by His grace, I'm not just a nice person. I'm His person.

For the time will come when men will not put up with sound doctrine. Instead, to suit their own desires, they will gather around them a great number of teachers to say what their itching ears want to hear. They will turn their ears away from the truth and turn aside to myths. But you, keep your head in all situations, endure hardship, do the work of an evangelist, discharge all the duties of your ministry. 2 Timothy 4:3-5 NIV

A BROADER PERSPECTIVE

James W. Thomas
Professor of English
Pepperdine University
Malibu, California

AS I WAS FINISHING my doctoral studies, my wife and I were also expecting our first child. She had just completed her master's degree, and I had written my dissertation. Summer would bring our baby, my "terminal" degree, our move to my full-time teaching job, and, really, the beginning of our lives as professional educators and parents.

My wife's due date was July 15. The date for the oral defense of my dissertation was July 21. I jokingly told her that she could deliver the child any time that entire summer except for July 21.

She went into labor on the afternoon of July 20. I drove her to the hospital at breakneck speed, only to find that she was in the very early stages of labor. It would be quite some time yet. Her labor continued all that day and through the night, and our son was born shortly before 10:00 the next morning. I was due at my exam at 1:30 p.m.

All through the night, I was keenly aware of the potential conflict between my personal and professional lives. I was worried about missing either my fatherhood or my arrival at academic nirvana. Yet, as the night and the morning wore on, as I saw my wife in a strange kind of ecstatic agony, and as I entered the delivery room, everything changed.

When I witnessed the birth of our son, it was as if God had placed everything in perspective for me. "Speechless" is, ironically, the only word that describes the occasion.

I had a little more than three hours to go home, get dressed, review a few notes, and go to my exam. Yet I wasn't stressed or worried. I was calm, elated, even elevated. Despite my lack of sleep, I arrived for the exam cool, confident, and quite relaxed and refreshed.

My dissertation director announced to the committee that I had been up all night and, just hours before, had become a father. One committee member responded by saying that personal matters shouldn't be considered in such a situation and expressed fear that the objectivity of the exam may have been compromised.

I think I did well answering the questions that day; I passed the exam. The committee member who had objected to the birth announcement asked me some especially tough questions. When I couldn't answer, I calmly said, "I don't know" or "I have no idea." The fact that I had, hours before, experienced the miracle of my son's entry into the world made this man's questions and his attitude irrelevant, or at least allowed me to view them from a broader perspective. What I had seen and felt overnight made me immune to academic intimidation that day and every day since. I had learned what are and what are not matters of life and death.

As I write this, my son and his wife are now expecting their first child. I know the birth of their child in a different July will bring them a deeper appreciation of God's blessings and a new perspective, just as my wife and I were changed forever on that July day many years ago.

God has made everything beautiful for its own time. He has planted eternity in the human heart, but even so, people cannot see the whole scope of God's work from beginning to end. Ecclesiastes 3:11 NLT

NOT JUST ANOTHER STATISTIC

Ronda O. Credille
Associate Professor
of Business Administration
Southwest Baptist University
Bolivar, Missouri

THE BRIGHT SUNLIGHT streaming over my shoulder made that famous sixth letter of the alphabet at the top of my business statistics test very easy to read. The blood first drained from my face and then rushed back as I began to suspect that everyone around me had also seen my grade. Never before had I flunked an exam.

Maybe "they" had been right.

My mind drifted back four years to the night I met John, a young sailor who had returned to college after completing his tour of duty in Vietnam. We were introduced by an older couple who opened their home to students on the weekends. One semester after our marriage, John graduated and I quit school so that we could relocate. As family and friends heard that news, they predicted I would just be another statistic, one of those who would never finish college; it just would be too hard to go back to school after dropping out.

Straightening up in my desk, I tried to reconnect with the statistics professor, but my mind would not cooperate. Instead, it began to replay the discussion John and I had had about our future four months earlier. Neither of us was happy in our jobs. We had no children and no debts, except a mortgage. John said that he thought it would be a good time to sell our house and move so that I could finish school at the Baptist college where we had met. Within weeks we had changed addresses, John had changed jobs, and I was enrolled as a full-time student. God's direction seemed clear.

And now I'd failed the first college exam of my big comeback. How could I face John? Two stats courses were required for the business administration degree, and I had not even passed the first, and presumably easiest, exam.

Determined that I would earn a bachelor's degree of *some* kind, I went to my academic advisor's office and announced to him that I was changing my major to another field. When he asked why, I confessed to the failed exam and rationalized that statistics was just too demanding after being out of college for a while.

"Have you asked for help from your stats professor or any of your fellow students?" he asked.

"No," I admitted.

He paused for a moment. "Do you believe that 'where God guides, God provides'?"

"Well, yes."

"Then why do you think the answer to your problem is to run away from it?"

I had no answer.

Before I left his office, I had promised to seek assistance, and he had promised to pray for me.

Three months later, I anxiously waited while the stats professor graded my final exam. When he finished, his face was expressionless. He arose from his desk and walked toward me with my paper. As he handed it to me, he said "Congratulations," and a large grin spread over his face. At the top of the paper, he had written, "100%, A+."

I earned the bachelor's degree, then an MBA, and ultimately a Ph.D. I guess my family and friends were wrong. I have no doubt now that God guided; He certainly provided.

"For I know the plans I have for you," declares the LORD, "plans to prosper you and not to harm you, plans to give you hope and a future." Jeremiah 29:11 NIV

NO EXTRA CREDIT FOR A MODERN VIRGIN MARY

Crystal Downing
Professor of English and Film Studies
Messiah College
Grantham, Pennsylvania

I COULD'VE BEEN the Virgin Mary. At least this is what I thought during my student days at a Christian college. After all, I had all the qualifications: dedication to God, disciplined prayer life, volunteer work in a local church, sexual purity, knowledge of the Scriptures with numerous chapters expertly memorized, and, ummm, humility. Aye, there's the rub. Confidence in my qualifications disqualified me.

As I look back on those days with my mind's eye–brain matter wrinkled like my actual eyes–I see God working in mysterious ways. The first way mystified me for quite some time.

It happened in the middle of my college years while I was leading a Young Life Bible study across town. Because I did not own a car, a friend allowed me to use his green Volkswagen Bug for my Monday night ministry. While driving back to campus after Bible study one night, a yellow Mustang swerved in front of me, then braked suddenly as the traffic light turned red. Though I screeched my brakes, I was unable to stop in time. I rammed into the rear of the Mustang, rumpling its bumper. And with the impact, my head whipped forward and cracked the windshield of my friend's Bug.

Several days later, insult was added to injury, quite literally. When I went to the Mustang owner's business to sign insurance papers, she looked at me, for the first time in daylight, and exclaimed, "Oh! I didn't realize that you broke your nose in the impact!"

With barely disguised chagrin, I replied, "I didn't break my nose."

But she wouldn't let it alone. "You need to go to a doctor! I know someone who broke her nose and it looked exactly like yours."

I signed the papers with a sigh and said, "My nose always looks like this."

And then things got worse. My friend told me that his parents had not properly insured the Volkswagen. This meant that I had to pay for the repair of both vehicles out of my own pocket. The repair costs took my entire life savings, which I had been accruing for fifteen years, ever since I started putting a dime a week into the bank in first grade.

My prayers turned angry: "It's not fair, God! I was serving You, using the car not to party, not to shop, but to do Your work! And because of that, my life savings (not to mention my dignity) is gone! I was even reciting a Bible verse out loud when the Mustang swerved and stopped in front of me. Shouldn't that have given me extra credit?"

Of course, extra credit before God is precisely what Jesus taught against. But it took several other painful experiences–significantly more devastating–to finally imprint on my wrinkly brain matter that my God (Thank God!) is a God of mercy rather than justice, that Christ-credit supplants extra-credit.

And Mary said, "My soul magnifies the Lord, and my spirit rejoices in God my Savior, . . . [who] has brought down the powerful from their thrones, and lifted up the lowly." Luke 1:46, 47, 52 NRSV

A MODEL FOR SPEAKING OUT

Lee Royce
President
Mississippi College
Clinton, Mississippi

I WENT TO COLLEGE as a conservative Christian and encountered all the diversity one might expect at an elite university. You could stroll through the Student Center and pick up a Communist newspaper, receive an invitation to the Gay Alliance Dance, or find opportunities galore to sign petitions against U.S. government policy, foreign or domestic. Even the university chaplain, who had started out as a Baptist and converted to Buddhism, got into the game. I remember hearing him expound at length on the sins of Christian America. All in all, the university seemed to be indifferent, or at times even hostile, to mainstream Christian belief.

There were few professors of my acquaintance who openly identified themselves as Christian. Professor Leech, an American history scholar, was one of those few. I learned from him that a person can have an impact for Christ in quiet and gentle ways. As a history major, I enrolled in all three of the courses he offered in Colonial American history; he was always an engaging lecturer, and I enjoyed the subject.

I can still remember the day that I got my copy of *Newsweek* from my mailbox just before going to Professor Leech's class. To my amazement, I saw that the magazine had published a letter to the editor from Professor Leech. He was responding to a *Newsweek* article that had called into question the historical truth of the resurrection of Christ. In his letter, he maintained that, as a professional historian, he believed that there was as much evidence to support the resurrection as there was for many other events in history that we all accepted without question. I was greatly heartened to read that my professor had taken a stand for Christ in a national news magazine, and that he had done so with scholarship and humility.

I rushed to class and waited eagerly to speak with him. He invited me to his office, and we spoke about the Christian witness at the university. He offered me a copy of *Good News for Modern Man* from a stock he kept on the corner of his desk. His humble witness, gracefully employing his scholarship in defense of the faith, is an example for all in the academy who call themselves Christian.

Always be prepared to make a defense to any one who calls you to account for the hope that is in you, yet do it with gentleness and reverence. 1 Peter 3:15 RSV

TAMING OF THE SHREWD–AND LONELY

Mark A. Tatlock
Vice President for Student Life
The Master's College
Santa Clarita, California

"A MAVERICK CHRISTIAN." These were the words our student body president, Kelly, used to describe me as a sophomore in college. I was tempted to respond defensively, but I knew his words were motivated out of love. Just three weeks earlier Kelly had invited me to join his discipleship group. As we studied the theme of servant leadership in the book of Philippians, Kelly began to demonstrate a level of concern and interest for me that I had not experienced before from a friend.

Having moved thirteen times before coming to college, I had developed the ability to manipulate others in order to become accepted. Whenever I arrived at a new place, I had to work to become a part of a group of friends who had grown up with each other, had a shared history, and were always on the inside of jokes. I learned to quickly assess new acquaintances and endear myself to them through the use of humor and kindness.

By my sophomore year of college, using this strategy, I had been voted "Class Clown" and "Most Spirited." I had obtained a position in student government, joined several theater and music groups, and successfully maneuvered myself into many leadership positions on campus.

But Kelly saw through me. He discerned that, though I had become popular as a student, I was not allowing myself to be known by or to depend on anyone else. He wisely asked me to make a covenant with him to let him speak honestly about my life. In return he promised that no matter what became exposed in my life, he would always be my friend and extend love to me.

These two longings had always been in conflict with each other:

friendship and vulnerability. Kelly's offer of unconditional friendship allowed me for the first time to be completely honest about who I was and what my struggles were, while at the same time experiencing rest and acceptance. It became evident to me that this was a picture of God's love for me.

Since that time I have come to understand the power of unconditional love. Conflict in a relationship is no longer something that places the relationship at risk; rather, it presents an opportunity to grow and forgive. God's unconditional love has now become the definitive standard for my relationships with my family, my friends, the lost in my community, and even "maverick Christians." The knowledge of being secure in God's love is what frees me to pursue others.

Now, as a college administrator, each fall I look forward to meeting our incoming students. I often recognize many who are longing for real relationships. I welcome these students, praying that they will encounter the authentic love of God through the pursuant and unconditional love of upperclassmen like Kelly. The adage says that you will make the best friends of your life in college. I learned from Kelly that not only can you make the best friends, but you can also discover the heart of true friendship.

But God demonstrates His own love toward us, in that while we were yet sinners, Christ died for us. Romans 5:8 NASB

THE THIRD MEETING

"Come and hear, all ye that fear God, and I will declare what he hath done for my soul."

Psalm 66:16

Annie Olson
Chair, Department of English, LeTourneau University

Paul Freitag
Vice President of Advancement, North Central University

Rich Brown
Vice President for Spiritual Formation, Simpson University

Rod Janzen
Distinguished Scholar and Professor of History, Fresno Pacific University

Robin Hasslen
Professor of Education, Bethel University

Betty Jane Fratzke
Chair of Behavioral Sciences, Indiana Wesleyan University

Michael S. Stewart
President, Emmanuel College

Dwayne Uglem
President, Briercrest College

Paul Jordan
Professor of Computer Science, Southern Wesleyan University

Eddie K. Baumann
Professor of Education, Cedarville University

GRACE IN A CLASS AND A CROSS

Annie Olson
Chair, Department of English
LeTourneau University
Longview, Texas

SLEEPING IN CLASS is never a good idea, but that day I just couldn't help it. It was that time in the semester, about two weeks before graduation, when all the final projects were due. As a working mother with three small children, I was trying to balance school, homework, job, and family. I had been working frantically to keep the high GPA I wanted. To accomplish everything, I had been sleeping only two or three hours a night. That day it finally caught up with me.

Unfortunately, this was not the sort of large lecture class where I could hide. Eight or nine students and the professor sat around a table in close discussion of the subject, and I could not stay awake. I think I might have even snored a bit. Finally, the professor said, "Annie, I want to see you in my office after class."

Okay, I thought, *I'm in trouble now. There goes my grade. One major project left, and I blew it.* I sat in his office and waited for the lecture to begin.

It started with questions. "What's going on in your life? How much sleep are you getting? How much progress have you made on the final project?" It was due Thursday, only two days away. I hadn't started yet, but I assured him that I planned to start that night. I would get it done.

The professor just looked at me and shook his head. Then he said the most amazing thing. "You have already earned your 'A.' Even if you don't do the final project, you will still have an 'A' in the course. Don't do the project. Just go home and get some sleep."

I'm sure I sat there with a dumb look on my face for a full minute before responding. I couldn't believe I had heard him right. But I had. I walked out of his office realizing what it felt like to have a burden lifted and grace poured all over me.

This experience helped me to realize that my strength and my available hours just weren't enough to meet all the demands and to make the grade. That grade seems far less important to me now, but at the time, it was monumentally significant. I've finally learned, though, that life makes very real, eternally important demands that I can never be enough or do enough to satisfy. Praise God, I don't have to! When Jesus died on the cross, He cried out, "It is finished." All demands were satisfied. My burdens were lifted, and grace was poured out all over me, at the cross and in a class.

But he said to me, "My grace is sufficient for you, for my power is made perfect in weakness." Therefore I will boast all the more gladly about my weaknesses, so that Christ's power may rest on me. 2 Corinthians 12:9 NIV

FROM LOSING LEADER TO WINNING SERVANT

Paul Freitag
Vice President of Advancement
North Central University
Minneapolis, Minnesota

ELECTIONS WERE COMING soon for the next year's class officers. As a freshman at North Central Bible College in the spring of 1984, I was excited about the possibility of being a class officer. At that time, I thought that leadership meant having a position more than it meant actually being a servant. Because I wanted to be a leader, I decided I wanted to be a sophomore class officer and I prepared for the election.

When my opponent won, I felt as though I had just lost a popularity contest. I wrestled with God about the disappointment. I had been so sure that this office would be good for me. Now what was God doing? How could I be used by Him when I couldn't even be elected as a class officer?

At the same time, some other leadership positions were open to whoever was willing to fill them. I was less than excited when one of the college leaders encouraged me to take one of these unglamorous roles. I don't think he perceived leadership skills in me; he just needed to recruit volunteers to fill the slots. It wasn't much of a consolation prize, but I agreed to help out.

As summer approached, I heard about all the exciting things that the class officer team was planning for the next year. They were sharp students; they were going to make a difference. It pained me to hear all this when I had wanted so badly to be a part of that leadership team. I still didn't understand why God hadn't put me on the team.

One day early in August, as I was preparing to return to school, the telephone rang. It was the sophomore class president. He asked me to consider serving in the role that I had pursued in the spring. The person who had been elected had had a change of plans and would be unable to fulfill his term. Since I had been the other candidate, they decided to ask me to take the position rather than to hold another election. I gladly accepted the invitation.

So during my sophomore year, I served as a class officer after all. I also served in the other volunteer position that I had been reluctant to accept. As it turned out, I really enjoyed it. Though I had thought the job to be beneath me, I learned the joy of serving. And the experience I gained in that position opened up the opportunity for me to be chosen to serve as a resident advisor during my junior year. Then as the time came to elect senior class officers, it looked like no one was interested in running for senior class president. My classmates nominated me, and I was elected unopposed.

So my senior year in college, I enjoyed serving my classmates as their president. I thank God for what He taught me: seeking a position does not make one a leader of others; serving them does.

He who calls you is faithful, who also will do it. 1 Thessalonians 5:24 NKJV

MY OWN RELATIONSHIP WITH GOD

Rich Brown
Vice President for Spiritual Formation
Simpson University
Redding, California

I WAS LOOKING forward to leaving home to finish my college education. Raised in a healthy Christian home with loving parents, I was active in a local church fellowship during my junior college years. Yet I was eager to get away. I felt like I needed to find out who I really was when Dad, Mom, and my Christian friends weren't around. I wanted to find out if the Jesus I had known in grammar school was worthy of my young adult commitment. Could He handle my college-age questions?

It felt a little risky to rebuild my faith, and my identity, from near scratch. I wasn't sure I'd be safe stepping out from all that was familiar to me. It helped me to assume the role of a seeker. I wanted to know about Jesus "once again for the first time."

I was introduced to the writings of C. S. Lewis, Francis Schaeffer, and J. B. Phillips. Their books, *Mere Christianity*, *The God Who Is There,* and *Your God Is Too Small* challenged me to think for myself about who God is and what I believed.

I bought myself a copy of J. B. Phillips's paraphrase of the New Testament and read the life of Jesus as I had never read it before. I placed myself in the crowd of five hundred disciples who were curious about Jesus.

I began attending a different local church. I had read about Pascal's "habit of faith," which said that the time when you are having questions about your faith is not the time to quit going to church. I agreed with Pascal. It didn't make sense to stop spending time in the place where I was most likely to find answers. It made more sense to hang around people who had some of the same questions as I did.

This was all going pretty well. I felt like I was growing in my personal spiritual experience. Then, during the summer after my junior year, I took a job a thousand miles from home. No familiar faces, no Christian activities, no church. It was just me and God. For the first time in my life, I would really find out what God and I had going.

I found out we had a lot going. I could talk to Him without the distracting chatter of others' expectations. I could ask Him for the help that my peers and parents couldn't provide. That summer, I sensed myself developing my own personal spirituality. He was my God. I was *His* follower.

One of the developmental tasks during college is to "individuate" one's point of view in many areas of life, and especially spirituality. Each person's journey to "individuated spirituality" will look different. In my journey, I felt that I had to get away and find out if I could be my own spiritual person, independent from what family and friends said or thought. Reading books by great Christian thinkers, reading the Bible for myself, staying in touch with the community of faith–I found all of these to be vitally important contributors to my developing faith. And because I had the courage to take this journey, I now have a relationship with God that is my own.

Jesus told those who were asking questions, "If anyone chooses to do God's will, he will find out whether my teaching comes from God or whether I speak on my own." John 7:17 NIV

MERE CULTURE AND A REAL CHRISTIANITY

Rod Janzen
Distinguished Scholar
and Professor of History
Fresno Pacific University
Fresno, California

DURING MY JUNIOR YEAR at Pacific College (now Fresno Pacific University), I was in residence at Regent's Park College, a Baptist-affiliated institution that is part of Oxford University. There, in the heart of England, I was introduced to a vast array of new cultural experiences.

For example, I learned to navigate a punt on the River Cherwell, to discern the true meaning of words like "torch" and "bog," and to appreciate English cuisine like steak and kidney pie and Cornish pasties. At The Eagle and Child, a pub located just around the corner from the college, a plaque positioned above one of the booths indicated that C. S. Lewis, J. R. R. Tolkien, and others had often conversed there over a pint of ale.

I also spent many hours preparing for weekly tutorials in English history and literature. At these intimidating one-on-one intellectual encounters, students read their personal essays aloud, to be critiqued by well-read professors–in their own homes. One week my assignment was to read Jane Austen and write an essay discussing what she had to say about late eighteenth- and early nineteenth-century English society. When I asked which of the writer's books to read, the professor responded, "All of them."

Life at Regent's Park was exciting, stimulating, and all-consuming. There was reading to be done; there were essays to be written; there were new cultural traditions to figure out. This left little time to think about home, the past, or old relationships. It was also easy to forget about my relationship to God and the church, and about Christian commitments in general. There were too many new experiences and overwhelming academic requirements.

Between terms, however, the Oxford system had scheduled two six-week "vacations." On the heels of the hustling busyness of school, during these times I often found myself in a state of social isolation and personal angst. This was particularly true during the Christmas season. I was confronted with issues of foundational meaning and purpose in my life. I had been so busy during the school terms, soaking up every aspect of this fascinating new culture, that I was in danger of forgetting my own personal Christian culture.

This is when C. S. Lewis helped me to rediscover the power of God's presence. I purchased a copy of his *Mere Christianity* at a Church of England bookshop near the Thames. Lewis's words provided me a creative and intellectually stimulating way to deal with complicated issues involving the supernatural dimension of my existence. This reconnection with God was essential to the sustaining of my life, holding things together.

I still have that book. It has continued to be of great value to me over the years, because through C. S. Lewis's words, God brought a renewed spiritual focus to my life. During an interlude in a cultural learning extravaganza, God reconnected me to my Christian culture. His culture.

The heavens are telling the glory of God; and the firmament proclaims his handiwork. Day to day pours forth speech, and night to night declares knowledge. There is no speech, nor are there words; their voice is not heard; yet their voice goes out through all the earth, and their words to the end of the world. In the heavens he has set a tent for the sun. Psalm 19:1-4 NRSV

LEARNING BY SERVING

Robin Hasslen
Professor of Education
Bethel University
St. Paul, Minnesota

BEING A COLLEGE STUDENT in the 1960s was both captivating and discomforting. The world seemed to be falling apart, roiled by racism, war, poverty, assassination, gender strife. I wrote letters home to my mother asking where God was in the midst of this chaos. Who had the answers? What was right? What was wrong? Could I live out my faith in ways that would be true to what I had been taught to believe during my first eighteen years?

My faith faltered. The world was too dismal and out of control. Neither the preachers nor the professors seemed to be able to give me the answers I sought. Halfway through my freshman year, I decided I really didn't need the church.

I determined that perhaps I needed to experience firsthand some of the suffering of the oppressed and figure out the answers for myself. So in the summer of 1964, following my freshman year of college in Pennsylvania, I went to South Carolina. I waited tables at an upscale restaurant that catered to businessmen. That was the summer of the civil rights legislation, and the restaurant's owner had threatened that anyone who dared to wait on any Blacks who might enter would be fired.

On the second of July, in the middle of the noontime rush, the place suddenly became dead silent. I turned and saw two young Black men enter and sit at a table near the door. No one moved as the boss assumed a defiant stance in front of them. I picked up menus and waited on the men. We had a subdued conversation as I tried quietly to put them at ease. When they left, I cleared their table and took their plates to the kitchen. I was fired on the spot.

What a rude awakening! I was horrified to think that I had willingly participated in such a racist system for my first eighteen years. That day, I vowed to do my part to work for social justice.

When I returned to college, I spent every weekend in Philadelphia working in the areas of greatest poverty, or in south Jersey in the fields with the migrant workers. The next summer I went to West Virginia to teach in the first Head Start programs. After I graduated, I traveled to eastern Kentucky and built a hut out of a pigpen in a "holler" called Little Creek.

My father, who had financed my education, was dismayed at my "career" choice. "Didn't you learn ANYTHING in college?" he would ask over and over. Of course I had learned the basics for earning my keep. But the most important lessons were the ones I learned outside of the classroom. I learned that education can be gained through interacting with the lives of others, whether they be professors or the poverty-stricken. I learned that oppression and affliction fall on all of us. And I learned that, following Christ's example, we can minister to and continue to learn from one another.

Blessed be the God and Father of our Lord Jesus Christ, the Father of mercies and God of all comfort; who comforts us in all our affliction so that we may be able to comfort those who are in any affliction with the comfort with which we ourselves are comforted by God. 2 Corinthians 1:3, 4 NASB

PLAYING FOR GOD

Betty Jane Fratzke
Chair of Behavioral Sciences
Indiana Wesleyan University
Marion, Indiana

I LEARNED TO PLAY basketball in a hayloft. Since we were farm kids, my brother and I spent a fair amount of our free time playing basketball upstairs in our barn. I longed for a day when I, a girl, could play on a real team. Then I learned that I could–in college. So as a twelve-year-old, I voiced a promise to God while pushing a lawnmower one summer afternoon: "If you will let me play basketball on a real team someday, I promise I'll play for You."

I began to dream about going to college. But during my senior year in high school, tragedy struck. A tornado destroyed our home and farm buildings. As we tried to rebuild our lives, I was certain that my dreams had been blown away by the financial loss. But God had other plans. He gave me Psalm 50:10, a reminder that "the cattle on a thousand hills" belong to Him; He would provide enough "cattle" for my education bills.

And He did! And money was not the only "cattle" He provided. I experienced spiritually-rich mentoring from my professors and coaches, and the college chapel services inspired me.

Two years later, while attending Greenville College, I was given the opportunity to play on a Sports Evangelism Team traveling in Mexico. Again, God provided the necessary "cattle" for trip expenses. And during nearly every day of that trip, we all saw God's "cattle" in the form of some type of miracle. For example, one day as we traveled from one large city to another, a tire went flat on our bus. We were forced to stop in what seemed to be the middle of nowhere beside a run-down old shack. To our amazement, there was a large tire behind the shack that fit our bus wheel. The miracle, however, was that during the forty-five minutes we had stopped for repairs, a man who lived near the shack talked with our interpreter. The Holy Spirit had prepared this man ahead of time with a hunger for peace; he accepted Christ right then while we waited.

We saw lots of "cattle" as we traveled through Mexico; God revealed His power and mercy in vivid ways, and many souls were won for the Kingdom. My dream of playing for God had come true in far greater ways than I had ever hoped! We were keenly aware of His presence working through us. I was sorry to see the tour come to an end.

All through the years since college, God has continued to provide "cattle" in many ways. He faithfully continues to give me opportunities to see His power at work, to share His mercy with others, and to help other college athletes experience His "cattle" too.

For every animal of the forest is mine, and the cattle on a thousand hills. Psalm 50:10 NIV

GOD WITH ME AT EMMANUEL

Michael S. Stewart
President
Emmanuel College
Franklin Springs, Georgia

ENTERING MY FRESHMAN YEAR at Emmanuel College was a frightening experience. Several factors increased my anxiety about starting college. First, I had not been a shining star in high school. Studying was not a problem, but many times I felt bored with the whole notion of school. Second, my grandfather had died just a few months before. He and my grandmother had raised me. His death left my grandmother alone, and I worried about how I was going to pay for this venture. Third, although I was excited about attending Emmanuel in rural Georgia, I did not know any other person on the campus.

When the time came, Grandmother packed me up, tearfully said goodbye, and waved vigorously as I sped away to college, driven by an uncle whom I barely knew. But he gladly drove me the long distance from Maryland to Georgia and helped me to disembark my suitcases at the front doors of my new home—Wellons Hall.

There I was, a frightened young man alone in a sea of strangers, overwhelmed by feelings of inadequacy. It seemed as if all the baggage of my life was unpacked in that small college. Fears that I had kept well hidden for many years came forcefully to the surface. Abandonment, inadequacy, loneliness, and paralyzing fear overtook me. These feelings, though they were not unlike what many freshmen experience when they first arrive on a college campus, were my overwhelming reality.

At that small college named Emmanuel, which means *God with us*, God met me. The first way I encountered His grace was through the simple demonstration of Christian community. I found friends, not just among fellow students, but also among faculty and staff members. Some of these friendships have lasted to this day. The feelings of aloneness left as I found mentoring relationships with faculty who cared about me and my future. God was truly revealing Himself to me through the simple kind acts of people with lofty letters like Ph.D. and Ed.D. behind their names.

My second direct encounter with the grace of God came when I realized that I would be unable to complete my junior and senior years because I could no longer afford the tuition. My funds were limited, and Grandmother could not contribute. Though I was working as much as a student can, it was evident that I could not pay the bill.

At a critical moment, by the grace of God, I was asked to meet the college president in his office. He told me that if I would stay to complete my final two years, he had found an anonymous donor who would pay my entire bill. Of course I stayed. To this day, I don't know the identity of that generous person. But in gratitude for this life-changing gift, I have always tried to pass it on by helping other struggling students.

Today, that once-frightened young man who showed up at Emmanuel over thirty years ago now serves as president of that very college. The place where God met me still stands as a place where God meets young men and women in order to empower them to fulfill their destiny.

Humble yourselves, therefore, under God's mighty hand, that he may lift you up in due time. Cast all your anxiety on him because he cares for you. 1 Peter 5:6, 7 NIV

A LESSON IN NEED

Dwayne Uglem
President
Briercrest College
Caronport, Saskatchewan

THE THOUGHT of having to share my dorm room with someone else was one of the anxieties that troubled me most as I headed off to college as a freshman. I was already well acquainted with dorm life from my high school experience, but I had never had a roommate. I soon discovered that sharing a room was both better and worse than I had imagined.

As the year began, it became clear my interests and those of my roommate hardly overlapped. Our relationship was defined by, and essentially confined to, a common desire to study and learn without distraction from others, especially from a roommate. And so we separately lived our lives in a twelve-by-twelve-foot room for eight months. Today, I can't even remember the fellow's name, which says a lot about the nature of our relationship.

While I am naturally introverted, I always had friends, and in high school I considered myself to be moderately social. But in college it was all too easy to be focused on myself. Complicating the issue was the fact that I had already found the love of my life during high school. College was simply something that needed to be finished before we married. This understandably short-circuited some of the natural social interactions that often take place during college years. The other, larger part of the problem was I simply did not think I needed people.

In my second year of college, I had the chance to choose a roommate, and we actually built a relationship that deeply affected me in that year and in the years to come. An impetus for this came from a professor's direct challenge that I needed to include in my educational journey at least one chapter where I would invest in relationships and not just in studies.

My experiences raised new questions about the role people would play in my life. Even though I was stridently independent, I began to realize that all through that first year of college dorm life I had been consciously choosing to ignore something that God meant for good. I have no idea what I missed out on in that first year. In my second year, with a different perspective and a different roommate, I received a wonderful taste of what relationships could do for me. By the third year, I was married and a new circle of relationships emerged.

Thus, college became a journey of sorting out the role that I would allow people to play in my life and deciding whether I really needed people at all, beyond a very small group of friends. It was in my second and third years of college that my expanding circle of relationships enabled me to begin to see a picture of the body of Christ for the first time. I saw how being in relationship with God and with others completes me and gives me a context for life. I saw that relationships are not just instruments to be used when I need something, but that they actually shape the way I see myself and my world. I actually need relationships to live a full life. And that is one of the most important things I learned in college.

But woe to the one who falls when there is not another to lift him up. Ecclesiastes 4:10 NASB

THREE MEN AND A KNOCK ON MY DOOR

Paul Jordan
Professor of Computer Science
Southern Wesleyan University
Central, South Carolina

I WAS ON MY OWN for the first time at Appalachian State University in North Carolina. It had a reputation for stong programs in education, business, and computer science–and for partying.

Now what do I do? I thought. I could go where I wanted to go with little or no accountability. *Who do I want to be*? I could be my own person.

There was a knock at the door to my room on the third floor of Frank Hall. Hugh Whitfield and Mark Hodges had come to invite me to join them for church the next Sunday, followed by a meal for college students. Having grown up in church, I knew this would be a good move. *But I'm free. Is this what I really want to do*? I agreed to go.

Sunday came, and Mark pulled up in a van to pick me up, along with my girlfriend Vicki (now my wife) and other freshmen he and Hugh had reeled in. We were off to a church on a hill about ten miles from campus. When we arrived, I met the man who is, to this day, the inspiration of what I do as a Christian professor.

Roger Critcher, owner of Critcher Brothers Produce in Deep Gap, North Carolina, is a humble man. At five foot ten, his stature didn't get my attention as much as his character. His ability to reflect the love of Christ in a humble manner was immediately apparent.

During my years in college, I watched Roger Critcher. The man had built a multimillion-dollar produce business in Nowhere, USA. He only had a high school diploma, but he taught the College and Career Sunday school class at church. He's been teaching that same class since 1984.

I don't know the statistics, but I'd guess Roger is responsible for sending more people to seminary, to follow a calling into full-time Christian ministry, than any other person in North Carolina. Yes, because God has blessed him, he has financially helped students through school. But more than that, young people just want to be like him and do what he does–influence generations for Christ.

How different my life would be if Hugh, Mark, and Roger hadn't taken an interest in me at that critical time of my life. Roger says that he sells produce. He does, but he also plants seeds. Roger doesn't know the difference he has made in my life, but he influenced that young college student and has continued to influence me to become the man I am today. I am the spiritual child of this godly Christian man that I've watched over the years. And I'm grateful for that life-changing knock on my door.

The righteous man walks in his integrity; his children are blessed after him. Proverbs 20:7 NKJV

EDIFICATION FROM UNBELIEF

Eddie K. Baumann
Professor of Education
Cedarville University
Cedarville, Ohio

AS AN UNDERGRADUATE, I studied history and philosophy at a public university. Because I had served in the military, I was slightly older than most undergraduates starting college. Having come to Christ at fourteen, I had been nurtured in a strong fundamental church. Throughout high school and early adulthood, I was a voracious reader of the Word and of many godly proponents of the faith. Thus I believed I was prepared for the challenge of being a Christian philosophy student at a public university.

During discussions in class, I defended my faith against perceived challenges, soon developing a reputation among my peers as the "resident theologian." This provided me with opportunities to discuss Christianity and Christ. Often my classmates and I would convene in the Student Union to discuss the relevance of Christianity to life. These were serious discussions about serious issues, involving people with bright minds and sensitive, searching hearts.

I suddenly found myself an apologist for the social responses of contemporary evangelicalism. It was the early 1980s, a time of serious shifts in environmental policy, deregulation of business, and cuts in social spending while military spending was increasing. My peers started to ask how these policies aligned with the Bible; they wondered how the church could be silent or acquiesce to such policies. My response was to defend the stance of most evangelicals, though my peers' concerns caused me to start questioning some of my church's positions.

Soon the Lord began to teach me some significant lessons. It became apparent that I was not connecting with these people, that by defending the faith and trying to win the argument, I was losing the very people that God desired me to reach. I may have been speaking the truth, but it was not in love (Ephesians 4:15). My peers had been asking genuine questions and seeking valid answers; my response had been to treat them as the enemy, rather than as victims of the Enemy. The Lord impressed on me the need to show grace and mercy as I sought to show my peers the truth of the Good News.

I had been feeling compelled to answer all their questions; it was difficult for me to accept not knowing the answers. The points my peers raised represented serious shortcomings in how I applied my faith, causing me to doubt the answers I had previously learned.

Through this experience, God impressed on me the need to humbly submit to His teaching, even if He chose to use unbelievers, at times, to edify me. God showed me that these unbelievers often cared for the victims of sin in a more compassionate way than I did. Through these peers, God taught me that sin creates social injustices. And He impressed on me that I needed to act for justice, just as Christ acted for justice, to show Christ's love to a watching world.

He has showed you, O man, what is good. And what does the LORD require of you? To act justly and to love mercy and to walk humbly with your God. Micah 6:8 NIV

THE FOURTH MEETING

"Come and hear, all ye that fear God, and I will declare what he hath done for my soul."

Psalm 66:16

Pamela Coker Browning
Chair, Department of Early Childhood, Elementary and Special Education, Lee University

Stephen Woodworth
Chaplain, Montreat College

Bryce Jessup
President, William Jessup University

Martha Bradshaw
Associate Dean and Professor, Louise Herrington School of Nursing, Baylor University

David Wilkes
Dean, School of Arts and Humanities, Mount Vernon Nazarene University

Jerry Falwell
Chancellor, Liberty University

Leslie J. Van Dover
Professor and Graduate Chair, School of Nursing, Azusa Pacific University

James W. Mohler
Chair, Christian Ministries Department, Trinity International University

John Pate
Chair, Communication and Visual Arts, California Baptist University

Christina Sinisi
Professor of Psychology, Charleston Southern University

COMPREHENSIVE CONFIDENCE

Pamela Coker Browning
Chair, Department of Early Childhood, Elementary and Special Education
Lee University
Cleveland, Tennessee

WALKING DOWN the hill toward my office at the University of Tennessee, Knoxville, I saw him standing on the busiest corner of campus. He had a smile on his face and greeted each person who approached him. I recognized who he was and felt my heart drop. I didn't want another one of those little green New Testaments. However, as I watched student after student ignore him, I felt sorry for him and decided to let him add one more to my collection.

So I arrived at my office with two new acquisitions–the green Gideon Bible and the third set of questions for my doctoral comps. I was exhausted. It was Friday, the third of four days sitting at my computer writing for four hours. I had carefully chosen the sequence of exams so this day would be my easy day. The committee member who had prepared these questions had told me ahead of time what questions to expect, word for word. I had studied. I knew it.

I sat down at the computer and read the first question. Confusion hit. I read the second question. Panic hit. The third question was even worse. I was clueless. Anger quickly replaced my confusion and panic. Why would she tell me to study certain topics and then ask me completely different questions? I had actually studied additional material to impress her. Instead, I now found myself not even understanding the questions.

I picked up the telephone to call my chair and complain. A little voice said, "Stop." I replaced the receiver and decided that as a highly-stressed female, my next best option was to cry. The little voice spoke again: "Stop." My eyes fell on the little green book on my desk.

That New Testament I had reluctantly taken from the Gideon just moments earlier became my lifeline. A verse came to mind that I knew was somewhere in the fourth chapter of Philippians: "And my God shall supply all your need . . ."

I began at verse one in search of my "supply your need" verse. However, before I found it, I discovered verse 6: "Be anxious for nothing; but in every thing . . . let your requests be made known to God."

Verse seven offered more encouragement. "And the peace of God, which surpasses all understanding, will guard your hearts and minds through Christ Jesus." Then I arrived at verse 13. "I can do all things through Christ who strengthens me."

In that moment, God showed Himself to me. Feeling His peace, I prayed and returned to the computer. I decided to answer a question, even if it was not the question the professor had asked.

Somehow, I answered all three questions. Four hours later, I stopped writing and made the trek to my chair's office to return the much thicker envelope. I didn't say a word about the questions. I consider that to be one of my finest moments.

Several days later in my oral exams, the time came for me to defend my answers to the professor who had given me those questions for my written comps. She simply said, "I was very pleased with Pam's answers. I have no further questions for her." Obviously, God had given me the strength to do something I could not have done on my own.

I can do all things through Christ who strengthens me. Philippians 4:13 NKJV

THE CRISIS OF THE PERFECT HYPOCRITE

Stephen Woodworth
Chaplain
Montreat College
Montreat, North Carolina

I GREW UP in East Kingston, a picturesque but too- small coastal New Hampshire town that had a one-room schoolhouse, fishing derbies, and an annual lobster festival. I often felt as if the potential for my life was too large for the town's boundaries.

In my first attempt to escape, I was denied entrance to the one and only college I applied to. After spending the next year in an upholstery shop, thinking about my life's end while pulling tacks from old sofas, I was accepted into a college located in another too-small town: Montreat, North Carolina.

I had chosen Montreat College because it was a Christian school, and despite my casual approach to life, I had convinced myself that I was a Christian. I had been raised in a nominal Christian home. But like many teenagers, I was a perfect hypocrite, living one life during the week and another on Sunday mornings.

When I took my double standard to college with me, many people there quickly recognized it. Three such people were a beautiful Southern belle named Carrie, a worship leader named Jon, and Ed, the college chaplain. At the close of my freshman year, these three were planning to spend the summer leading a small-group ministry at youth conferences. The group needed another member, and the voice of God persistently badgered Ed until he reluctantly invited me to come along.

During the second week of the summer, far from home, friends, and vices, God broke me. Following a late-night meeting in Ocean City, New

Jersey, I was approached by a young girl who asked how to become a Christian. I lowered my head to walk her through a prayer I had mouthed myself many times before. But somewhere between "Jesus, I know I am a sinner," and "Will you come into my heart?" I realized with a profound conviction that my faith was a sham, and that this very prayer needed to become my own for the first time.

Later that night, I shared the experience with the whole ministry group. Ed invited the team to gather around me for prayer. Through tear-soaked eyes, I saw them come. Jon literally fell at my feet and embraced them with his forehead resting against my bare toes. I felt Ed's hands pressing hard on my shoulders. Carrie gently held my hand. It was one of the most tangible experiences of God's love I had ever known.

When we returned to school in the fall, my new family embraced me as their new brother. I moved into a house with Jon, Ed became a strong mentor to me, and Carrie eventually became my wife.

What did I learn in college? I learned in the most concrete way that faith cannot develop in a vacuum. As much as I had prided myself in my ability to go it alone, God showed me another way. As I sit today on the other side of the chaplain's desk at Montreat College, I smile in wonder at the availability of a few people, sold out to Jesus, who determined to be the body of Christ to a sinner in need.

Two are better than one, because they have a good reward for their toil. For if they fall, one will lift up his fellow. But woe to him who is alone when he falls and has not another to lift him up! Again, if two lie together, they keep warm, but how can one keep warm alone? And though a man might prevail against one who is alone, two will withstand him—a threefold cord is not quickly broken. Ecclesiastes 4:9-12 ESV

THE BLESSING OF A BIG DISAPPOINTMENT

Bryce Jessup
President
William Jessup University
Rocklin, California

I HAD PLAYED baseball in high school and some semi-pro baseball during my Bible college days. I had a strong yearning to play professionally. I had been given an opportunity to play with a farm club of the Pittsburg Pirates, but I hesitated. My Christian worldview made me hesitate. But the desire to play did not go away.

Following college, I headed for Oregon to take on my first full-time youth ministry. I was nervous, challenged, insecure, yet hopeful. The youth ministry work went very well. I grew and so did the youth group, but it soon became evident that I needed more education to develop the potential God gave me. As I explored graduate possibilities, I discovered I could get the graduate studies I wanted at Pepperdine University, and they had a highly ranked NCAA baseball team. The coach encouraged me to enroll and play. It seemed a perfect fit–graduate school and baseball. I could have the best of both because I was still eligible under the NCAA rules at that time since my undergraduate degree was from an unaccredited college.

I moved my family to Southern California to play baseball and pursue a graduate degree at Pepperdine. But to my great disappointment, the NCAA rules changed that same summer to state that any undergraduate degree, whether from an accredited or unaccredited college, disqualified a player from collegiate sports. I was devastated.

I talked with one of my professors about it. I told him of my deep passion to play baseball and how I had become ineligible to play for Pepperdine. I also told him I still could exercise my option to play professional baseball, as it had a five-year window of opportunity. His comment startled me. He said, "Why don't you go do it?"

It was the first time I fully realized I had a choice. It was all up to me. If I wanted to play pro ball, there was nothing stopping me. But deep down I felt it would be wrong to do it. That professor's challenge forced me to seriously consider the ramifications of abandoning graduate school and ministry. By so doing, it clarified for me that I really *did* want to preach. From that day on I never looked back.

The change in NCAA rules that summer forced me to quit struggling between two options. I either had to give my life fully to baseball or fully to ministry. I no longer could have it both ways. In forcing me either to quit baseball or to go pro, the rule change clarified for me that my real passion was to serve the Lord by helping people to know and grow in Him. That hugely disappointing situation turned into a huge blessing that gave me needed direction for my life.

Trust in the LORD with all your heart and do not lean on your own understanding. In all your ways acknowledge him, and he will make your paths straight. Proverbs 3:5, 6 NIV

THE HIGHEST FORM OF SERVICE

Martha Bradshaw
Associate Dean and Professor
Louise Herrington School of Nursing
Baylor University
Waco, Texas

I LOVED being in college. As a student at Baylor University, I enjoyed every minute of it. I particularly enjoyed being in the band because I made a lot of cool friends, played some great music, and got to go to all the football and basketball games and show my true school spirit. Yes, college was a great place to be.

But I loved it so much that at times I was in danger of forgetting why I was really there—I wanted to become a nurse. I had made that decision in high school. So I had come to Baylor for its nursing program. When the coursework began, however, I discovered that I preferred my English courses and playing in the band. I was doing better in those than the hard pre-nursing courses like microbiology and anatomy and physiology.

This made me stop and think about my future. Should I switch my major to English or music, which I was enjoying so much? Or should I stick with nursing, even though my grades were not as good in the science courses? After a bit of deliberation, I chose the path that would ensure me a job after graduation: nursing.

Once I entered the actual nursing courses, I still felt a little unsure of myself, but I began to feel a peace that this was what I was supposed to be doing. As I started working with patients, I realized how much I liked making a difference in their experiences in the hospital. I gained satisfaction from helping them recover from illness or surgery. I was happy being a servant to others.

When I graduated and began working as an RN, I was able to work with students from Baylor's School of Nursing. I felt a compassion for these students because I knew what they were going through. My desire to help them have a pleasant learning experience was the beginning of my life in nursing education.

After working elsewhere in nursing education for more than twenty-five years, I've now come full circle back to Baylor, a faith-based university that places Christian service at its core. But in every place that I've taught, I've had the opportunity to support and encourage students who are struggling as I once did. I can understand and empathize with young people who are academic "late bloomers" like I was.

My college dilemma was whether to make the effort to follow my dream of becoming a nurse in the face of other enjoyable interests. At the time, I couldn't see how God was using my predicament. Now I know that that experience has made me a better mentor to student nurses. Because I stayed the course that He progressively revealed to me, and let Him work out His will, I am reaping genuine rewards; by being a servant to my patients and my students, I enjoy engaging in the highest form of service, serving my Lord.

You did not choose me, but I chose you and appointed you to go and bear fruit–fruit that will last. Then the Father will give you whatever you ask in my name. This is my command: Love each other. John 15:16, 17 NIV

PORTRAIT OF A CHRISTIAN AS A YOUNG MAN

David Wilkes
Dean, School of Arts and Humanities
Mount Vernon Nazarene University
Mount Vernon, Ohio

I WAS A JUNIOR transfer student at a secular university when Stephen Dedalus declared himself a "monster" and walked away from his religious convictions, right there in the novel class. It didn't matter that Dedalus's world was a fictive one or that James Joyce, the author, was a Catholic while I was a non-denominational Young Lifer with no church tradition to reject in the first place. What mattered was that Stephen's experience had broken into the inner sanctum of who I was as a young believer. Only God had been allowed to go that deep; so when this confident apostate with his radiant "whatness of a thing" invaded my inner space, it really rattled my cage. I had never experienced such a willful denial of God before. How could I read books like this and still grow in my faith?

Not having much of a religious background had its pros and cons, I suppose. Although I wasn't bound by certain expectations, I also didn't have a sounding board off of which to bounce new or challenging ideas. And none of my dorm friends was the least bit interested in my faith and literature problems. They were budding chemists, political scientists, and biologists. Life seemed so simple and organized for them, and here I was starting to get desperate. Strangely enough, it never occurred to me to ask my pastor. Maybe deep down inside, I was afraid that he couldn't relate to my concerns.

So I did the next best thing. I got up the guts to visit one of my English professors whom I knew to be a high-church believer. She was an Americanist with a passion for the poetry of T. S. Eliot. (That had to count for something.) I actually drove my '65 Chevy pick-up with the oversized off-road tires into her groomed neighborhood and knocked on her very imposing medieval door. To my surprise, she was glad to see me. More than anything else in the world, I wanted to hear her say that I was on the right path, that God was larger than any fictional character I ran into, and that my fears of being infected were groundless.

I must confess, so many years later, that I can't remember a single word she said. What I do remember is her kind and generous spirit, her guidance and consolation. I would be fine, her presence told me. I was in God's hands. I wasn't a traitor to my faith. It would be all right. Just keep reading, keep learning, and keep processing.

I am grateful for that undergraduate encounter. Joyce's novel now has lasting significance for me. To this day, it reminds me of the spiritual hurdle I leaped over and of the professor who helped me, in Jesus' name, to do so.

And my God will meet all your needs according to his glorious riches in Christ Jesus. Philippians 4:19 NIV

MY FIRST GREAT FAITH EXPERIENCE

Jerry Falwell
Chancellor
Liberty University
Lynchburg, Virginia

WHEN I BECAME a freshman at Baptist Bible College in the fall of 1952, I began attending High Street Baptist Church. It was a big church, with more than two thousand members. I knew I would be lost in that church if I didn't get involved. The pastor suggested I work in the junior department.

The junior class superintendent said, "I don't have much hope for you Bible student types. You start strong and fade fast." After I pled for a chance, he gave me one eleven-year-old boy to work with. "That will be your test," he said. "If you can handle one student, just maybe you can handle more."

On my first Sunday, Daryl and I sat in two chairs in a corner of a large room with a curtain drawn around us. I taught from the Bible and he listened. After two weeks, the poor kid got desperate or bored enough to bring a friend for company. The weeks crawled. Nothing happened. After six Sundays, I told the superintendent I was quitting.

"Give me back the roll book then," he said, reaching out for the book. "I didn't think you would make it. I didn't want to give you a class in the first place, but did it against my better judgment."

"No," I shot back, my pride touched with hurt and anger. "I'm not going to quit." I grabbed the roll book back.

I went back to the college and got the dean of students to give me a key to an empty dorm room on the first floor of my building. Each afternoon for the remainder of the year, I went in there and prayed from 1:00 to 5:00 p.m. There was no mattress on the bed, so I just stretched out on the springs. During my first few sessions in that room, God broke my heart over my failure with the small Sunday school class. I realized if I were unfaithful in little things, God would never bless me in big things.

In that room I read books that motivated me to greater prayer challenges and faith commitment, books by Andrew Murray and a biography of George Mueller. Mueller's story taught me to think big, to tell God what I wanted and believe God for miracles. These and other books challenged me to pray confidently so I could minister confidently and changed my whole attitude toward serving Christ.

The next Saturday morning I began what became a regular practice of trying to recruit any eleven-year-old I could find to my Sunday school class. And every Sunday I loaded my '41 Plymouth with children and drove them to High Street Baptist Church. Soon I had to get my fellow college students who had cars to help transport children to Sunday school.

I gave the children Bibles and taught them how to mark and study them. I taught them the great stories from the Old and New Testaments. I held memorization contests where the boys would quote the verses they had learned by heart and receive prizes for their work. Of course, I found that teaching the Bible was the best way to learn it for myself.

Each Sunday morning at 11:00, I'd march the whole class into the sanctuary for the morning sermon. At the end of almost every Sunday worship service, I stepped forward with one or more boys, led them to pray to receive Christ at the altar, and then recommended them for baptism or church membership. On weeknight visitations to their homes, I led parents or older brothers and sisters of my eleven-year-olds to faith in Christ.

When I quit teaching a Sunday school class at the end of my first school year at Baptist Bible College, I had fifty-six regular members, and attendance in special class activities often swelled to more than a hundred eleven-year-olds. I was blessed to see so many of those boys become followers of Christ, as did many of their mothers, fathers, and friends.

There are many things I learned from this experience. One of the most important was that I truly realized for the first time that if I would pray and work, in that order, there was unlimited potential in the service of Christ.

If you can believe, all things are possible to him who believes. Mark 9:23 NKJV

FEARING FAILURE AND FINDING GOD

Leslie J. Van Dover
Professor and Graduate Chair
School of Nursing
Azusa Pacific University
Azusa, California

THE FIRST STATISTICS EXAM of the semester was coming, and I was worried. Failing it might end my career as a graduate student. Feeling weak and vulnerable was unusual for me; I was used to being successful in academic life.

But a lot was at stake. I had moved from Nova Scotia, Canada, to the University of Michigan in Ann Arbor to study for my Ph.D. in nursing. I loved working with student nurses as a classroom teacher and clinical instructor in the hospital and community. Failing this course would shatter my dream of furthering my career in nursing education.

In the small town where I grew up, life for my two sisters and me had revolved around our loving parents, school, and church. I had made a profession of faith, becoming a church member at age fourteen, but somehow faith had never come alive for me. So in the years after I left home, God crossed my mind only occasionally, and I seldom attended church.

Now at age thirty-one, I suspected I was in big trouble. Math had never been my strong subject, and my statistics professor seemed to delight in pitching lectures at a level of abstraction that left me struggling. Finally I got a tutor and began to learn more effectively, but I worried that it would be too little, too late.

A couple of nights before the fearsome exam, I was in the grad student lounge chatting with David, a man I had dated. Knowing he was a person of faith, I asked him to pray for me. To my surprise, he took my hand, bowed his head, and quietly offered a simple prayer on my behalf. I was amazed at the depth of feeling this experience gave me. For the first time in my life, someone spoke to God as if God was someone who loved me and sincerely desired to help me.

When I passed the exam, I was grateful to David, and his God, for being there for me. Several months later, when David had finished his degree and was preparing to head home to Dallas, he said to me, "You really should find a home church."

I took him seriously, and soon I began attending a warm and friendly church in nearby Ypsilanti. This action changed my life. The God who had seemed so real when David had prayed to Him became real to me. His loving power replaced my doubt and denial with newborn faith.

I had become a student in order to "seek truth" by learning how to do research. Ironically, I instead came face-to-face with the truth that God, who created me and loves me with an everlasting love, is real.

More than twenty years later, I am still amazed that God allowed me to experience His transforming love in such a tangible way. He used that simple prayer encounter to break down my wall of resistance to Him. Today I give thanks for all the gifts of faith, and especially for my husband–David.

Do not remember the sins of my youth or my transgressions; according to your steadfast love remember me, for your goodness' sake, O LORD! Psalm 25:7 NRSV

MY $65 EDUCATION

James W. Mohler
Chair, Christian Ministries Department
Trinity International University
Deerfield, Illinois

AS A YOUNG MAN just out of high school, I found the cost of a college education to be very daunting. My parents were unable to help me pay for tuition, so I knew that I would bear this financial burden alone. Though I wanted to attend a Christian college, I didn't see how I could ever afford it. Even so, I applied and was accepted at the Christian college of my choice. But about a month before school was to begin, I began to be filled with doubts about how I would be able to pay for school. Instead of going to the Christian college, I ended up attending the local community college.

This certainly was not what I had envisioned for my life. But within the year I had realized that it was God's plan for me to be at that community college. My faith grew and I was able to impact several lives for Christ. Also, during that year God put into my heart a desire to attend a different Christian college. I just knew I was supposed to attend this school, that God was going to do something special in my life.

So after a couple of years at the community college, I applied and was accepted at the college God had placed in my heart. But as the time for school to start neared, my doubts about finances plagued me again. How could I ever afford the tuition? I certainly did not have the resources. About one month before school was to begin, I was ready to pull out and find a state college to attend. But then God intervened.

One day I found an envelope on my desk at my church, where I was working as a ministerial intern. Inside the envelope was a letter from "a sister in Christ" and sixty-five dollars in cash. This anonymous "sister," also a student, had felt compelled by God to give me this gift. I never found out who she was, but that sixty-five dollars gave me the confidence to trust God with the costs of college. It was God's confirmation that I was to go to the Christian college to prepare for His work.

I worked hard to pay for as much as I could, and trusted God for a lot more than I could make. And God provided. I eventually earned a bachelor's degree and a master's degree, all without having to take out any loans for my education. The only loan I ever needed for my education was the very last semester of my Ph.D. work.

It was difficult for me to trust God for all of that money. I am so thankful that God compelled my "sister in Christ" to give me that gift. That sixty-five dollars strengthened my faith, and "paid" my way through college! These days, when I face financial challenges, I look back to that sixty-five dollars. It still gives me confidence that as long as I strive to remain in God's will, He will continue to faithfully take care of the details.

I have received full payment and even more; I am amply supplied, now that I have received from Epaphroditus the gifts you sent. They are a fragrant offering, an acceptable sacrifice, pleasing to God. And my God will meet all your needs according to his glorious riches in Christ Jesus. To our God and Father be glory for ever and ever. Amen. Philippians 4:18-20 NIV

A RAINCOAT AND A SMILE

John Pate
Chair, Communication and Visual Arts
California Baptist University
Riverside, California

THE ILLNESS had reached its zenith around 2:00 a.m. that Saturday morning in the spring of my sophomore year at Auburn University. I was sweating from a 102-degree fever, and my head hurt terribly every time I moved. The taste of blood in my mouth told me this was much more than a bad common cold. I had to get help.

I managed to roll out of bed and walk to the front door of my apartment, hoping that if I could make it that far, I might make it to the campus doctor. Struggling to put on a raincoat, aching with every movement, I stumbled out into the rainy night. Perhaps the motion of walking, combined with the sounds and coolness of the rain, allowed me to make it to the infirmary alive. I was feeling a bit better, but only for a brief moment. The front door was locked tight. I pounded on the window a few times, 99 percent sure no one would answer at 2:30 a.m., and I was right. So I began the long trek back home.

As I walked back through the village of Auburn, I stopped to rest in the park beside our Baptist Student Union. I sat on a cool, wet, concrete bench, and leaned my head back on the large round table slab. The raindrops felt so welcome on my face; they seemed to bring calm and healing. I rested there in a semi-comatose state for about two hours, praying to God to either kill me now or heal me soon.

Eventually a crinkling sound told me that I wasn't alone. I opened my eyes and blinked back the raindrops. Another poor soul sat about four tables over, a trash bag pulled tightly around his head and shoulders. I began to study his sad face. Deep wrinkles marked his forehead and brow, and his anxiety was of a more permanent ilk. I began to hurt for this man. I would soon recover from my malady; his would certainly continue. Beside him stood a shopping cart, filled with a bag of clothes, several stacks of aluminum cans, and a sign asking for food and work. He smiled briefly, and then leaned over the table to rest his head. Soon he was sound asleep.

I began to wonder how a culture allows this disparity. Here we both sat in the same lonely, rainy park, society granting me such privilege, and him such pain. I suppose I had known, somehow, that hurt comes in all forms; I just had never realized it until now. As we both sat in this helpless state, even my nineteen-year-old sophomore mind understood that I could not cure his problems, and he could not cure mine. But God's instructions are clear. I quietly walked over, laid my raincoat on the man's cart, and headed toward home. It was a simple transaction. He had given me a smile. I gave him my raincoat.

The rain was stopping, the first light of dawn was appearing over the horizon, and I was feeling no pain. I smiled, thanking God for my recovery and for the lesson He taught me in this exchange of a raincoat and a smile.

If anyone has material possessions and sees his brother in need but has no pity on him, how can the love of God be in him? 1 John 3:17 NIV

MONOPOLY ON HURT

Christina Sinisi
Professor of Psychology
Charleston Southern University
Charleston, South Carolina

I ATTENDED Hollins College on scholarship, multiple summer jobs, and the money that came in from Daddy selling the cows. Though I had grown up only half an hour away, the school and my house with the tin roof might as well have been worlds apart. Hollins catered to girls who came from "old money" and good families. I came from neither.

My roommate and I met when we were interviewing for that scholarship I so desperately needed. As we spent the day on campus, we found that we were interested in the same things. When we arrived at Hollins for our freshmen year, we realized both of us had found a place we belonged.

During our sophomore year, she started planning on a semester abroad. I ached. Even if I could have scraped the money together, I couldn't afford not to work. I had visited her family the year before, and the memory of their beautiful house and of her summer spent at their cabin in Maine made me cold with envy, even when the old radiators in our dorm room banged out so much heat that we opened the windows.

One night she told me about the dresses she had bought for the cotillion at nearby Washington and Lee. The conversation brought all my shallowness to a head. How could she talk about such things when she knew I couldn't afford one dress, much less three? The only dress I owned was a thrift store treasure.

I can't remember her answer. Something to the effect that she hadn't thought anything of it; she was sorry. Then, I was sorry that I'd said anything. And we made up.

We drifted apart. We stayed friends, but the next year she was an R.A. and I found a roommate from a less affluent background.

Several years later, I was in graduate school half a country away. She had taught English for a few years in Japan. The letters were few. So, my having a dream about her being ill and the terror with which I scrambled out of that dream and into wakefulness shocked me. I called her, which, with my penny-pinching ways, shocked me again.

She had cancer–a brain tumor. Had we remained close friends, I could have been walking through the black tunnel with her. It hurt to realize that. Instead, jealousy had eaten at me, for what? Now, I had a husband and I lived, if not in ease or wealth, at least in comfort. And so what good had the jealousy done me?

When Jesus told us not to judge, I always thought of others' sin. But we can just as easily judge others' good fortune. God does not promise us an easy path, but neither should we feel superior in our hardship. We are all poor in spirit at some point in our lives, and we are better for having had those times of weakness. The memory of those times will help us to lift up others when they are down.

Judge not, that you be not judged. Matthew 7:1 NKJV

THE FIFTH MEETING

"Come and hear, all ye that fear God, and I will declare what he hath done for my soul."

Psalm 66:16

Mark Davis
Dean of Students, Pepperdine University

Charles White
Professor of Christian Thought and History, Spring Arbor University

James P. Helfers
Professor of English, Grand Canyon University

Barbara Howard
Professor and Director, Academic Support Center, Northwest Nazarene University

Lucile C. Lacy
Professor of Music, Oakwood College

James A. Borland
Professor of New Testament and Theology, Liberty University

Karen Lea
Professor of Education, Trevecca Nazarene University

Glenn E. Sanders
Professor of History, Oklahoma Baptist University

Deborah Gayle Copeland
Chair, Department of Education, Geneva College

Beatrice Hill Holz
Professor of Music Education and Voice, Asbury College

NOT THE HAIR BUT THE HEART

Mark Davis
Dean of Students
Pepperdine University
Malibu, California

HOW COULD THIS HAPPEN? My first day on campus and I landed in the Dean of Students' Office. Dean Campbell seemed just as surprised. "What brings you here today?"

"Well, I don't know," I said with an innocent shrug. "I was in line at New Student Orientation, and when I tried to turn in my registration card, the woman at the counter gave me a funny look and said I'd have to see the dean before I could complete my enrollment."

"Oh," he said, and gave me the same "once over" scan that had landed me in his office. "It must be your hair. It's over the collar. You're going to have to get it cut."

Dean Campbell must have read the you've-got-to-be-kidding look on my face. So he quickly followed with a response that I didn't expect from the dean. "Hey, you need to know that being a Christian has nothing to do with the length of your hair."

"So why am I here?" I asked.

"The truth is," he said, "some of our board members feel very strongly about our students having a well-groomed look, and on the heels of the hippie movement, we have a dress code that I have to enforce. I've got a feeling the code will change one day. But for now, we really don't have a choice. You're going to need to get your hair cut."

Looking me in the eye, he continued speaking. "But what I'm most concerned about is not your hair. It's your heart. I don't want this encounter to embitter you or to cause you to think that we believe Christianity is all about externals."

And from there we had a friendly conversation about campus life and all the good things I could expect to experience during my college years. Dean Campbell transformed an awkward encounter, which could have ended in a heavy-handed enforcement of rules, into a teachable moment to extend grace and to help me understand my new campus culture. I left his office feeling valued as a person.

Dean Campbell's kind and gentle manner not only smoothed a bumpy start for me, but also made a lasting impression. Today, as a university Dean of Students myself, I'm grateful for the lesson I learned from Dean Campbell about the importance of treating students with special care when discussing university rules and policies.

Looking back at my haircut ordeal, I am also reminded that although we often get caught up in outward appearances, God goes much deeper. It's easy for us to be overly impressed with how people look, and miss the heart of the matter. It's good to be reminded—especially by the dean—that college is more about the heart than the hair.

But the LORD said to Samuel, "Do not consider his appearance or his height. . . . The LORD does not look at the things man looks at. Man looks at the outward appearance, but the LORD looks at the heart." 1 Samuel 16:7 NIV

WHAT I LEARNED AT HARVARD

Charles White
Professor of Christian Thought and History
Spring Arbor University
Spring Arbor, Michigan

AS I CROSSED the bridge over the Charles River on the night of April 15, 1969, I could see there was trouble. Students were running up and down the streets while shouts and sirens filled the air. On my way to my fourth-floor room, I stopped at the room of my radical friend, Dave. He had been out demonstrating and now was back to get protection from the tear gas the police were shooting. He said if you soaked your bandana in water and then put it across your nose and mouth, the tear gas wouldn't hurt you.

Like most of the things my radical friends believed, this idea was nonsense. Tear gas immobilizes you, wet bandana or not.

They were also wrong to think that throwing rocks at the Cambridge cops was a blow for freedom, that breaking the windows of the local bank would bring capitalism to its knees, and that shutting Harvard down would liberate the oppressed people of Vietnam.

But while my radical Harvard classmates were wrong about politics and economics, they were right about one central truth: "living room liberalism" was dead. Being moderate, endlessly balancing both sides of the question, being sympathetic to all sides, yet doing nothing—that was worthless.

Being at Harvard radicalized me. I learned that either Jesus is God and I must follow Him passionately, or else there is no god and no passion in life. I discovered that the Bible is either God's Word, truthful in all it affirms, or else it is an infantile illusion. I found that money is either a trust from God to be used to feed the poor and extend His Kingdom, or else it is a cruel master that makes people its slaves. I realized that sex is either God's good gift to a married couple, or else it is a nasty trick evolution has played on us.

Harvard taught me to think hard about an issue, to examine it from all perspectives, ask all the hard questions, and follow the truth wherever it leads. That's where I learned that when I have found the truth, I must obey it at the cost of my life. Only then can I begin to love the Lord with all my heart, soul, mind, and strength, and start to love my neighbor as myself. Only then will I be a real radical.

"Love the Lord your God with all your heart and with all your soul and with all your mind." This is the first and greatest commandment. And the second is like it: "Love your neighbor as yourself." Matthew 22:37-39 NIV

COLLEGE AT THE CROSSROADS

James P. Helfers
Professor of English
Grand Canyon University
Phoenix, Arizona

I WAS AT A CROSSROADS in my Christian life when I graduated from high school in Arkansas. As a kid, I'd lived in my head, in my imagination as I read books, and also in my rational mind. I enjoyed using my brain. Because of this intellectual bent, I was often a slightly bemused spectator of the emotional aspects of the revivals that were part of church life. Yet I also felt the contradictory pull of my heart to participate in these emotional outpourings. I wasn't sure I could be a committed Christian *and* be a serious intellectual.

But my head kept nagging at me. As I considered college, I felt as if I was living two lives: the conventional evangelical life of considering missionary work, and another life of wondering if there was anyone out there with a sharp mind who embraced Christianity. Because nothing in my church experience had ever acknowledged the great Christian intellectual heritage that attempts to "bring every thought captive to Christ," I couldn't reconcile the intellectual with the spiritual.

I chose to attend Wheaton College in Illinois. It was there that God met me at the crossroads. I signed up for the Vanguards wilderness program, thinking that it would just be a romp in the forest. I should have known better. The course readings challenged me intellectually and spiritually–I and II Kings, *Your God Is Too Small*, and *Man's Search for Meaning*. The program included active pursuits like backpacking, camping, climbing, and rappelling. But we also spent quiet time fasting, praying, thinking, and examining ourselves.

This program gave me a unique opportunity to reflect on my goals. I had wanted to become an engineer or a missionary pilot. But as I got to know myself better, I became convinced that my gifts were not primarily in mathematical understanding or practical flying skills. Instead, I discovered a talent for writing.

Having a clean slate of career goals, I embraced my undergraduate experience with an open mind and heart. I found my professors to be people who thought deeply, yet who were deeply committed to teaching, to getting to know me, and to Christ. They lived out for me the insight that they taught: "All truth is God's truth, wherever it may be found." They also attempted to bring every aspect of their lives into consistent obedience to God's truth. I'd never seen this kind of committed education before; I was used to the public school system, where my learning method was to sit quietly in the back of the classroom, read all I could, and make furtive critical comments about class proceedings. Wheaton professors made me participate.

Ultimately, my college experience convinced me that God is the author of truth. My love for the exercise of my mind deepened, but I also developed an ideal of integrating my Christian faith with my academic knowledge. I entered college thinking that the life of the mind and a genuine Christian faith were two unrelated roads. But only after I worked in the business world for some years did I comprehend how my four years at a Christian college had radically altered my perspective and my sense of purpose. Those two roads are one as God calls me to commit my heart and my mind to Him.

See to it that no one takes you captive through hollow and deceptive philosophy, which depends on human tradition and the basic principles of this world rather than on Christ. Colossians 2:8 NIV

ONLY A FIVE-DOLLAR BILL

Barbara Howard
Professor and Director
Academic Support Center
Northwest Nazarene University
Nampa, Idaho

I WAS INSTANTLY attracted to the little wooden plaque. The decoupaged picture on the front portrayed an old-fashioned lamp, an open Bible, parchments, and a pewter dish of walnuts sitting on a rugged old table. It reflected my life at that time as a full-time graduate student.

The lamp in the picture would have fit perfectly in the tiny room I rented in the old Victorian home near campus. The open Bible reflected my studies in Christian education and my love for God's Word. And the nuts symbolized the nutritious but simple meals I ate with my fellow graduate students.

Even though the plaque was only $4.99, my wages from a part-time job did not cover such a luxury in 1974. With sadness over my financial situation, I continued perusing the gift shop while waiting for my clothes to dry at the nearby laundromat. *Maybe some day I'll be able to purchase items to dress up my little room*, I thought with a sigh. Then, trying to dispel any hint of self-pity, I added, *Hasn't God provided wonderfully for me to attend graduate school?*

I walked back to the laundromat to retrieve my clothes and meet up with my housemates. *I don't even have a car*, I whined to myself as we rode home in my housemate's car. Sitting in the backseat, I could sense myself slipping into a mood of discouragement. It seemed ridiculous that the little plaque could have such power to sway my attitude and spiritual walk. Fortunately, the conversation at dinner that night was lively and spirited. Enjoying my friends lifted the gloominess I had experienced in the gift shop.

As the busy days rapidly progressed, I didn't have time to remember my self-pity. Toward the end of the week I received a letter from my sister. I opened it, anticipating a newsy letter catching me up on her life. Much to my surprise, she had enclosed a $5 bill. In her note she said that she wanted me to use the money on something "extra"–something just for myself. My sister had never sent me money before, nor has she ever since. I just stood there staring at that $5 bill. *How did she know? Why would God care if I had that little plaque or not?* God's sensitivity and His desire to surprise me with this little gift amazed me.

I still have that little plaque. It has graced all of my offices, reminding me of my housemates, and of the wonderful experiences I had in graduate school. But it also serves a much higher purpose than just helping me to recall those long-ago days. It reminds me of my Lord Jesus' desire to delight me with His love. It is amazing what an ordinary $5 bill can mean when it comes from the hands of God.

The LORD your God is with you, he is mighty to save. He will take great delight in you, he will quiet you with his love, he will rejoice over you with singing. Zephaniah 3:17 NIV

PROFESSOR X AND THE LIBRARY BOOK DROP

Lucile C. Lacy
Professor of Music
Oakwood College
Huntsville, Alabama

WHEN I WAS A TEENAGER, a high-school teacher told me that I would never be a success in my life and that I'd be a detriment to society. It was the first time anyone had made such a sweeping negative evaluation of my potential, and I was devastated.

After completing a master's degree in music teacher education from George Peabody College for Teachers, I taught college for several years. Then I prayed, "Lord, if it is Your will for me to pursue the doctorate degree, prepare the way." Unexpectedly, I was awarded a United Negro College Fund Teaching Grant for $10,000, renewable annually. This to me seemed a notable honor for one who had been told by a professional educator that I had no future.

I wanted to get my doctoral degree from Ohio State University. From a pool of 400 applicants, I was one of the ten accepted into the program. Soon I met Professor "X" who told me that, as a Seventh-day Adventist, I had no chance of succeeding as a doctoral student at OSU. The graduate music program was impossible to complete while missing the Friday night and Saturday sessions. He said I should either attend the classes as required or withdraw from the program. I left his office determined to complete the program and keep the Sabbath.

One Friday afternoon at the end of one semester, Professor "X" gave the class an almost impossible "take home" final examination. It was due the following Monday and would require exhaustive research in the library all weekend.

Two hours before sunset on Friday, I closed up all my studies and prepared for the Sabbath. Saturday evening some of my classmates called to wish me success. They had spent all Friday evening and all day Saturday in the library and were far from finished.

By Sunday evening, after ten hours of research, I had answered three of the exam's ten questions. I stopped and communed with God for one hour. Then, one hour before the library closed, I was impressed to walk down the stacks. Praying silently, with tears running down my cheeks, I felt nothing but despair when suddenly, in front of me, a book dropped from the shelf and fell open to a page of information I needed. I quickly picked up the book and continued to walk down the aisle when another book fell from the shelf. Books began falling from high and low, faster and faster. Each book was opened to an exact answer.

I grabbed a cart and moved quickly down the aisle picking up books. The library assistants heard the sounds of the books falling from the shelves and asked if I knew who was throwing the books. I just smiled through my tears, rejoiced in the Lord, and kept on picking up those books.

I was the only student in the class who completed the entire exam. Professor "X" was shocked.

I have found that people cannot set limits for us when we pray and completely depend on a loving God who honors those who trust in Him.

Thou hast commanded Thy precepts to be kept diligently. O that my ways may be steadfast in keeping Thy statutes! Then I shall not be put to shame, having my eyes fixed on all Thy commandments. Psalm 119:4 6 RSV

HE CALLED, I ANSWERED, HE PROVIDED

James A. Borland
Professor of New Testament
and Theology
Liberty University
Lynchburg, Virginia

DURING MY SOPHOMORE YEAR at UCLA, I lived at home and attended every service at my local church. I even participated on church visitation night. I was so interested in the Bible that I read it completely through in three months, notes and all while keeping up with school. I was thinking about transferring to a small church-related Christian liberal arts college just to study the Bible for a year, and then perhaps return to UCLA.

One day on campus I visited my Sunday school teacher in his office in the UCLA physics department, where he was a professor. I told him what I was thinking. He suggested that I hear guest Bible teacher, Frank Logsdon, at a nearby church. That Friday I went. The message spoke to my heart. I sensed a deep call to serve Christ full-time. With a crowd of others I went forward to publicly express my call to full-time ministry. At age nineteen, I honestly felt that my life would be wasted if it were not used full-time to serve Christ. I might have forty years left to serve Christ in the ministry, and I wanted them to count.

Returning home, I continued to pray and fellowship with the Lord over this decision. My parents were out for the evening. The next day I shared my decision with them. Sometimes parents are not so eager to see their offspring enter the ministry. Other options seem more secure or financially rewarding. My father asked, "The ministry? Do you want to starve to death?" I suppose he was aware of the meager salary that many churches paid their ministers.

After satisfying my parents about ministry as a career, I faced the second challenge to my new heartfelt sense of call to service: money. The "incidental fee" I paid at UCLA was just $83.00 per semester. Since I lived at home, that was my only expense. My father wanted to know who was going to pay for this new educational venture at a private Christian college, including room and board, and he asked in a way that made it clear it wouldn't be him. The costs were substantially higher. I imagined getting a job. The minimum wage was about $1.25 per hour. I would have to trust the Lord for His provision. I have since heard the phrase, "Where the Lord guides, He provides."

Before long I was enrolled at the Christian school. By then, my father had softened and was willing to pay half the costs. A school bus driving job paid me $2.60 per hour and covered my share of the expenses. It is hard to describe how excited I was to have godly men and women teaching me the Bible, theology, and Greek in formal college classes. Later came three seminary degrees and more life-long learning and studying. God has graciously allowed me to serve him beyond the meager forty years I had anticipated. At age sixty-one with good health, I do not envision retirement anytime soon, just continued full-time service as God gives me the strength and the abilities to continue.

I know that God inspired that UCLA physics teacher to tell me to go hear Frank Logsdon. And He inspired Frank Logsdon with just the right words that planted the call to ministry in my heart. He worked on my father's heart to help pay the bill. In short, God called me when I was a nineteen-year-old student at UCLA. I answered. And He has provided for me all the way.

He who calls you is faithful, who also will do it. 1 Thessalonians 5:24 NKJV

MY SUCCESSFUL FAILURE

Karen Lea
Professor of Education
Trevecca Nazarene University
Nashville, Tennessee

WHEN I STARTED my freshman year of college, I signed up for sophomore mathematics courses, feeling very confident of my abilities. I did great that year, thoroughly enjoying the challenge and fun of the higher-level mathematics. The time spent in study groups, solving problems and discussing multiple solutions, was like brain candy for me.

During my sophomore year, as a mathematics major, I earned my first "F." I was devastated; my ego was crushed. I was sure the professor had made a mistake and I couldn't wait to show it to him, so I spent hours poring over that graded exam. Yet, as I compared my exam with the exam of a friend, I realized the professor was right.

Eventually I found the courage to stand in the door of his office. Close to tears, I held up my paper for him to see. I will never forget the look of compassion on his face. "I don't know of anyone who doesn't need to back away sometimes and try something again, at least once in life," he said. "That does not reflect on you or how smart you are. In fact, it makes you smarter." He then suggested that maybe I had jumped ahead by taking on an upper-division course before I was ready.

I dropped the class that semester. When I took it again the next year, I was ready for it. And that time, I earned a good grade.

I didn't fully appreciate or understand my circumstances in that moment of failure. But in the intervening years since that time, I've reflected on how God turned those circumstances into good in my life, shaping who I am as a teacher.

My professor's words come back to me when a student sits in my office, distraught because she has failed a test, or devastated because she has not passed a course, or even a required state exam. While I can't change the grades they have earned, I can offer reassurance that trying something again is not always negative. It may be the most important lesson they need to learn at that moment in their lives—much more important to their future than the particular momentary failure.

If I hadn't gone through that devastating experience of failure myself, I might not understand what my students are feeling in those moments. Or I might be tempted not to hold them accountable. I'm glad that God used my caring professor to teach me to require accountability, but with compassion, encouragement, and hope.

And we know that in all things God works for the good of those who love him, who have been called according to his purpose. Romans 8:28 NIV

PROVIDENCE THROUGH PUZZLEMENT AND LIVING THE QUESTIONS

Glenn E. Sanders
Professor of History
Oklahoma Baptist University
Shawnee, Oklahoma

I FIRST READ Leo Tolstoy's *The Death of Ivan Ilych* in a sophomore course on existentialism. My first semesters at Baylor University had introduced me to the intellectual exhilaration of studying history and literature. But this course showed me how significant ideas really could be.

Tolstoy's story proved particularly potent. It challenged my comfortable, lower middle-class lifestyle with its tale of how the worldly and ambitious Ivan grows sick and confronts death. Ivan finally comes to the shattering realization, "Maybe I did not live as I ought to have done."

I know now that such concerns are part of becoming adult. Over the last thirty years, I've helped twenty-somethings have the same experience, because I believe that "living the hard questions" serves God's Kingdom. Living the hard questions reminds us of human finitude and the need for faith; it suggests new ways to love God and neighbor; it clarifies the character of injustice and impels us to right action.

But when I was learning to think about such matters, I could only feel overwhelmed, uncertain, and disoriented. I grew dissatisfied with what I then saw as the superficial religiosity of church life. I sometimes felt distant from God.

Strangely enough, even as I started confronting these hard questions, I continued to participate in a Friday afternoon mission program for local children that I had joined during my first year. A group of five or six of us would travel to a low-income area to spend a couple of hours playing tag, telling Bible stories, and singing "Father Abraham" with the children.

I don't know why I continued to participate. I was not consciously enacting an authentic faith to which I felt drawn. I didn't see the mission as a "real world" to counterbalance my heady world of ideas. I just liked the kids and the friendships that I shared with the other student volunteers.

As a historian, I know that while the past must be interpreted in its own terms, its significance usually becomes clearer when examined in the context of the present. And yes, historians have to deal regularly with the "made up" quality of the past. Memory and desire play tricks on the "realities" of our experience. Even so, I have come to understand my own past better as I've looked back. Now I can see that my early adult questioning and my mission work actually complemented each other. The two experiences suggest to me that thought and living go together. Today I see God's providence in the way these two experiences paralleled one another.

I still read Tolstoy. In "A Confession," as he reflects on how his search for faith drew him to the peasants, I remember my own question-asking and my mission work. The real world was a fitting counterpoint to my best thinking, guiding that thinking to productive ends. Now, as the Tolstoy of my youth continues to pose hard questions, I can be assured that, in the midst of puzzlement, God always provides.

And my God will fully satisfy every need of yours according to his riches in glory in Christ Jesus. Philippians 4:19 NRSV

FINDING THE ULTIMATE FRIEND

Deborah Gayle Copeland
Chair, Department of Education
Geneva College
Beaver Falls, Pennsylvania

SITTING IN THE DARK closet with scissors in hand, I was thinking how tired I was of trying to be everybody's friend. Maybe if I just hurt myself, I thought, I would know who really cared about me. I didn't want to kill myself. I just wanted to feel loved.

I had been extremely popular in high school. But now, in a small Christian liberal arts college, I felt isolated. These people were certainly different from the Californians with whom I had grown up. Why were they so hypocritical? The guy that I really liked barely knew I existed. What was wrong with me? I was the good college student that I was supposed to be, wasn't I? I was really trying to live a faithful and obedient Christian life, only to feel extremely lonely.

This time was a turning point in my faith and life. I had been negotiating my faith in my head for the two and a half years I had been in college. I had thought through several alternative faiths and philosophies, even atheism, only to arrive at being unable to dismiss the personal nature of God. Whoever God was, He had to be a personal Being. I could not rid my mind of the obvious place of a personal Creator in this universe. But in the midst of this mental debate, I felt as if my view of a personal God was somehow disconnected from my attempt to live a faithful and obedient Christian life.

As I huddled there in the dark, hiding from everyone, I cried uncontrollably, questioning God's ways. Why did He bless others who weren't trying to live faithful and obedient Christian lives with an abundance of friends?

Time passed, and eventually it dawned on me that I was focusing on others and what they were doing or not doing. I had lost sight of why I was to live an obedient and faithful life. I had lost sight of what I thought a personal God was to be. I began to feel more like a lonely Pharisee. I knew I was a Christian, but I wasn't feeling that the Lord was the "joy of my salvation." I had been trying to make my life in *my* image of Christian success.

At that moment in the dark, God brought into my mind some famous words He spoke to Jeremiah. As those words went from my mind to my heart, I continued to cry out to God, but rather than wailing and complaining, I now asked Him to forgive me for my selfishness. I emerged from that dark closet with a desire to fully surrender my whole heart to God, who loves me more than I can fathom.

"For I know the plans I have for you," declares the Lord, "plans to prosper you and not to harm you, plans to give you hope and a future. Then you will call upon me and come and pray to me, and I will listen to you. You will seek me and find me when you seek me with all your heart." Jeremiah 29:11-13 NIV

THE FALSE ACCUSATION AND THE MISSED WITNESS

Beatrice Hill Holz
Professor of Music Education and Voice
Asbury College
Wilmore, Kentucky

IN MY FIRST freshman English class at the University of Cincinnati, the professor gave us the most predictable of assignments imaginable: write a short essay (two pages, double-spaced) on something memorable about your summer. I wrote my essay as assigned and handed it in at the next class. The professor returned our essays to us at the beginning of the third class. When she handed my paper to me, I was shocked to see large scrawling red ink across the top that read, "See me after class."

I'm sure I didn't hear a single bit of the remainder of the class lecture. I couldn't imagine why I needed to see the professor after class. An introvert by nature, I was apprehensive about speaking to her. When the class finally ended, I walked nervously up to the desk, paper in hand and heart pounding, to find out why I didn't have a grade on the top of my assignment like everyone else did.

"Did you copy this story from somewhere?" the professor asked. My throat was so constricted I could hardly speak. The story was a simple description of an experience at a music camp I had attended just a month before, the place where I had fallen in love with my husband-to-be. How could she think I had plagiarized such a personal event?

After I assured the professor of my innocence, she gave me a look of serious doubt before placing an "A+" at the top of the paper and handing it back to me in surly silence. She dismissed me with a peremptory hand gesture. I was humiliated at having been falsely accused of plagiarism, and even more embarrassed by the flaming cheeks and the threatening tears that I was sure everyone could see as I left the building.

It was the last day of the first week of classes; drop-add would not end until five o'clock. I ran across campus to the office where class changes were being processed, and I promptly signed myself up for a different English class. I wonder to this day if that professor took my dropping her class as a confession of guilt.

I was a Christian then, but certainly not one who read the Bible and took it to heart for my daily life. Had I been, I might have remembered that Scripture teaches us to expect suffering. Then maybe I would have thought more about being a witness in that situation rather than running away from it. But I was far too concerned about how I looked to others and desirous of making good impressions. I shied away from "shining my light" because I feared offending the professor or being further shamed by her disapproval. Had I placed God's approval first and let Him lead me, I might have seen Him use the situation to His glory and for my good.

Today, I pray for protection against that desire to blend in to the point that others can no longer see Christ in me. I pray that, rather than pulling away from challenging situations in which He sometimes places me, I will let Him work in the midst of those circumstances to see His purpose fulfilled.

I pray also that the eyes of your heart may be enlightened in order that you may know the hope to which he has called you, the riches of his glorious inheritance in the saints, and his incomparably great power for us who believe. Ephesians 1:18, 19 NIV

THE SIXTH MEETING

"Come and hear, all ye that fear God, and I will declare what he hath done for my soul."

Psalm 66:16

Dan Struble
President, Montreat College

Charles L. Quarles
Vice President for the Integration of Faith and Learning, Louisiana College

Jeff Kisner
Professor of Religion, Waynesburg College

Lydia Huffman Hoyle
Associate Professor of Church History, Campbell University

David R. Smith
President, Brewton-Parker College

Margaret Britt
Associate Professor of Management, Southeastern University

Doyle J. Lucas
Professor of Management, Anderson University

Brenda Duckworth Bradford
Business Division Chair, Missouri Baptist University

Pamela L. Bryant
Chair, Department of Physical Sciences, Howard Payne University

Steve Badger
Professor of Chemistry, Evangel University

A SUMMER OF GODLY DESIRE

Dan Struble
President
Montreat College
Montreat, North Carolina

I WAS RAISED in the Presbyterian Church but walked away during my teen years. As a rising junior at the United States Naval Academy, I began searching for answers to the fundamental questions of life. The more I searched, the deeper my sense of ennui.

The summer after my junior year was filled with more travel and excitement than most people experience in a lifetime–piloting and jumping from airplanes, combat simulations in the Quantico forests, diving submarines, driving destroyers, classified briefings on the Soviet threat, and European travel. Amid all that excitement, I still felt empty.

In the middle of that amazing summer, God in His wisdom sent two key people into my life: a fellow midshipman with an evangelistic bent and a young woman named Karen. My midshipman friend sensed that I was searching, so he invited me to church (the first time I had been in several years). I listened closely to the pastor's sermon. It was based on Psalm 37:4: "Delight yourself in the Lord, and He will give you the desires of your heart." The sermon touched me because God had recently given my heart a desire I had never known before.

Just a few weeks earlier I had met Karen. It was on July 4, 1981, in Paris. I fell in love that very day and felt confirmed in that love when she and I (and a half dozen of her friends) went to dinner the next evening. Unbelievably, I had to leave Paris later that night to continue with my summer training. And Karen was going to Denmark for the rest of the summer and would then return to Texas, far from Annapolis, Maryland.

It seemed impossible for two people who had spent only a few hours together in Paris and who lived more than a thousand miles apart to build and sustain a relationship. Nevertheless, my heart was filled with a God-given desire. Karen, however, was cautious. She wanted to be sure that I shared her faith before she would risk getting close. She answered my long letters of that summer with one short one. At the end of it, along with her signature, she appended an item in the shorthand with which we Christians are so familiar–a simple Bible reference: "Ps. 37:4."

I received that letter from Karen on a Monday, the very day after hearing the sermon on that same text which had so touched me.

I was astounded. With so many verses to choose from, could it possibly be a coincidence? Was it possible that my life-search for meaning, my first-ever Godly desire for a woman, that pastor's sermon, and this woman's probing for a shared faith could all coincide by chance? Or was

God working to change my life and call me to Him? I thought both possibilities were long shots, so I committed myself to reading the New Testament through during the next week. When I finished, I declared that God was sovereign and I committed my life to Him. And sometime later I committed my life to Karen, who became my wife.

Delight yourself in the LORD and He will give you the desires of your heart. Psalm 37:4 NIV

THE RAGING PROFESSOR AND THE FREEDOM OF TRUTH

Charles L. Quarles
Vice President for the Integration of Faith and Learning
Louisiana College
Pineville, Louisiana

WHILE ATTENDING a state university, I took a course called "Sociology of Death and Dying." My professor, whom I will call Dr. Gary, was a staunch secular humanist. Dr. Gary and I developed a close relationship during the semester. I frequently visited his office to discuss the various theories he had introduced in class.

On one of these visits, I objected to a sociological theory that disagreed with my Christian convictions, defending my position by quoting the Scriptures. Our discussions had always been very friendly, but at my mention of Scripture, Dr. Gary flew into a rage. "Don't ever quote that book in my presence," he shouted. Reaching up to his bookshelf, he pulled down a copy of Karl Marx's *Communist Manifesto*. Waving it in the air, he screamed, "You have your Bible and your God. Here is my Bible and I am my own god!"

I walked out of his office trembling, both wounded and baffled by his reaction. I replayed the conversation in my mind, trying to understand why he had acted so aggressively. I concluded that our interchange that day was not the result of a personality clash. He clearly liked me and I loved him. Our sharp disagreement was the result of a clash of two very different worldviews, two very different ideologies, two very different gods, and two very different books. I sought to view reality through the lens of the Holy Scriptures, in light of the truths revealed by the God of the Bible. But Dr. Gary interpreted reality through the lens of a contrary human philosophy that deifies humanity and elevates human philosophies above divine revelation. Because each of us appealed to two very different gods and two very different books, our views on reality were light years apart.

That experience was foundational to the development of my commitment to distinctively Christian education that integrates the truths of the Christian faith with every aspect of learning. Some institutions permit Marx to speak but refuse to give Jesus a hearing, but Christian professors in the classrooms of Christian colleges can compare and contrast the views of Marx and Jesus. Claims that compete with Christian views can be clearly and fairly presented because Christian professors are confident that their faith is true and that the truth will prevail.

Dr. Gary's response to my use of Scripture is just one example of how the Bible is banned and God is muzzled in many secular settings. Education that takes place in such settings, because it is not grounded in Christian faith, all too often produces students who are "ever learning, and never able to come to the knowledge of the truth" (2 Timothy 3:7). But as a Christian professor in a Christian institution, I am grateful that I have the opportunity to unleash God and His Word and let Him speak. After all, the greatest learning takes place at the feet of Jesus, the Master Teacher.

In [Him] are hid all the treasures of wisdom and knowledge. Colossians 2:3

A CAR OR A KINGDOM

Jeff Kisner
Professor of Religion
Waynesburg College
Waynesburg, Pennsylvania

LIKE MANY YOUNG MEN of my generation, I made my car an extension of my identity. Between high school and college, by working for a small business in my hometown, I had earned enough cash to buy my car and modify it to race at the local drag strip. The success I enjoyed at the drag strip, and the prestige of owning a race car that I could drive on the street, gave me a measure of status and pride I had not experienced before.

At the same time, I became involved in my home church and made a commitment to follow Christ's way. I grew close to the pastor of my home church. Apparently he saw something in me that I did not see in myself; he encouraged me to think about college.

About a year and a half later, I began my undergraduate journey. Preparations for the journey included trading in my race car for a more responsible car, one that got great gas mileage and had a few creature comforts like air conditioning and an eight-track player.

In spite of the amenities, the 450-mile drive to college was difficult. I was excited to begin this new chapter in my life, yet I shed tears of grief along the way. The emotional turmoil continued for several days; I wept about leaving family, girlfriend, friends at work, and my short-lived notoriety for my "hot car."

Then it got worse. As I was going through college orientation, a kindly and soft-spoken gentleman, whose intimidating title was "Controller," informed me that I could not afford to make payments on my new car and pay my tuition, too. Give up my car?!

I soon called my pastor back home and poured out my burdened soul to him. Then, after regaining my composure, I walked to the office of my faculty advisor, whom I had met briefly just the day before. Soon, as I explained my dilemma to him, I was again drowning in a pool of tears. The decision to leave all behind had been excruciating enough; but I was now being called to give up the palpable extension of my identity: my precious wheels! At that moment, I prayed as I had never prayed before for God to empower me to make the right decision.

I did. I drove my car to a dealership an hour away and sold it for the "payoff," that is, the amount I owed the bank for the loan. I was car-less for an entire academic year. But as a result, I invested myself deeply in campus life, my studies, and new friends. I often tell my own students today that my college experience was an opportunity to be "born again," to give up an old way of being and doing and take on a new way of Kingdom life. The sacrifice was well worth it.

Another said, "I will follow you, Lord; but let me first say farewell to those at my home." Jesus said to him, "No one who puts a hand to the plow and looks back is fit for the kingdom of God." Luke 9:61, 62 NRSV

ONE STEP AT A TIME

Lydia Huffman Hoyle
Associate Professor of Church History
Campbell University
Buies Creek, North Carolina

MY BEST FRIEND when I was a child was Greg, a boy who lived down my street. For as long as I can remember, Greg knew that he wanted to be a pharmacist when he grew up. His favorite toy was a chemistry set. He dispensed "pills" from his candy stash. As he grew older, Greg took lots of science classes, knowing that he would need them to study pharmacy. Eventually, he went to college and became a pharmacist.

All along the way, I longed to share Greg's certainty about the future, but my prayers for direction brought no answers. No vocation ever seemed quite right. Everything was a possibility, and I could not rule out many options. Even after selecting a major in college, I had no idea what I might ultimately do.

As a college senior, I attended the Urbana Student Mission Convention sponsored by InterVarsity. I was fairly certain that I was not called to missions, but I desperately wanted direction. So I jumped on a bus full of strangers and journeyed six hundred miles to Urbana.

One day while I was there, as I was walking across the University of Illinois campus, a young guy with a beard appeared beside me. Without sharing the usual niceties or introductions, he asked me, "So, where are you headed next?"

"I'm going to seminary," I answered. My own words shocked me. I am not sure that I had ever even known a woman who went to seminary. I cannot remember consciously considering the option prior to that moment. By the time I could see through the cloud of shock that surrounded my words, the bearded guy was gone. I was left with an odd mixture of peace and excitement.

That day, I began to realize that my understanding of God's will would only come in small increments. I only knew that I should go to seminary; I did not know why I should go. But as I was faithful in following the limited light in front of me, I would always find more light to reveal the next step. Sometimes, my foot would already be in the air, searching for a place to land, before there was light to guide the way.

Today, I still feel that the journey would have been easier if I had known my direction before I started down the path. But perhaps then I would have missed the joy of looking back and seeing how God has used all the twists and turns in my life to prepare me for this moment.

Commit your way to the Lord; trust also in Him and He will do it. Psalm 37:5 NASB

A WAKE-UP CALL AND A CALLING

David R. Smith
President
Brewton-Parker College
Mount Vernon, Georgia

AS A FIRST semester freshman, I quickly learned that college students enjoyed much more freedom than high school students. No parents demanded that we keep a schedule, and no truant officers enforced mandatory attendance in class. Enjoying this newfound freedom, my evenings began to consist largely of spending a lot of time meeting girls in the student center and taking late-night snack trips to a popular hamburger restaurant on the far side of town.

Unfortunately, those late nights made it difficult for me to get up the next morning for my 8:00 a.m. history class. But because I had always enjoyed history, I already knew most of the material that was being covered in class, so I didn't mind missing an occasional morning lecture.

I was fast asleep in my dormitory room one morning when a loud knock shook the door. I stumbled groggily out of bed, noting that it was

7:15 as I went to open the door. The shock of seeing my history professor standing outside my room registered clearly on my face.

"Is there any reason that you have missed my last three lectures?" he asked.

"No, sir," I stammered, now fully awake.

"Are you ill this morning?"

"No, sir. Just a little tired."

"Then I expect to see you in my history class in forty-five minutes," he said. Then he turned and walked away.

I never missed another class. In fact, I began to meet that professor for coffee and conversation at 7:00 a.m. a couple of mornings each week. We developed a fast friendship that continues to this day. Now in his mid-eighties, this fine man still corresponds with me and encourages me in my work on a Christian college campus.

My history professor taught me that freedom, for people of faith, comes with responsibility. He showed me the importance of always looking for ways to help others develop good habits of godly living, just as we've been mentored by those who have served as our examples. Through my history professor, God woke me up to the responsibilities of my calling to serve Him.

Be strong in the grace that is in Christ Jesus. And the things which you have heard from me in the presence of many witnesses, these entrust to faithful men, who will be able to teach others also. 2 Timothy 2:1, 2 NASB

SEEDS SOWN IN AN AGE OF RAGE

Margaret Britt
Associate Professor of Management
Southeastern University
Lakeland, Florida

I WAS NOT a practicing Christian during my college years at the University of Massachusetts. It was the age of rage. Angry, rebellious students, ostensibly protesting the Vietnam War, would shut down campuses on the slightest of pretexts. Although I never participated in those events, I watched the chaos from the sidelines and wondered, "Is this all there is to life?"

A group called Campus Crusade for Christ held weekly meetings in our Student Union. There were other students who read the Bible and were not ashamed to say so. This made a lasting impression on me because these students were so different from those who were caught up in the political events of the day.

Although I went to church on Sundays, Christ was never a part of my daily life. God was an intellectual concept and someone very remote. The idea of a personal God could not be found on my radar screen. The Bible was just another book that was filled with stories.

During my sophomore year, I was required to take a course in biblical literature. The professor stated many times during the course that she could not interpret the meanings because this was a literature course and not a "religious" Bible course. This was my first real exposure to the Scriptures. I became curious to know what kind of book the Bible really was.

What I didn't realize then was that seeds were sown into my life at a state university that would germinate six years later. At the age of twenty-six, I had a conversion experience and began to read the Bible, not merely as an intellectually curious bib-lit student, but as a devoted follower of Jesus Christ. As I tell both undergraduate and graduate students now, the Bible is the only book that forever changed my life, and it all started imperceptibly at a very secular state university.

And we know that all things work together for good to those who love God, to those who are the called according to His purpose. Romans 8:28 NKJV

A HEART FOR SERVICE, A MIND FOR BUSINESS, AND A CALL TO TEACH

Doyle J. Lucas
Professor of Management
Anderson University
Anderson, Indiana

I WAS BORN into a blue-collar working-class family in rural western Pennsylvania. It seemed likely that I would follow a path similar to that of my father or my uncles, all of whom spent their working lives as general laborers on a farm or in coal mines, glass plants, and steel mills. However, encouraged by my pastor, my high-school teachers, and my mother's persistent prayers, I applied and was accepted to attend my "church" college in Indiana.

My outlook on life changed significantly during those four years of college. I didn't have a "road to Damascus" experience, but I was changed by the patient care of people who served God and who had my best interest at heart. I gradually came to understand that to fully love God, I needed to love and serve Him with my mind as well as with my heart and hands.

Like many college students, I struggled with finding God's purpose for my life. I believed that people who wanted to serve God were called into the pastoral ministry, and I was wondering why this wasn't happening to me. I prayed, watched, and listened, but I saw no handwriting on the wall, nor did a voice from a cloud disclose God's calling for me.

I've always loved learning, but I didn't know what to study. Eventually I settled on a major in business management, reasoning that a business degree would help me to get a job after graduation.

One day in the fall of my junior year, the still small voice of God spoke to me through the calm tone of a beloved Christian business professor. I had just given a short classroom presentation. After class, the professor called me aside and quietly asked me if I had ever considered going on to graduate school and then teaching at the college level. Given my family heritage, this had never crossed my mind. It didn't really register that day either.

However, that simple encounter with my godly professor began to simmer in my mind. It eventually worked its way into my heart as well. I began to realize that, given my love of learning and my desire to serve God, it was possible that He was actually calling me to serve Him vocationally as a business professor at a Christian college or university.

During my senior year I explored this calling further and received nothing but encouragement from my professors, my friends, and, most importantly, my parents. After graduation, I returned to Pennsylvania, got married, and began a job in industry. But the call to love God with my mind and serve Him as a professor had not left me, so I intentionally sought employment that would permit me to also begin graduate studies and to accept a part-time faculty position. Some time later, I was offered a full-time faculty role at my alma mater.

After twenty-five years, through God's grace and call, I find myself having the opportunity to come alongside students who desire to discover and prepare to fulfill God's purpose for their lives. Like my professor and mentor did, I listen for God's prompting; when appropriate, I quietly speak what I sense God wants me to say.

Jesus replied, "'You must love the Lord your God with all your heart, all your soul, and all your mind.' This is the first and greatest commandment." Matthew 22:37, 38 NLT

I WASN'T SUPPOSED TO BE THERE

Brenda Duckworth Bradford
Business Division Chair
Missouri Baptist University
St. Louis, Missouri

AT THE BEGINNING of my senior year at Soldan High School, I talked with my senior counselor about my future. I was excited and ready to hear what he suggested for me. As I sat there anticipating positive affirmations, he told me that I needed to learn how to type so that I could be someone's secretary. He said that I was "not smart enough to go to college." He never even looked at me.

I walked out of the office feeling like I was too dumb to even exist. In the hall I ran into my friends, who were all excited because they had been given applications for college. They asked me what college I was applying to. I couldn't tell them what my counselor had just said. So, spying a brochure for Washington University in St. Louis on the floor, I picked it up and acted like I had dropped it. I told my friends that my counselor had given it to me. It was a lie, but at the moment I was too crushed and embarrassed to allow anyone to know what I had just experienced.

The brochure had a pre-stamped tear-off, and I filled it out and mailed it. Shortly afterward I got a letter telling me the dates to take the ACT exams. I had no idea what that was, but I went to take the test. It was hard! I figured I'd never hear from them again, so I put it out of my mind.

However, God had another plan. About seven months later, I was sitting in the school auditorium on Senior Awards Day telling jokes to my friends. I was startled when Mr. Brasfield, our principal, called my name. I went up on stage, thinking that I might be in trouble for not paying attention. Surely I wouldn't be getting any award–I was "not smart enough." But when I got there, he presented me with a Career Scholarship from Washington University.

I started my freshman year at Washington University with tremendous difficulty because I just wasn't academically prepared for college. My advisor arranged for me to get help with my reading and math skills. I withdrew from two of my classes and got intensive tutoring in math, reading, and study skills. By second semester, I was ready to take a full load of classes.

From that point on I was on the Dean's Honor Roll. After completion of my undergraduate degree, God opened a door for me to receive a full paid fellowship for graduate school.

God allowed my challenges to prepare me to minister to young people going through life's journey. God turned my weaknesses into His tools to reach people who feel that they'll never be good enough. His love made it possible for me to go beyond what I could have ever dreamed.

We also glory in tribulations, knowing that tribulation produces perseverance; and perseverance, character; and character, hope. Now hope does not disappoint, because the love of God has been poured out in our hearts by the Holy Spirit who was given to us. Romans 5:3-5 NKJV

HARD WORK LOST, GOD'S GIFT RECEIVED

Pamela L. Bryant
Chair, Department of Physical Sciences
Howard Payne University
Brownwood, Texas

A YOUNG PERSON at my church calls me "Smiley," because I am always upbeat. That is exactly how I started my first semester at Augusta College in Augusta, Georgia. I was ready to conquer this new world. Math had always come easy to me, so I decided to get a math degree. I was fascinated with my classes, and was getting great grades. I loved the college life, even if I did have to live at home and bum rides to school.

Financing this great adventure was challenging. My parents didn't have the money to pay my college fees, nor would they allow me to apply for loans or grants. But somehow I just knew that God would provide if I trusted in Him. I put that trust into action by babysitting, tutoring, working part-time in the church office and at youth camps, and working in the math department at school. All of this work combined covered the expenses for that first year.

I worked all through the next summer at a Christian-oriented conference center. By the Sunday before school started, I had made just enough money to cover tuition and expenses for the fall of my second year. I could hardly wait for school to start.

That Sunday, when I sang in the choir at church, I left my purse in the choir room. For some reason, I had all the money I had earned in my purse, ready to pay tuition Monday morning. While we were singing, my purse was stolen, along with all my tuition money. My whole summer's hard work gone! Now what would I do?

I went home discouraged, but not devastated, because I remembered that I still had money that my aunt had sent to me. That should be just enough to get me started for the fall. I told my family what happened and asked Dad for the money from my aunt. He said he was sorry but he had spent it. I would not be able to attend college that semester.

I don't really remember or understand how it happened, but my church quickly raised money to help me go back to school. My mother asked her boss for help, too, and he gave her some money to help with my tuition.

So I got to go back to college that fall semester. But it wasn't my hard work that got me there; it was God's love, poured out to me through the gifts of His people, that provided for me that semester. And God continued to provide for my needs. He gave me all that I needed to complete my bachelor's degree in math. Later he supplied the resources to help me through a Ph.D. degree in chemistry at Louisiana State University, and post-doctoral work at MIT. I will never forget the love God showed me at that critical time in my life, through the generosity of my church family and the courage my mother had to solicit her boss's help on my behalf. That's why I can keep smiling–because God keeps on loving and caring for me.

Delight yourself in the LORD; And He will give you the desires of your heart. Commit your way to the LORD, Trust also in Him, and He will do it. Psalm 37:4, 5 NASB

THE DEPRESSED WITNESS

Steve Badger
Professor of Chemistry
Evangel University
Springfield, Missouri

DUSK SLOWLY turned the colors in my living room to shades of black and gray, just like my dark mood. My depression was not so much from loneliness as it was from the painful scars of a recently abandoned sinful lifestyle. I prayed for relief, but God didn't seem interested in my feelings. Instead of comfort, I felt His Spirit directing me to visit a fellow graduate student, my friend Steve.

Steve and I had been friends through most of graduate school. We'd shared a sinful lifestyle, and he'd watched, much closer than I'd realized, as God changed my life.

Now God was urging me to visit Steve, but I was paralyzed with self-pity. And I was annoyed with the Lord, because rather than comforting me, He was saying, "Go tell Steve that I love him."

I silently argued with God. "I'm going to tell him just how depressed I've been. Don't expect me to hide that." I dreaded arguing "religion" with this Catholic-turned-agnostic scientist. His brilliant mind had an amazing knack for ferreting out faulty logic. Couldn't God see I was in no condition to witness to Steve?

But with a heavy heart, I obeyed God and drove across town. Steve was pleasantly surprised to see me. After a few minutes of chatting, he asked me, "How are you doing?"

Speaking slowly, and with conviction, I fulfilled my threat. "Today has been the most depressing day of my life."

"I thought Christians didn't get depressed," he responded. "I thought life was a bed of roses for Christians."

"It hasn't been like that for me," I replied. "And I don't think faith in Christ guarantees a carefree life." Instead of preventing a significant witness, this comment provoked an amicable discussion about faith. He told me about his childhood in parochial schools and his concept of Christianity. I explained that my trusting God included trusting Him during depression.

When our conversation ended, I felt that Steve was no closer to finding God's salvation. So I challenged him before I left. "Read the New Testament. Ask God to reveal Himself to you." He gave no indication that he'd do it.

More than a year later I heard that Steve had come to faith. I was skeptical, but it was true. Christians and non-Christians alike were impressed with the way God transformed his life.

A few years after that, my friendship with Steve was rekindled when we began attending the same church. One night, as we rode home together after church, we were reminiscing about how God had worked in our lives. I asked him what he'd thought the night I'd visited him during my depression. Steve didn't even recall that I had been depressed.

I couldn't believe my ears as he told me that, instead, he remembered that he'd been alone and lonely, feeling unloved, and I'd knocked on his door. Steve's eyes filled with tears as he thanked me for loving him enough to come over and visit him. He told me that that was a pivotal night in his life, the beginning of a months-long odyssey culminating in his new life in Christ.

And I'd almost missed it!

But in your hearts set apart Christ as Lord. Always be prepared to give an answer to everyone who asks you to give the reason for the hope that you have. But do this with gentleness and respect, keeping a clear conscience, so that those who speak maliciously against your good behavior in Christ may be ashamed of their slander. 1 Peter 3:15, 16, NIV

THE SEVENTH MEETING

"Come and hear, all ye that fear God, and I will declare what he hath done for my soul."

Psalm 66:16

Michael Wilkinson
Associate Professor of Sociology, Trinity Western University

Karen G. Doenges
Assistant Vice President for Academic Administration, Mount Vernon Nazarene University

Malcolm Russell
Vice President for Academic Administration, Union College

Steven R. Cramer
President, Bethel College

Sydney N. Giovenco
Associate Professor of Languages, Northwestern College

John D. Booth
Professor of Music, Hannibal-LaGrange College

Walt Mauldin
Vice President for Student Life, Lee University

Larry V. Ort
Vice President for Academic Affairs, University of Sioux Falls

Ron Walborn
Dean of Bible and Christian Ministry, Nyack College

Kent Olney
Professor of Sociology, Olivet Nazarene University

THE PROFESSOR AND THE OPEN DOOR

Michael Wilkinson
Associate Professor of Sociology
Trinity Western University
Langley, British Columbia

IT WAS LATE Friday afternoon and I needed to get the reading for next week from my anthropology professor. I made my way to the university campus and into the old building where my professor had his office. As I walked down the hall, I could see that his door was ajar. I could hear him talking quietly on the phone, though I couldn't overhear the conversation. I waited patiently a few steps away from his door until he hung up the phone.

"Michael, is that you?" he called out. "Please come in." He motioned for me to sit down, which I didn't really have time for. I only wanted to get the handout for next week's class. But before I knew what was happening, he began to tell me how his son was in trouble with the police. He was obviously distraught.

Only six months before, I had begun my graduate studies at the university, having just completed my undergraduate degree in sociology and anthropology. This professor taught one of my favorite classes, anthropology of religion. We were reading about new religions, old religions, unfamiliar rituals, magic, priests, and prophets. There was a certain energy in the class. Everyone participated and we knew that our professor thoroughly enjoyed the weekly exchanges.

Following one of those classes, the professor and I were having an extended conversation about religion. "It's obvious that you are a Christian, but there's something different about you," he said. "I had a student last year who only wanted to argue with me about what he believed, and why I needed to reject evolution and become a Christian. I don't know why he thought I believed in evolution. I never talked about it in class. He just assumed I did. I just want to say, I appreciate your contribution to the course."

Now here I was, late on that Friday afternoon, sitting in my professor's office, listening for nearly an hour as he talked about his son in need. As the conversation was coming to an end, he said, "My son needs God. He needs God like you've got Him." I couldn't believe what I heard. My self-proclaimed Jewish agnostic, Oxford-trained anthropology professor was asking me to pray for his son.

As I walked to my car that afternoon, I thanked God for the open door. Through that door, my unbelieving professor had sensed God in my life, and in his time of need, had begun to reach out toward what he saw of God. Today, as I reflect on my university experience, I thank God again for the many doors that were open for me to live faithfully for Him.

On arrival, they got the church together and reported on their trip, telling in detail how God had used them to throw the door of faith wide open so people of all nations could come streaming in. Then they settled down for a long, leisurely visit with the disciples. Acts 14:27, 28 *The Message*

CONFIRMATION IN THE TRASH

Karen G. Doenges
Assistant Vice President
for Academic Administration
Mount Vernon Nazarene University
Mount Vernon, Ohio

IT WAS A COLD November evening as I made the all-too-familiar trek to Columbus from my home in Mount Vernon. Already tired and discouraged after a long day of teaching, driving through the snow and wind in the dark was not helping matters. I was trying to balance being a wife and mother of three teenagers, being a full-time mathematics teacher, and being a Ph.D. student at Ohio State University. I was more than halfway through my doctoral program, but at times I wondered if it was really the Lord who had brought me to this point. This quarter was proving to be especially difficult, with a night class in qualitative research. It was held, of all places, in the Aviation building, far from any student parking.

When I arrived on campus, the usual ritual of finding a parking place was exceptionally difficult, and so I was running late when I finally parked the car. As usual on these winter nights, I had not worn my coat in the car. When I climbed out of the car, before I could turn and reach back in for my coat, the fierce winter wind blew the door shut. I was locked out–my purse, keys, coat, and backpack inside.

Stunned, I didn't know quite what to do. Obviously, I would need to get into the car sometime. But if I worked on that right now, I might miss the whole class period, for which I was already late. This class met only one night a week, and since it was early in the quarter, I didn't know anyone in the class to call for notes. So there was no option–I headed to class.

I will never forget that night. Walking half a mile in the cold without a coat was very disheartening. Was God trying to tell me something? I finally got to the building, colder and even more discouraged.

Since I didn't even have a pencil or paper to take notes, I snatched some paper out of a trash basket outside the classroom. To my surprise, there was also a sharpened pencil lying on the floor. I grabbed the pencil and stepped into class.

As I slipped into the only empty seat in the room, embarrassed because I was late, I looked down at the papers from the trash and could hardly believe my eyes! There in my hands were ten copies of the hymn "Trusting Jesus."

"Simply trusting every day, Trusting thro' a stormy way;
Even when my faith is small, Trusting Jesus, that is all.
Trusting as the moments fly, Trusting as the days go by;
Trusting Him what-e'er befall, Trusting Jesus, that is all."

I still did not know how things would end that evening, or what would lie ahead as I worked to finish my doctoral program. Never before or after that night did I ever see anything to do with a Christian hymn at OSU. But I knew that I was where God wanted me to be. He had used papers in a trash basket to tell me.

Trust in the LORD with all your heart and lean not on your own understanding. Proverbs 3:5 NIV

SAFETY IN NUMBERS

Malcolm Russell
Vice President
for Academic Administration
Union College
Lincoln, Nebraska

GRADUATION from college provided me with very little immediate gratification after shaking hands with the college president on Saturday night.

The next day I moved out of the dorm and started working at the only job I could find immediately: cleaning up construction sites with a crew whose specialized vocabulary made one word serve as verb, subject, and adjective.

Soon, however, notification of my acceptance into graduate school the fall term suggested that the rough hands and mental boredom would only be temporary. A few days later my *alma mater's* misfortune became my opportunity. Columbia Hall, the graceful administration building at Columbia Union College, had burned down a few months before, and Gordon Madgwick, the dean of students, needed help in organizing records that had escaped the flames but suffered water damage.

This being a task far more suited to my recently completed history major than picking up trash around new condominiums, I eagerly applied for the position and was hired. That summer taught me much about life, both from my fellow workers and from odd bits of information in the files themselves.

However, the most vivid lesson that summer came from Dr. Madgwick himself. He stopped to chat one day while I was recording some data, a task that required only modest attention, and he soon addressed the topic of life in graduate school and the professional world.

The discussion began about a recent sermon that had inspired us; then, it drifted to sermons and church services that left no discernable effect. Despite the quarter-century since then, Dr. Madgwick's chat seems clearer in my mind than this morning's lecture.

Education and graduate school might change me, he said, and very possibly my local pastor's sermons might fail to interest me spiritually or intellectually. But beyond any arrogance that such a conclusion might suggest, it was simply too dangerous to cultivate the idea that as an intellectual I would benefit more by staying home from services to commune with God privately through study and prayer. The slope, he said, very quickly became treacherously steep, and soon the Sabbath and other vital aspects of the church and faith would seem insignificant.

Simply put, he made it plain that someone who stayed away from church too often strayed from church. By contrast, even if the sermon was boring, the music was flat, and the "discussion" during the Bible education hour amounted to reading notes from the study guide, attendance brought a vital renewal in the truth.

To this day, I cherish that advice from Dr. Madgwick. Living in areas quite densely populated with church members, my family and I have been fortunate both in the pastors we have heard and the convenience of an alternate congregation.

On occasion, I have missed church, particularly while traveling. But Dr. Madgwick's advice to a young graduate student has been a guiding light in my life, and one I am obligated to share with others.

Not forsaking the assembling of ourselves together, as is the manner of some, but exhorting one another, and so much the more as you see the Day approaching. Hebrews 10:25 NKJV

A SOLID FOUNDATION

Steven R. Cramer
President
Bethel College
Mishawaka, Indiana

MY FATHER was a bricklayer by trade while I was growing up. Occasionally he received calls from customers, asking him to fix a crack in a wall he had built—what had been a small thing at first had become a major flaw in the building.

One day as we traveled to one of those jobs, I asked my father what had happened. He explained that although he could make the wall look acceptable, the problem was not in his work. It was in the foundation. The foundation had not been rightly laid, and until it was fixed, the problem would only reappear and get worse.

That conversation wouldn't come back to me until the middle of my sophomore year at a small Christian college. I had enrolled at that school only to fulfill the expectations of others. Lacking any focus in my life, I had performed poorly and had decided to drop out. I hadn't told my parents of my decision, but the college's concert choir director noticed I had not enrolled for the next semester. He summoned me to his office.

We spent an hour talking about life, the future, and faith. He helped me see that this decision would lay the foundation for my future. It would set a pattern. He talked of my potential and of the talents that God had given me. I remember very little of the actual conversation, but it came at a time when I needed encouragement, when I needed someone to believe in me, before I even believed in myself.

During this time I was reminded of Jeremiah 29:11, with its assurance that the Lord has a plan for each us, and of 1 Corinthians 3:10-13, which says there is only "one foundation" on which to build my life.

Suddenly my father's words about bricklaying came to mind with new meaning. I chose to stay in school and allow a strong foundation of faith and learning to be established in my life. The faith that professor had in me and a reawakened faith I placed in the Lord became the strong foundations for a life of service.

For no one can lay any foundation other than the one already laid, which is Jesus Christ. If any man builds on this foundation using gold, silver, costly stones, wood, hay or straw, his work will be shown for what it is, because the Day will bring it to light. It will be revealed with fire, and the fire will test the quality of each man's work. 1 Corinthians 3:11-13 NIV

TWO KINDS OF SERMONS

Sydney N. Giovenco
Associate Professor of Languages
Northwestern College
St. Paul, Minnesota

IT WAS AN EARLY September morning. The note from the Dr. Erickson, a vice president at North Park College, was brief and to the point: the loan I had requested had not come through. I had forty-eight hours to vacate the dormitory, unless I paid the four-hundred-dollar balance of my tuition, room, and board for the fall semester. That was a large sum of money in 1962. I had been depending on that loan because I knew my parents could not help me.

That night I couldn't concentrate on my studies. How would I even *continue* my studies? Where was I going to find a place to live in forty-eight hours?

The next morning, I was too upset to go to classes, so I took a stroll just off the edge of the campus. As I walked, I came to the North Park Covenant Church. Stopping to admire the majestic gray stone Protestant church, I felt that perhaps someone there might help a Catholic like me.

I climbed the stairs, entered the church, and went to the secretary's office. "Good morning," she said, recognizing the North Park College sweatshirt I was wearing. "What can I do for you?"

"Could I speak to the pastor?" I asked.

Soon I found myself in Pastor Cedarleaf's office, explaining my situation. I asked him if the church could hire me for a month or two, or if there was someone in the church who could use my services. He said he would think about it. "I'll let you know by tomorrow," he reassured me. His answer was all I had for hope.

On Wednesday morning I found a brief note in my mailbox: "Sydney, be sure to see Dr. Erickson this afternoon." That was all. No signature. No date.

That afternoon, after waiting for an hour, I was ushered into the vice president's office. "Sydney," he said, "you may be allowed to finish the semester. You have my support, but this cannot happen again. I don't know who you talked to, but your financial situation, though resolved for the time being, is serious." Dazed at the unexpected turn of events, I thanked him and left his office elated. I was allowed to remain in my classes, and I did not have to move out of Burgh Hall.

The following Sunday morning, I worshipped for the first time at the North Park Covenant Church of Chicago. At the end of the service, as I was exiting through the massive doors, Pastor Cedarleaf shook my hand, smiled, and asked me how I was doing. He said nothing to acknowledge the part he apparently had played in keeping me in school.

After that, I saw Pastor Cedarleaf every Sunday morning. The day I joined his church he invited me for lunch at his home. His powerful sermons were clearly inspired by the Spirit of the Lord. Those sermons that he preached, and the one he acted out in my behalf, provided spiritual guidance for me, profoundly shaping the course of my life.

Fear not, for I am with you; Be not dismayed, for I am your God. I will strengthen you, Yes, I will help you, I will uphold you with My righteous right hand. Isaiah 41:10 NKJV

FROM PROBATION TO "MOST IMPROVED"

John D. Booth
Professor of Music
Hannibal-LaGrange College
Hannibal, Missouri

MY FIRST WEEK at college was the most exciting yet most devastating time in my life. That one week helped define much of what happened in my college experience. This being before the age of advisors, students were expected to arrange their own class schedules and figure out the maze of college life after one week of orientation.

Not only was it a new academic world for me, it was also a brand-new world of faith. Just a month before coming to this Baptist college, I was born again. I grew up a preacher's kid who said all the right words and did all the right things, but I had never made my faith truly personal until I was eighteen. I came to college as a new convert.

During freshman orientation, I learned that because of my major, I had to audition for the music department. I hadn't known I needed to audition, so I had nothing prepared. But I was the best singer in my church, so I thought I should be able to do this. On my way to the appointment, I picked up a hymnal from a classroom. For my audition I sang "In Loving Kindness Jesus Came." It was bad. I was put on probation for my first semester as a music major.

I went back to my room and cried out to God. "I thought you wanted me to go into music ministry. They are telling me that I cannot sing well. Are you sure?" The answer came back clearly. "I have a plan for your life. If I call you, I will equip you."

I thank God for the encouragement of my roommate, Chris, during that tough time. His deep, sincere faith bolstered my own growing faith in this trial and others throughout my college experience. Chris mentored me in the Christian walk before we knew what mentoring was.

Three years later, I had just finished performing my junior music jury when a member of the voice faculty confessed that at my freshman tryout the committee had laughed after I left the room. He also said that I was the most improved student they had.

Today, as head of a music department, when I sit in on auditions, I often become quietly emotional when an uncertain student "bombs" a song. It is even more emotional to stand (as is our faculty graduation tradition) for the "most improved student" as he or she walks across the stage to receive a diploma. And I see how my painful experience enables me to help work out God's plan in the lives of such students. God has a plan and He is faithful.

"For I know the plans I have for you," declares the Lord, "plans to prosper you and not to harm you, plans to give you hope and a future." Jeremiah 29:11 NIV

FOLLOWING THE GREAT CONDUCTOR

Walt Mauldin
Vice President for Student Life
Lee University
Cleveland, Tennessee

IT WAS ONE of those hot, humid Indian summer days in Cleveland, Tennessee. Everyone on campus seemed to be enjoying this last ditch effort of the "too warm for comfort" climate of the South–except me. I was far too occupied with the plans for the rest of my life. Everything was unfolding much too quickly. The final semester of college had just begun, I was newly married, and all I had left to do was complete my student teaching, perform my senior recital, and find a job. Yet the thought of having to deal with all of these situations in the span of three months was almost overwhelming.

I had always thought that I would make a career of being a band director. To be on the sidelines of a huge marching band seemed like the next best thing to heaven. Oh yes, I also could see myself "blessing congregations" on the weekends by serving as a part-time minister of music in a local church. In some strange way, I guess this was my method of "tipping" God. But, God had other plans for me.

Throughout that grueling semester of rollercoaster emotions, I sensed that the Lord was leading me in a path that was uncomfortable yet calming all at the same time. In a retreat setting, one of my professors had mentioned that it was not enough for me to merely "tip" God in the area that He Himself had gifted me. Hundreds of thoughts raced through my mind in a split second. Was I guilty of doing just that? God had gifted me in ministry and music, but was I really recognizing that fact?

During many weeks of prayer and soul searching, I came to the realization that God was calling me into full-time Christian ministry. Several factors confirmed this for me. First, something within me was drawing me to this particular calling; I felt a deep excitement and calming inside me all at the same time. Second, as I read the Bible, I was drawn like a magnet to particular verses that changed my thinking and thus changed my life. Third, other people were aware that God was doing something in my life. Individuals confirmed in daytime conversations what God was speaking to me in the still of the night. And fourth, I listened to the voice of the Lord in the circumstances of life.

After graduation, my first job was in a church that had enjoyed a long line of veteran ministers of music, each much more qualified than I was. After all, I was fresh out of college with no experience. It seemed an improbable starting place, but the Lord works in mysterious ways. He blessed my experience in that church, and in other places since then. I found then, and continue to find to this day, that as long as I follow Him, I find myself in the exact place, in the exact moment, that He has orchestrated all along.

In his heart a man plans his course, but the LORD determines his steps. Proverbs 16:9 NIV

TO WILL, TO BE, AND TO SURRENDER

Larry V. Ort
Vice President for Academic Affairs
University of Sioux Falls
Sioux Falls, South Dakota

DURING MY COLLEGE YEARS, I embraced existentialism by immersing myself in reading its major authors and philosophers. At the same time, I was also reading a number of the works of C. S. Lewis. While lying in my bunk and reading *Surprised by Joy*, I encountered the following quotation from George McDonald: "The one principle of hell is 'I am my own.'"

I recall thinking, "But wait a minute: that's exactly what I believe!" My conscience was pricked a bit by the thought that my philosophy might be aligned with hell. But I was extremely self-sufficient (or so I thought). I was carrying a full academic load, working the night shift as an auditor in a hotel, and paying my own way through college. It was a grueling schedule, but I was meeting the challenge.

As I continued to reflect on McDonald's words, I decided that it was time to throw out my "profession" of Christianity. So I did. At the same time, I vowed that if and when I would commit to Christ, that commitment would be authentic.

The next day, I discussed my decision with my philosophy professor, Dr. Darrel Moore. I half expected that he would argue with me and encourage me to recommit. But Dr. Moore surprised me when he said, "Good. Now we are getting somewhere." What a powerful testimony of his trust that God would work in His own time!

Over the next few years, I resisted God. The return of this prodigal was a long, slow process. It took time to teach me that I was not self-sufficient. I am happy to say that the time came when I experienced the power and depth of God's love in a profoundly meaningful way, and I surrendered my life to Jesus Christ.

I still read some existentialist philosophy. But for philosophical reading I stay primarily with the works of Søren Kierkegaard, such as *Purity of Heart Is to Will One Thing* and *The Acts of Love*. Those works have taught me that surrender and commitment is an ongoing process. As Kierkegaard points out, our efforts to will only one thing are daily influenced by "delay, blockage, interruption, delusion, corruption." And deep in the center of Kierkegaard's philosophy I see God's philosophy, that I really am not my own, that He is calling me to surrender to Him.

Submit yourselves, then, to God. Resist the devil, and he will flee from you. Come near to God and he will come near to you. Wash your hands, you sinners, and purify your hearts, you double-minded. James 4:7, 8 NIV

THE PHILOSOPHER, THE DRUNK, AND THE KINGDOM

Ron Walborn
Dean of Bible and Christian Ministry
Nyack College
Nyack, New York

IN THE WINTER of 1983, I was a Nyack College junior studying in London for a month. It was a Sunday afternoon and we had the day off from our various trips and course work. I found my way to Hyde Park to observe the amazing exercise of free speech that took place every Sunday afternoon in this beautiful setting. Near the world famous "Speaker's Corner," there were people standing on makeshift platforms declaring their philosophies and ideologies.

One gentleman caught my interest with his engaging discussion of the philosophical pursuit of truth. Though I was a history major at Nyack, I had developed a great love for philosophy and thus began to dialogue with this obviously brilliant man. I could tell from his gentle spirit and the way he was presenting his arguments that he was a follower of Jesus. But try as I might, I couldn't get him to come right out and say it.

After ten or fifteen minutes of our discussion, a fairly large crowd had gathered around us. At the height of one of our most interesting moments, we were rudely interrupted by a loud, cursing Englishman who began to lash out at this gentleman in an obviously drunken rage. The quiet philosopher simply folded his hands in front of him and refused to react to the rantings of his inebriated countryman.

After a moment or two, I decided I should step into the fray and put this drunk in his place. I touched him on the shoulder and said, "Excuse me, sir, but we were having an intelligent conversation before you got here." Hearing my obvious American accent, the man now turned his attention on me. "Oh, what do we have here? A —— Yankee!" And then came a tirade, rich with expletives, mocking my country of origin.

I could feel the fire of anger growing within me. At that time of my life, I was much more devoted to my nation than I was to the cause of Christ. Grabbing the Englishman by the lapels of his jacket, I shouted, "Listen here, you ungrateful jerk! If it wasn't for us Americans you'd be speaking German right now." The crowd around us roared with laughter, and to my surprise the drunk retreated. But what I heard most clearly in that moment was the quiet voice of the philosopher as he spoke words that pierced my spirit and changed my life forever: "Ah, son, you have just forgotten your true citizenship."

I looked into the gentle eyes of the speaker that were now brimming with tears. It seemed for a moment that I was staring into the face of God. Immediately I was struck by a conviction that I had grieved the heart of my Savior and lost sight of what was truly important. I walked away from the crowd weeping quietly, but forever transformed. While I am still proud of my country, I have never again allowed myself to be ruled by a nationalism that keeps me from remembering where my ultimate loyalty lies: I am first and foremost a citizen of the Kingdom of Heaven.

For, as I have often told you before and now say again even with tears, many live as enemies of the cross of Christ. Their destiny is destruction, their god is their stomach, and their glory is in their shame. Their mind is on earthly things. But our citizenship is in heaven. And we eagerly await a Savior from there, the Lord Jesus Christ, who, by the power that enables him to bring everything under his control, will transform our lowly bodies so that they will be like his glorious body. Philippians 3:18-21 NIV

FROM FAR AWAY ON THE VERY DAY

Kent Olney
Professor of Sociology
Olivet Nazarene University
Bourbonnais, Illinois

"YOU'RE WRONG!" The words stung as Dr. Johnson punctuated his comments with an outstretched finger pointed right at me. I slumped in my chair, humiliated and defeated. I had just spent a grueling hour responding to question after question on multiple books and theories, but now I stumbled in my attempt to explain yet another author's thesis. The three-member committee had a brief discussion, and then told me that I had not passed my comprehensive exam.

I slunk out the door and began my seventy-mile drive home. Was this the end of the road for me? Had I come this far in my doctoral program at the University of Oregon only to be disappointed and turned away?

When I arrived home on that April afternoon, my wife came bounding out of the house to greet me. She and my two young sons had planned a celebration to mark this next achievement in my academic goals. When I told her that I had failed, she laughed half-heartedly, certain that I was only teasing her. When she finally realized that I was serious, we embraced and cried.

We had felt God's guidance all along the way in this graduate school endeavor, even though it had meant several sacrifices. I had strongly sensed that God was leading me to teach in the college classroom. I'd even signed a contract to join the faculty at Olivet Nazarene University for the upcoming fall, and plans were already under way to move across the country.

As I sat glumly pondering my options, feeling every bit the failure that Dr. Johnson's pointed finger and thundering voice had indicated, the mail arrived at our home. I was surprised to receive a letter from Columbia, South America. It was from Margaret Brabon, an acquaintance who had spent most of her life as a missionary.

Back during my undergraduate years, I had spent a summer with Margaret and her son on the mission field. We hadn't been in contact for more than fifteen years, but here was a handwritten note from her. "I am thrilled to hear how God is leading you," I read. "Be sure I will pray for your ministry now and in the future. How we need godly professors. These are awesome days to watch God work. Knock . . . and keep knocking!" Though her letter was written a month earlier, it arrived on the very day when I needed it most.

Though my response to the committee in the morning had been wrong, God's afternoon timing proved just right. Margaret's letter of encouragement led me to do two things. First, I placed the letter in a secure place, from which I continue to pull it out and refer to it often as a reminder of God's sovereignty, care, and timing. Second, I contacted my committee, restudied the book that had tripped me up, and scheduled a retake of my comprehensive exam. I passed it, and completed my doctoral degree and became a professor. God's encouragement came just in time.

I trust in you, O Lord . . . . My times are in your hands. Psalm 31:14, 15 NIV

THE EIGHTH MEETING

"Come and hear, all ye that fear God, and I will declare what he hath done for my soul."

Psalm 66:16

Michael Gough
Professor of Business Administration, MidAmerica Nazarene University

Hazel Arthur
Social Work Program Director, Lipscomb University

Richard B. Steele
Professor of Moral and Historical Theology, Seattle Pacific University

Elmar P. Sakala
Professor of Gynecology and Obstetrics, School of Medicine, Loma Linda University

Debbie Snyder
Associate Professor of Accounting, Mount Vernon Nazarene University

Troy D. Riggs
Chair, Department of Mathematics, Union University

John T. Maple
Chair, History and Political Science Department, Oklahoma Christian University

Matthew Lucas
Director of Graduate Studies in Education, Corban College

Eugene B. Habecker
President, Taylor University

Gregg Chenoweth
Dean, College of Arts and Sciences, Olivet Nazarene University

A SHEPHERD IN A WRINKLED SUIT

Michael Gough
Professor of Business Administration
MidAmerica Nazarene University
Olathe, Kansas

ONE WEDNESDAY NIGHT when I was a junior in college, I went to a midweek prayer service. It was just another ordinary Wednesday evening service, the way they were thirty years ago—a few songs, a time for testimonies, a prayer, and a homily. Yet that ordinary service has had an extraordinary impact on my view of things later in life.

When it came time for the homily, our pastor announced that we had a special speaker. Maybe we're in for a treat, I thought. He might be a good speaker. But then I saw him. He was short, overweight, and bald. His suit looked like he had slept in it. The collar on his shirt stuck up, exposing his poorly knotted tie. I couldn't help but think that this, along with the rest of his disheveled appearance, caused him to resemble Otis, the town drunk on the Andy Griffith Show.

What could this guy say to me? Though I wasn't the brightest student in college, I was just smart enough to have an attitude. This showed up, when, of all things, he picked the Twenty-Third Psalm as the text for his sermon. Surely he could have picked a more difficult text to expound on, I thought. After all, this was a church near a college.

I sat there listening, checking my watch over and over again to see when church would be finished. He began to go through the psalm verse by verse. Strangely, as he spoke, I realized I was slowly drawn into what he was saying. He had a very simple style. Though he didn't quote any Old Testament scholars, he spoke as one who had walked beside quiet waters, and also through some valleys. I was drawn in even more.

Then the man in the wrinkled suit came to the last verse. He quoted verse 6 from the King James Version: "Surely goodness and mercy shall follow me all the days of my life: and I will dwell in the house of the Lord for ever." Then he concluded by interpreting this verse in a way unlike any I had ever heard before. He said that Goodness and Mercy were the names of the Good Shepherd's sheepdogs. Like well-trained sheepdogs, Goodness and Mercy were constantly encircling us to keep us protected from evil, to keep us in the fold, and to keep us heading in the right direction.

I heard that sermon over thirty years ago. And I have heard thousands of sermons since that night. I recall very few of them. But I do remember that one from a man I thought didn't have much to say to me. Many times I have pictured Goodness and Mercy encircling me. I have been comforted by the thought of knowing the Good Shepherd's great provisions for me. I have also been slower to judge and quicker to listen to those who have gone before me and have something to say. Even if their suits are wrinkled.

Listen to advice and accept instruction, and in the end you will be wise. Proverbs 19:20 NIV

POSTCARDS OF HOPE

Hazel Arthur
Social Work Program Director
Lipscomb University
Nashville, Tennessee

I LIVED the first thirteen years of my life in an inner- city housing project. I first learned of David Lipscomb College (as it was called then) when I was ten or eleven years old. With my church youth group, I visited the campus, ate dinner, and watched a basketball game. Before that night, I'd never seen a college, eaten in a public cafeteria, or watched a formal ball game.

The "college people" I knew were my teachers; I knew (unfortunately) that children from the housing project didn't go to college. But that first visit to Lipscomb's campus was a postcard of a better life for me. It was my first conscious awareness of a place full of people who loved God and loved learning, who had a sense of hope not common in the inner city. And just as postcards of beautiful places leave you longing to be there, I longed for this God-filled, learning-filled place of hope. I "went to college" at ten or eleven, and my heart never really came back home.

Some time after that visit to Lipscomb, I remember sitting at the drug store soda fountain next to our church with Miss Polly Sheldon, telling her that I wanted to be a social worker and asking her if I had to go to college to do that. When Miss Polly said that I'd need to go to college to be a social worker, I asked her if she thought I could go to Lipscomb. Without hesitation, she told me that *of course* I could. That was very significant because others had often reminded me that "people who live here, don't go there." Miss Polly's words were a second postcard. And just as postcards from Florida convinced me that it was real and a few states away, Miss Polly convinced me that college was a reality just a few years away.

Federal grant programs made it possible for me actually to attend Lipscomb. Once there, I met Jeanne Bowman, the first social work program director. She had spent her professional career in Tennessee's public welfare system, and had actually been a social worker for my family many years earlier. As I sat in class daily, aware that Ms. Bowman knew "where I came from," I never feared judgment or exposure. In her eyes, I saw unquestionable love, unwavering belief, and unmatched passion for me, for my family, and for all whose lives I would touch in the future. Another postcard.

The earlier postcards planted and nurtured hope in my own heart. But that postcard in Jeanne Bowman's eyes gave me the passion to plant and nurture that hope in the hearts of others, first as a Christian social worker in public welfare and ultimately as a social work professor. Today, I'll enter the office and sit at the desk that once belonged to Jeanne Bowman. And in the quiet of the morning, before I encounter the first students of the day, I'll pray that each will see in my eyes what I saw in hers so many years ago—a postcard of hope.

"I know the plans I have for you," declares the LORD, "plans to prosper you and not to harm you, plans to give you hope and a future." Jeremiah 29:11 NIV

A REDEMPTIVE HUMILIATION

Richard B. Steele
Professor of Moral and Historical Theology
Seattle Pacific University
Seattle, Washington

I WAS A CHRISTIAN when I went to college, but I wasn't much of one. I was interested in God, but chiefly as a metaphysical problem that I wanted to solve rather than as a living reality to whom I was accountable. Occasionally I prayed and attended Sunday services, but these habits of my religious upbringing were gradually eclipsed by insatiable academic curiosity and overweening intellectual arrogance.

After college graduation I went to seminary with a plan to study philosophical theology, proceed straight to graduate school, and then find a college teaching job. But God had other ideas.

One day, I visited one of my professors in his office. I told him about a paper on the doctrine of the church that I had just finished for another professor. No doubt I was expecting him to applaud my cleverness. He listened with solemn attention, but finally looked me in the eye and told me that my argument was "indecent." I was thunderstruck. How could a theological argument be "indecent"? He told me that in attempting to "explain" a holy mystery, I was delighting in the exercise of my own powers of reasoning instead of marveling at God's presence among His people.

Deeply humiliated, but not yet properly humbled, I wandered around campus in a funk. Soon I saw another professor coming in my direction. I stopped him and asked if he thought solitude was a good thing for someone who was experiencing spiritual turmoil. "That depends," he said, "on whether you feel lonely when you are alone." Again I was stunned by the evident wisdom of this simple distinction, and ashamed of my apparent inability to see such obvious spiritual truths.

He saw my anguish and invited me into his office. I poured out my heart to him, describing my growing realization that I didn't understand the first thing about theology. Finally he said, "It is good that you feel this pain. And you must let it hurt more. Good night." And with that he showed me the door.

I stumbled out into the night, once again flabbergasted. I had expected him to cheer and reassure me. Instead he simply told me the truth: for the sinner, there is no consolation without repentance.

It was then that God Himself intervened. Speaking to me wordlessly in the depths of my heart, He showed me that although He had given me some modest gifts as a thinker, I had been misusing them. I had only been flattering myself and trying to impress others. Such arrogant trifling had to stop if I was ever to become the teacher of theology that I had always yearned to be.

My lifelong dream has come true; I am now a teacher of theology. Every day I pray for the humility to carry out my duties according to God's stern instructions. And as I remember how God used those two wonderful professors to bring about my "conversion," I pray daily for the courage to be as honest with my own students as my professors were with me.

But we appeal to you, brothers and sisters, to respect those who labor among you, and have charge of you in the Lord and admonish you; esteem them very highly in love because of their work. 1 Thessalonians 5:12 NRSV

A BATTLE OVER FIGHTING

Elmar P. Sakala
Professor of Gynecology and Obstetrics
School of Medicine
Loma Linda University
Loma Linda, California

THE WHEAT FIELDS of the Pacific Northwest were a universe away from the killing fields of Vietnam. Yet in the late 1960s, when I was a graduate student in education and psychology at Walla Walla College, the war could be as close as the next day's draft notice. The military was not a volunteer organization as it is today. All young men of appropriate age and health had to register for the military draft and a lottery decided who would actually serve.

In my view, serving one's country in a just war was one thing, but being sent to a distant Asian jungle to fight in a futile war that could not be won was quite another. My male classmates were faced with deciding what classification they would request for their military draft status: combatant, conscientious cooperator, or conscientious objector. This was not a trivial matter, since American boys were being brought home from Vietnam in body bags. This choice could literally mean the difference between life and death.

As a Canadian citizen, I didn't have to register for the draft, but my heart ached as I put myself into my buddies' position and agonized with them over the many questions that begged for answers. How does one convince the local draft board of the sincerity of one's choice? How about the morality of the war? What about bearing arms? Is there any fundamental ethical difference between a rifle-carrying combatant (who pulls the trigger killing an "enemy" soldier) and a non-combatant medic (who carries no weapon but helps restore to health the soldier who pulls the trigger)? Maybe the best choice was to refuse any participation in the military and seek alternative service in a hospital in the United States. Or is that merely a coward's way out?

My friends spent countless hours working through these very personal decisions, agonizing over the merits and weaknesses of the various options. I agonized right along with them. Myriads of prayers ascended to heaven seeking guidance and direction. Yet often the issues still remained hazy.

So we turned to a truly valued resource–Walla Walla College faculty members from many disciplines: English literature, history, physics, biology, theology, psychology, business, fine arts, engineering, and sociology. What those late 1960s Walla Walla College teachers had in common–as demonstrated clearly in their classrooms and in their personal lives–was both a solid spiritual grounding and a willingness to be challenged to the very basic assumptions of their beliefs.

Those Friday evenings in my apartment, when we fellows would bare our souls and voice our fears to trusted faculty, were times of inestimable support. While not imposing their personal positions on us, they provided the accepting environment that allowed my collegiate contemporaries to come to grips with some of the most serious decisions they would ever make. I suppose those professors were only faintly aware of the invaluable contribution they were making in our lives.

Plans fail for lack of counsel, but with many advisers they succeed. Proverbs 15:22 NIV

MY ARROGANCE, HIS ACHIEVEMENTS

Debbie Snyder
Associate Professor of Accounting
Mount Vernon Nazarene University
Mount Vernon, Ohio

ONE MEMORABLE DAY during my senior year in college, I received a notice that I had been accepted into a top graduate program. I was pleased with myself for what I thought I had accomplished. To celebrate, I went out to dinner with a couple of friends, followed by a movie. As we sat in the theater seats waiting for the movie to begin, we had a discussion that I will never forget.

"So Debbie," asked one of my friends, "where do you want to work after graduate school?"

"I plan to work in one of the top CPA firms as a healthcare consultant," I replied.

"Do you think they would hire you as a consultant right out of graduate school with no experience?"

"Why wouldn't they hire me? I'm a top student, I'll be a CPA, and I'll have a graduate degree in health administration. It would be stupid for them not to want me!"

My friends were speechless. I could see my arrogance in the looks on their faces, and it shocked me too. I couldn't believe I had said it, yet knew I wouldn't have said it had I not thought it was true. I sat in silence until the movie began, a movie of which I remember nothing, because all I could think about was the depth of my pride and arrogance.

Throughout my undergraduate education at this non-Christian college, individualism and achievement orientation had been constantly reinforced. Now, near the end of my program, I had almost completely accepted these philosophies. The Lord clearly had some work to do on my worldview.

Dealing with pride and arrogance is no simple task. I had been perfectly happy to let the Lord have access to the parts of my life where He and I agreed; but in the areas where there was not agreement, I had chosen to go my own way. In going my own way, I'd seen any achievement as *my* achievement. I had not accepted the truth that anything I accomplished was only through God's grace and mercy.

As it turned out, after finishing graduate school, I did not get my dream job. I did not go to work in a CPA firm. I didn't even remain long in the healthcare industry. Every step I took in any of those directions proved fruitless.

Then, faced with what I considered to be a bleak future, my distorted worldview finally crumbled under God's truth. I had to accept that I had believed the lies and made decisions based on those lies. But in God's grace and mercy, He brought me back to Himself. I am grateful that, despite *my* so-called achievements, He opened up the door to a career that is very well suited for who He designed me to be.

The human mind may devise many plans, but it is the purpose of the LORD that will be established. Proverbs 19:21 NRSV

A GOD WHO WON'T BE BOXED

Troy D. Riggs
Chair, Department of Mathematics
Union University
Jackson, Tennessee

AS A BOY, I learned to recite the basic doctrines of the faith, along with supporting verses from Scripture. By high school, I could tell you that Jesus was my Savior and that He fulfilled the roles of prophet, priest, and king. But none of this meant much to me, apart from my confidence that by believing in these propositions, I had secured my ticket to heaven. I was also under the impression that with these simple doctrines, we had contained God within a nice manageable box.

Then I lost my mother to cancer. That kind of thing can really mess up a box. My grief over her loss turned to anger, my anger to rejection, and my rejection to apathy. Why believe in a God who had so little to do with this world?

However, my desire to understand the world and humanity's part in it grew stronger than ever. So when I entered the University of South Dakota, I was happy that the school encouraged students to take courses across the curriculum. This was my opportunity to sample from many different perspectives; philosophy, psychology, history, and anthropology each provided new insights into the human condition.

In the midst of this exploration, it occurred to me that perhaps I did not know everything I should about the message of the Old Testament. I wanted to be equipped to disarm religious proselytes by knowing the Bible better than they did. And I was also genuinely open to learning something new that might have been neglected in my sectarian education. I was happy to discover that the university offered an Old Testament survey course, taught by one of the campus ministers.

From the first day of class I was encouraged. The professor's goal was that we see God and the world through the eyes of the nomadic tribes that carried on these oral traditions for hundreds of years before writing them down. I looked forward to hearing a fresh (and informed) perspective on the old Sunday school stories.

It became vividly clear that dusty shepherds had a far richer and more challenging view of God than I had. It made sense that people had invented gods to serve their purposes, but this God refused to be contained in a box. This God was more wonderful than people are capable of inventing.

One day, as we were reading from the prophet Micah, for the first time I heard that what God most desires is not religious activity but a certain kind of people, people who "act justly," "love mercy," and "walk humbly" with Him. In that moment my eyes were opened; I realized that this wasn't a Sunday school teacher or even a prophet speaking, but the Lord God Himself.

The time had come to deal with God outside of my box. I wrestled with Him about my anger, and about the depth of His love. But like Jacob wrestling through the night, I found that God always prevails. And when I gave in, He emerged from my box and entered into my life.

He has showed you, O man, what is good. And what does the LORD require of you? To act justly and to love mercy and to walk humbly with your God. Micah 6:8 NIV

AN UNREASONABLE BOSS AND A CHAIN OF EVENTS

John T. Maple
Chair, History and
Political Science Department
Oklahoma Christian University
Oklahoma City, Oklahoma

I GRADUATED from Oklahoma Christian College in April 1972. The University of Virginia in Charlottesville had accepted me to begin graduate studies in history, but since classes didn't start until mid-September, five months stretched before me. Married and with a seven-month-old child, there was no question that I needed to get a summer job. Soon I was working in the shipping department of an automobile parts remanufacturing company. Everything seemed set, and I was thankful to the Lord for providing for my family and me.

As summer jobs go, it wasn't too bad–very busy at times and quite slack at others. But as the weeks passed and June approached, I gradually became dissatisfied. Lugging engine heads on the fourth floor of a non air-conditioned building in Oklahoma with summer heat approaching 100 degrees stifled my enthusiasm for this apparent blessing. But even more sapping to my spirit was the insufferable behavior of the head of the shipping department. Rather than accepting that at times there was simply no work to be done, he insisted that the crew had to be busy. We literally had to move parts from bin to bin just to meet his demands. Three more months of mindless busywork began to look like an eternity.

Wanting to escape this situation, my thoughts turned to the possibility of moving to Charlottesville early and taking a summer class in a foreign language. I decided to see if it was possible. Because I had to leave for work at 6:30 every morning, I asked my wife, Connie, to call the university for me during business hours. When she made the call, she was told that that very day was the deadline for enrolling in the language courses for Ph.D. students. Which did I want, French or German? Because I hadn't indicated a preference, Connie made a snap decision. I came home that evening to find myself enrolled in French for Ph.D. candidates, with classes starting in less than two weeks. Ten whirlwind days later, we were new residents of Charlottesville.

It was only later, in September, that I began to see how providentially guided these actions had been. The history department had not communicated two key requirements to me. First, I had to take one seminar class in my major field during my first year; the only one offered for the entire year was Medieval France, with 80 percent of the readings in French. Second, I faced a language proficiency exam in October. Having studied French for ten hours a day for two months that summer, I was able to meet both of these challenges successfully.

More than three decades later, I still marvel at this chain of events. If I hadn't had an unreasonable boss, if Connie had called one day later, if she had chosen German, if we had decided we just couldn't move so quickly, then a difficult first year of graduate school would have been more than just difficult; it would have been impossible. Surely this was the providential care of a loving God.

A man's steps are directed by the LORD. How then can anyone understand his own way? Proverbs 20:24 NIV

THE "A+" REBUKE

Matthew Lucas
Director of
Graduate Studies in Education
Corban College
Salem, Oregon

WITH ANTICIPATION and nervous excitement, I opened my campus mailbox. It was a week after midterms, and I was anticipating the first evaluations of my performance as a college student. While there were several tests waiting for me, there was one in which I was particularly interested–Old Testament Survey, the one course every freshman feared. I had internalized that course as a potential wrecker of my grade-point average.

After an underachieving and unmotivated high school career, I had determined that I would work to my full potential in college and earn nothing less than a 4.0. That first midterm became my proving ground: I was going to demonstrate to myself, and, if the truth be told, to everyone else, that I was a good student. No, a brilliant student! So I studied, for a whole week, with particular attention to professor Anderson's Old Testament Survey.

When Monday morning came and I sat down to take the test, I was quite confident that I was thoroughly prepared. As I answered the questions and flipped through the sheets, my confidence soared. I would not only pass this test, I would ace it. Before turning it in, we were required to write our name on the front sheet and draw a line on which the professor would place the grade. In my hubris, I not only followed the directions, but I also filled in the blank: "A+."

So here I was, a week later, fingering through the papers to locate the one test that concerned me. There at the bottom of the pile was a paper with a red circle highlighting the grade I had given myself. However, at the height of my greatest joy and proudest accomplishment, I received a shock. Next to the grade, in small red letters, was a short note: "A little humility may be in order." My face flushed. I was embarrassed, then angry. I wanted validation, not correction. But deep down I knew that it was an accurate assessment; slowly my heart began to soften, my motivations to change.

As the years go by, this little incident has taken on greater and greater significance. I think part of that is due to my life coming full circle: I now teach where I once was a student. And while I have yet to encounter a student as brash and over-confident as I once was, I am sometimes confronted by one who feels I have nothing to offer, who refuses to accept the grade he has earned, or who takes a defensive posture when her ideas are challenged. At these times I draw on this story–sometimes by sharing the experience to soften the confrontation, usually by softening my heart toward the student, but always by checking my own pride against my professor's understated counsel: "A little humility may be in order."

All of you, clothe yourselves with humility toward one another, because, "God opposes the proud but gives grace to the humble." 1 Peter 5:5 NIV

WHATEVER IT TAKES

Eugene B. Habecker
President
Taylor University
Upland, Indiana

AFTER SPENDING eight years as the dean of students at George Fox University in Oregon, I concluded that if higher education was going to figure prominently in my future, my law degree was not adequate. I needed another type of doctorate. My wife, Marylou, agreed. But where should we go for me to get a Ph.D.?

We couldn't make this decision haphazardly. We had three small children and hardly any financial resources. I was accepted to the top-rated Ph.D. program in my field at the University of Michigan, but it would be more practical to stay in Oregon and attend the University of Oregon in Eugene. I would pay a much lower in-state tuition rate, and we wouldn't have to move our young family.

Marylou and I truly wanted to know God's desire for us in this matter. We took several days alone, fervently seeking God's direction. We asked our friends to pray that God would speak into our lives. From all practical vantage points, the answer seemed to be "stay in Oregon," so I started to take classes in the doctoral program at U of O.

During one of my two-hour commutes to Eugene, I heard a powerful song on a Christian radio station. The message of the lyrics was something like this: "Whatever it takes to draw me closer to You, Lord, that's what I'm willing to do." As the song played, God whispered to me. "Are you willing to do 'whatever it takes' to follow my leading in your life in this matter? Or will you settle for only being practical?"

Then during one of the chapels at George Fox (where I was still working), we heard the visiting Men's Glee Club from Azusa Pacific University sing a powerful Ken Medema song called "Moses." The song told the story of Moses' ultimate willingness to let go of his walking rod and throw it down, where it became a hissing snake, and ultimately an instrument of God's great blessing. The refrain asked, "What are you holding in your hand today? To what or whom are you bound? Give it up. Throw it down. Let it go."

Marylou and I reconsidered our "practical" choice. We had no idea how God would meet the financial need and care for the details of moving our family back to the Midwest, but we "impractically" decided to follow God to the University of Michigan. But God soon showed us how He would provide!

Our house was on a .75-acre lot, which we learned was divisible into two lots. And "out of the blue" a man stopped by the house one day and asked us if we were willing to sell part of our lot to him. The price he offered was equivalent to the money we would need to attend the University of Michigan.

We went, of course. We're so thankful that God challenged us to "do whatever it takes" to follow His leading.

"For my thoughts are not your thoughts, neither are your ways my ways," declares the LORD. Isaiah 55:8 NIV

FROM THE FIELD TO THE WORD

Gregg Chenoweth
Dean, College of Arts and Sciences
Olivet Nazarene University
Bourbonnais, Illinois

TWO AND EIGHT. God indelibly etched those numbers on my memory in 1986, my first year of college. Then, "2-8" represented the win-loss record of the football team I quarterbacked. Now it marks the radical identity shift that God planned for me through sports.

Recruiters from a few large state schools had courted me during high school. I had size, stats, and a powerhouse team. We lost only three games in four years. I lived what little boys dream of: throwing buzzer-beating touchdown passes, plunging into the end zone to the roar of thousands, giving TV interviews before big games. A police officer in my town pulled me over for speeding and then waived the citation because of who I was. Life was good. I throbbed with confidence.

I decided to attend a Christian college where a new coach from a Division I system would begin a quintessential "re-building" program. Fifteen of the twenty-two starting positions were filled by freshmen, many of whom were high school All-Staters in key positions: tailback, tight end, linebacker. We were poised for prominence.

Then it happened. Older, stronger, smarter opponents capitalized on our youth. They toyed with us, mocked us, and even abused us. I felt like a boy among men, with injuries to prove it: broken left wrist, broken right thumb, and sprained shoulder all within a few months. We lost often and hard, one time 51-6. It was devastating. Our indomitable spirit became anemic. Following that dismal first season, it took us three years to break .500.

My identity was shattered. Who am I now? What do I do now? Big questions like these can bump any 20-year-old off his feet because to answer them demands a personal change in kind, not degree. Don't think Donald Trump must figure how to become Martha Stewart. Think Vin Diesel becomes Mr. Mom. Competence in one field is forcibly exchanged for apprenticeship in another. It was a big deal.

In the spring of my junior year, God sent me help that I didn't know to look for in the person of Professor David Kale. This man assured me that my talents for the football field–leadership, communication, and zeal–could combine nicely with my spiritual grounding. He asked if I would join him and five others to launch a campus-wide small group ministry. Without giving it much thought, I agreed.

How strange it was to approach my friends spiritually. It was daring. I remember feeling a pang of risk when I called them, one by one, laying out a plan to train the spirit as much as the body. My professor became a coach. My baker's dozen of friends grew to a bushel. My "2-8" became "28"—twenty-eight people, to God be the glory.

And now, twenty years later, an irony is operative even as I pen these words. Outside my office window, college men play catch on a lawn shadowed by our campus prayer chapel, and the shadow reaches even to a neighboring freshman dorm where I once lived and was forever changed. It is now my privilege to invite them from the field and the dorm to the Word, and to a life only God could've designed for them.

[God] determined the times set for them and the exact places where they should live. God did this so that men would seek him and perhaps reach out for him and find him, though he is not far from each one of us. Acts 17:26, 27 NIV

THE NINTH MEETING

"Come and hear, all ye that fear God, and I will declare what he hath done for my soul."

Psalm 66:16

Meighan G. Johnson
Professor of Sociology, Shorter College

Ronald W. Johnson
Professor of Mission and Evangelism, McAfee School of Theology, Mercer University

Ruth-Anne E. Wideman
Chair of General Education, School of Undergraduate Studies, Regent University

Scott C. Bryan, II
Professor and Chair, Exercise and Sport Science, Bluefield College

David W. Chapman
Dean, Howard College of Arts and Sciences, Samford University

Cheri L. Larsen Hoeckley
Associate Professor of English, Westmont College

Charlie W. Starr
Professor of English and Humanities, Kentucky Christian University

Craig McDonald
Director, The Jack E. Snider Center for Honors Study, King College

Gwen Ladd Hackler
Professor of English, Southern Nazarene University

Robb Redman
Dean, Simpson Graduate School of Ministry, Simpson University

BE STILL

Meighan G. Johnson
Professor of Sociology
Shorter College
Rome, Georgia

MY RELATIONSHIP with God grew during an otherwise awful high school experience. I graduated when I was sixteen, took the big leap to college, and found myself in a very different world.

College was full to the rim with new people, new schedules, new classes, new activities. All of it fascinated me. I felt as though I was finally beginning my life.

In the exciting and busy pace of my new life, my nightly prayers became little more than a routine. My former spiritual fervor got diluted by shifting priorities. I changed my major five times and settled on sociology. I was taking less and less time to talk with God, my most understanding Friend.

My senior sociology courses so absorbed my attention that I was surprised when my last semester suddenly showed up. I had been so focused on college life that I had no clear career goal. I attended all of the college-sponsored job fairs, but nothing clicked. Yet I had to find a job. My parents had made it clear that after graduation, I was on my own.

As finals neared, I became more and more anxious. I took my exams, trying to ignore the gnawing worry. After finishing my very last exam, I just sat in the desk in the classroom. "Oh, dear God, what am I going to do?" This pleading prayer rolled over and over in my mind. It was late in the afternoon, and the other students were moving toward the door as they finished the test. But I sat still. I just could not budge. I was emotionally frozen in my seat with my faith struggling weakly against my fear.

Suddenly, the chair of the sociology department came bursting through the door, or so it seemed to me. His eyes quickly scanned the room and fixed on me. "Whew, I'm glad you're still here," he said. "This took longer than I expected." He tossed several papers on my desk.

"What's this?" I mumbled.

"Doonie," he said, using my nickname, "you are accepted into graduate school at Ole Miss."

"Really, Dr. Bryant? But I can't afford that. I have to get a job!"

Amused, he said, "That's taken care of. You will have a teaching assistantship. It will cover tuition and give you a small stipend toward books and housing. The head of the department at Ole Miss has assured me that there are plenty of opportunities for picking up some extra cash on campus."

"Do you mean that Ole Miss is going to pay me to go to school?"

"Yep! But you do have to fill out these forms right now. They have to go out in the five o'clock mail, and it's four now."

I had prayed, and God made me sit still. And then He answered my prayer.

Be still, and know that I am God. Psalm 46:10

THIS LITTLE LIGHT OF MINE

Ronald W. Johnson
Professor of Mission and Evangelism
McAfee School of Theology
Mercer University
Atlanta, Georgia

TO BE IN COLLEGE in the 1960s was a blast: campus life, rock-and-roll music, new friends, and involvement in the social causes of the day. Of course, there were the normal challenges of academics, social life, schedules, work, and managing the freedom I had never really known. But add the reality of war and the draft into this mix, and college life suddenly had a very sober edge.

Vietnam threatened to snatch us away from college and we had nothing to say about it. Out of forty guys on my dorm hall when my freshman year began, only eighteen of us remained at the end of the year. The rest had been drafted. We knew that the local draft boards were tossing the dice daily and our number might soon be up.

Our dorm hall was like most: noisy and a bit "hung-over" at times. This made studying a challenge, as did the guys who teased me for my faith and the fact that I did not drink.

I had a lamp on my desk made out of an old-fashioned telephone. When I lifted the receiver off the hook the lamp would glow. My roommate and I would often keep our door open, especially in the summer, because the dorms were not air-conditioned. I would be at my desk studying beside the lamp. Occasionally, the guys would pass by the door, see the lamp, and ask, "Any phone calls from God today?" It became a joke on the hall that when my lamp was on, God was calling.

Almost thirty years later, I was a guest preacher in a church. Just prior to the service, I was surprised when Craig, who had been on my dorm hall in college, sat down beside me. He hadn't been the least bit religious as a college freshman, and I was surprised to see him in church.

Craig told me how God had worked in his life and how important faith was to him today. He said that he had secretly watched my life during those college days, and that how I had related to the guys on the hall had affected his notion of what Christians were like. He had noticed that I didn't retaliate when the guys teased me, not even when they all threw me in the shower one Sunday evening as I came back to the dorm from a preaching assignment. They all had a good laugh, and so did I, even though it ruined my suit. Little did I know then that Craig was watching to see how I would handle the taunts.

I still have the telephone lamp. Whenever I lift the receiver off the hook and the lamp lights up the room, I think about Craig. He and many of the other guys would slip into my room for a private chat when they were anxious about the draft, or when they feared they would flunk out, or when something happened that made them think about life's serious issues. I am reminded of many nights in that dorm room when the soft glow of my telephone lamp helped me to see their concerned faces. That lamp became a symbol that God was there, even in a noisy dorm hall.

But in your hearts set apart Christ as Lord. Always be prepared to give an answer to everyone who asks you to give the reason for the hope that you have. But do this with gentleness and respect. 1 Peter 3:15 NIV

CONVICTION WITH LOVE

Ruth-Anne E. Wideman
Chair of General Education
School of Undergraduate Studies
Regent University
Virginia Beach, Virginia

AS A VARSITY volleyball player at a Christian liberal arts college, it was my privilege to represent Jesus Christ while also trying to be an admirable representative of my college. Initially this seemed to be an easy task to accomplish. I had a tremendous head coach as a role model and several Christian teammates.

However, as I moved from first- to second-year status, I encountered an unexpected challenge. It became apparent that the issue of homosexuality was going to rear its head on our team. This was not something that I was familiar with, nor did I desire to know about it. My first response was paranoia, or, to be more specific, homophobia. I confess I was quite judgmental and kept my distance whenever I perceived a teammate or competitor might be gay. After all, wasn't this practice contrary to Christianity?

It became readily apparent that this phenomenon was gaining in popularity among female athletes. Nevertheless, in an attempt to gain the Lord's perspective on the matter, I was driven to Scripture and much prayer. It was ever so apparent that a battle was taking place over my mind and heart. At one point I even contemplated quitting college because I was tired of seeing it and having to deal with the issue.

Upon arriving home for Christmas break during my junior year, I took a long winter walk in the farm fields one night. It was here that the Lord met me in a very real and dynamic way. He seemed to provide reassurance that purity and holiness are required of His people, and that I needed to exemplify this despite those around me who desired to "prove" that one could be both Christian and gay.

My return to campus after Christmas brought with it the opportunity to share my thoughts and opinions with a teammate who was actively pursuing same-sex relationships. We talked and argued for quite some time as she vehemently disagreed with me, insisting that she could in fact be a Christian lesbian. We continued playing volleyball together the rest of that school year and all through our senior year of college. However, the very obvious differences in our lifestyles and opinions presented many challenges for me during the season. Despite these differences, we remained friends, even after college ended.

It was through this struggle that I truly grew to love my friend with the Lord's love. During alumni volleyball matches following college, I always looked forward to seeing her and playing together. We had somehow developed a respect and love for one another as people regardless of our opposing viewpoints. As far as I know, she lives the gay lifestyle to this day. And as the Lord brings my friend to my mind, I pray for her.

I continue to believe that Scripture clearly indicates that the gay lifestyle is not blessed or honored by the Lord. I also feel strongly that we are to love deeply and, in doing so, pray fervently for our friends who are caught up in anything that is contrary to purity. I thank God for giving me His perspective, based on His Word, to clear my vision.

Now that you have purified yourselves by obeying the truth so that you have sincere love for your brothers [and sisters], love one another deeply, from the heart. 1 Peter 1:22 NIV

COLLEGE TEACHING AND MY "ISAAC OFFERING"

Scott C. Bryan, II
Professor and Chair
Exercise and Sport Science
Bluefield College
Bluefield, Virginia

WHEN I WAS a college freshman, I desperately desired God's will. So I prayed, "Father, remove anything from my life that is not your will. Show me clearly your plan for my life."

As soon as I had said "Amen," my year-long dating relationship began to unravel at the speed of prayer. I knew God was answering my prayer, but that knowledge did little to dull the post-operative pain of this open-heart surgery He was performing.

After months of loneliness, another girl, Nancy, came into my life. I hadn't known her for very long when she said, "Scott, God is love. Anything that is not of God is not love, for God is love." As Nancy's words hit home,

God mended my hurting heart. I knew that God had, in His love, replaced good with best. I was now ready to once again open my heart and trust the will of God.

Meanwhile, I had given my heart to a new love. All my daydreams, all my desires, were of her. I knew that she and I must be eternally wed. Her name was College Teaching. But I had learned enough to know that I must have my Father's blessing on this union.

Again, I prayed, "Father, remove anything from my life that is not Your will. Show me clearly Your plan for my life." As soon as I had said "Amen," I heard the still small voice of the Spirit say to me, "I want you to serve me in Africa."

Africa! There is no way I am going to Africa! I could just see me, my blond hair, blue eyes, pale skin, and southern drawl, greeting the locals with "How are y'all?"

Africa? No fun, no friends, no cable TV. No way! So I did what Jonah did. I ran away from God. And away from Nancy. And away from true joy, real meaning, and deep peace.

Nearly a year later, tired of running and missing my Father's house, I dropped to my knees one night in an empty dorm room. "Father," I prayed, "if You want me to go to Africa, then I will serve You in Africa."

Then God's Spirit spoke to me again. "Son, I don't want you to go to Africa. I want you to be a college professor. I simply wanted you to be willing to go to Africa."

College teaching was my "Isaac offering." Just as God did not want Isaac to be an idol in Abraham's heart, neither did He want me to idolize college teaching. Both had to be surrendered on the altar of sacrifice.

Today, more than twenty years later, not only do I know the joy of college teaching, I also know the joy of being married to Nancy. Even more important than that, I now know the true peace that comes from making Jesus my Lord and making teaching my service to Him.

Delight yourself in the LORD and he will give you the desires of your heart. Psalm 37:4 NIV

THE MOST IMPORTANT REVOLUTION

David W. Chapman
Dean, Howard College of Arts and Sciences
Samford University
Birmingham, Alabama

IT WAS THE SUMMER of '72. Everybody was listening to Crosby, Stills, Nash, & Young, and there was lingering rage about "four dead in Ohio." Five burglars had just broken into the offices of the Democratic National Convention in the Watergate office complex, and though we didn't know it, the Richard Nixon presidency would soon begin to unravel. Revolution was in the air.

Things were quieter in Oklahoma, of course. That August, my parents helped me load up a few clothes, some linens, a handful of books, a typewriter, and a cassette tape recorder. Two hours later I was checking into my dorm room at the University of Oklahoma. Among my few books was a Bible my church had given to me at my confirmation a few years before. I dropped it into the lower drawer of the built-in student desk.

It wasn't that I was antagonistic toward religion. I was regular in my church attendance and had been active in my youth group. The fact that I was a Presbyterian seemed, well, predestined. My father didn't go to church and my mother didn't drive. If the Baptist church had been a block closer, I might have grown up singing "Just as I Am" instead of "Breathe on Me, Breath of God."

Still, I thought of religious experience as something deeply personal, and I was leery of emotional displays of religion. I would like to say this was based on an analytical approach to religious inquiry, but I think it was mostly because I thought religious people were embarrassing. They had big ridiculous hairstyles and spoke with strange cadences. They were often haughty and judgmental and seemed to be upset with anyone who was having fun.

Surely God enjoyed the irony of the first sounds I remember hearing after I moved into the freshman dorm. Two guys on my hall fell into a kind of New Age-Hippie-Jesus-Freak-700-Club dialogue:

"Isn't Jesus good?"

"Oh, praise God, brother!"

"I think we should pray."

"Amen! Let's do."

As one who grew up in the "First Church of the Frigidaire," this conversation nearly inspired nausea. And a few hours later, I met our resident advisor, who described himself as "Gung Ho for Jesus." This also brought together some discordant images of bayonet charges and Christmas pageants.

In spite of all the warning signals, I found myself drawn to these other Christians in my dorm. If they came across as superficial and shallow to me, I'm sure they saw me as proud and self-absorbed. Still, we shared a common bond in knowing that life had a deeper meaning than sex, drugs, and rock and roll (all of which abounded on the campus). Through that freshman year, each of these young men had a profound impact on my life. We shared not only our faith, but also our lives. And in the end, we learned that there is room in God's kingdom for extroverts and introverts, for clapping hands and silent prayers. And that the most important revolutions are usually the ones that take place in our own hearts.

There is one body and one Spirit–just as you were called to one hope when you were called–one Lord, one faith, one baptism; one God and Father of all, who is over all and through all and in all. Ephesians 4:4-6 NIV

LEARNING THE LANGUAGE OF GOD

Cheri L. Larsen Hoeckley
Associate Professor of English
Westmont College
Santa Barbara, California

"For Christ plays in ten thousand places,
Lovely in limbs, and lovely in eyes not his
To the Father through the features of men's faces."
–from Gerard Manley Hopkins, *As Kingfishers Catch Fire*

I DECLARED ENGLISH as my major early in my sophomore year and quickly decided to specialize in Victorian literature. In my junior year, one of the department's senior Victorianists offered a course in the King James Bible as Literature. I was a high-school convert, and though I was involved in InterVarsity Bible studies, even leading a small group, I still felt overwhelmingly ignorant about Scripture. This course seemed like an opportunity to turn my studies toward some of the places my faith was taking me. Besides, I had tremendous respect for this professor's knowledge, so I enrolled.

I knew the reading for this course would be different from the ways I had begun to read Scripture. Over that quarter, we covered territory that I had wondered about, and some I could never have imagined considering.

Beginning in the sixteenth century with the Great Bible and the Geneva Bible, we moved through the seventeenth to the Douay-Rheims Version and then the King James Version. We discussed how translation altered the power of poetry, and how it modified statements about the nature of God. We explored the intricacies of Hebrew parallelism, pausing to consider how parallelism of ideas made Hebrew the most translatable poetry in any language tradition. We considered the recurring metaphors of the Old and New Testaments—water, sheep, dryness, vineyards—and learned about particular resonances of those metaphors in the early civilizations of the deserts of Israel and the Nile Valley. And I had some of the most graphically violent nightmares of my college career as we worked through the narrative details of 1 and 2 Samuel and 1 and 2 Kings.

I was clearly engaged with the material of the course, but my enthusiasm could never match my professor's. I had plenty of clues that she might have been a believer: a Jerusalem cross in her office, the broad knowledge of hymns that she used as illustrations in all her classes, her deep enthusiasm for the poetry of the Old Testament, her willingness to meet me one afternoon in the summer to help with my revision of an essay on Isaiah for a campus writing contest.

Whatever her beliefs, this professor played a crucial role in strengthening my appreciation for the power and the beauty of Scripture. Through this course I came to understand that stewardship of my education was my responsibility to a God who continued to provide with surprising abundance in that education, and in educators. I also began to understand how I could honor God with diligent study of the English language. God was clearly using that course and that professor, and I was being prepared for a career that I couldn't fully fathom yet.

Open my eyes, so that I may behold wondrous things out of your law. Psalm 119:18 NRSV

ONE CRAZY SPRING BREAK AND SOMETHING ELSE

Charlie W. Starr
Professor of English and Humanities
Kentucky Christian University
Grayson, Kentucky

IN MARCH 2002 I was trying to graduate from college for the third time. With only a week left to finish my dissertation, I was glad to be on spring break from the university where I teach. I planned to use the time to finish off my 350-page monster. Unfortunately, my body just then decided to suffer from kidney stones.

If you've never had kidney stones, you won't understand the excruciating level of pain that I'm talking about. It hurt! The doctor said, "Either surgery or wait for the stone to pass." I told him that, as long as we could kill the pain, I needed to finish my dissertation.

By week's end I still wasn't finished, and my body could no longer handle the painkillers I'd been taking. The last pill on Saturday sent me to the bathroom to throw up. When I leaned down to heave into the toilet, bracing myself on the laundry hamper, the simple downward motion of the first puking popped my left arm out of its socket. Of course I was too busy to scream in pain, let alone scream for help. So I emptied my stomach, rinsed out my mouth, and went to tell my wife.

Whenever I'd dislocated a shoulder before (yes, I had done it to them both), it would go back in on its own. But this time it got stuck. So we headed to the emergency room, my kidney in spasms, my arm dangling at my side, and the painkillers wearing off. At midnight, the ER doctor fed a milky white anesthetic into my IV, meant to knock me out just a little bit so he could put my shoulder back in place. When I woke up an hour or so later, half a dozen concerned faces were staring down at me from all sides of the bed.

"Charlie? Are you alright?" someone asked.

"Yeah, I'm fine. I'm feeling good."

It turns out the anesthetic had knocked me out completely, so much so that I even stopped breathing. They had to call a code blue! My wife told me this after the ER staff had cleared the room.

"Cool," I said.

Early Sunday morning they sent me in for surgery. The shoulder was fine, but the kidney stone still had to come out. I made it home by Sunday night, but students were coming back for school, and my dissertation wasn't finished.

Thankfully, my dean told me to take another week off, and my dissertation director got his dean (who had just had kidney stones himself) to extend my deadline. But the craziest thing to come out of the whole experience was my attitude toward it.

I noticed it on Sunday night. During the whole time, I never once worried about the circumstances or my deadline. I was accepting and even thankful at times. I somehow knew in my heart that God would take care of everything. Maybe it was the drugs? Maybe it was Something Else.

Be anxious for nothing, but in everything by prayer and supplication, with thanksgiving, let your requests be made known to God; and the peace of God, which surpasses all understanding, will guard your hearts and minds through Christ Jesus. Philippians 4:6, 7 NKJV

CAN YOU HEAR ME NOW?

Craig McDonald
Director, The Jack E. Snider Center
for Honors Study
King College
Bristol, Tennessee

FOR NEARLY a quarter century, I have had the privilege of introducing undergraduate students to the Confessions of St. Augustine as part of the literary survey course at King College. The rewards for such long exposure to Augustine have been many, but perhaps the most powerful has been the recurring reminder of the saint's relentless confrontation with sin and his awe that the Lord of the universe can and will use any sin, faulty decision, or circumstance to draw an errant creature back to Himself. I can speak of this with conviction to my students because I have experienced it.

To describe my first two years at Davidson College, I could draw on Augustine's portrait of a similar time in his own life. I was absorbed in my studies, addicted to desire for a young woman, and deaf to the appeals of God's Spirit, despite the prayers (and perhaps tears) of godly parents. Augustine, however, was much more honest. While he rebelled openly, I lacked the courage to do so. I instead proclaimed a faith while denying its power. I also paid the price. Mine was a split and often miserable life.

During my sophomore year I decided that I would spend a semester of my junior year at University of North Carolina, Chapel Hill. The official reason was noble. I could round out my education by taking courses in literature not offered at Davidson. That my girlfriend was also at Chapel Hill or that I wanted to see what life in the big university was like–these, of course, were incidental.

One evening, as my sophomore year drew to a close, I was strangely prompted to utter a brief prayer. "God, do something in my life at Chapel Hill." There was no reason for me to pray this prayer; I had experienced no dramatic event or any outward call from God. The words simply came. I'm convinced that it was the Holy Spirit making intercession on behalf of a heart that couldn't even utter its true longings. The Lord answered His own Spirit's prayer.

I did enter UNC in the fall, but not before my relationship with my girlfriend ended abruptly (much to our mutual benefit). What filled the vacuum, besides some fine courses, were renewed friendships with some high school acquaintances whose lives had been changed by a living gospel. Through them, I joined a Bible study with InterVarsity Christian Fellowship. It was filled exclusively with freshmen, but they were gracious and didn't discriminate against a wizened old junior. Through them, the Master began to blow life again into my dry bones.

When I returned to Davidson the following spring, that same irrepressible Master who had pursued Augustine had also prepared a royal welcome for me: a living, vital community, which eventually included my future wife, Karen.

Other periods of spiritual deafness have followed, some of them embarrassingly and painfully long. But just as often, sometimes through the words of St. Augustine as I "teach" him each year, God's still small voice has screamed in my ear, "Follow me!" What an ardent and eloquent lover our Lord God is.

In the same way, the Spirit helps us in our weakness. We do not know what we ought to pray for, but the Spirit himself intercedes for us with groans that words cannot express. Romans 8:26 NIV

A DIFFERENT WAY TO OXFORD

Gwen Ladd Hackler
Professor of English
Southern Nazarene University
Bethany, Oklahoma

IN THE STATE ROUND of the Rhodes Scholarship competition, I had been one of the two students chosen to represent Oklahoma, my home state. Now I was on my way to the final round interviews in New Orleans, where it would be decided who would become a Rhodes Scholar at Oxford University.

I had been feeling confident, but now I felt a touch of apprehension. I was up against students from the best universities in the country. Surely they had a better chance than me, a student from a small Christian school where only one student before me had ever made it to the first cut. But surely none of them had a stronger determination than I to use the years at Oxford to prepare for a life's work of teaching English literature to promising students at the college level, opening their minds and inspiring them to grapple for their intellectual best. Clearly God was calling me to this. I saw the competition as a critical step for me, the Rhodes Scholarship at Oxford being the best possible preparation for a life of academic service.

I remember bits and pieces of the interview, and the one question I hadn't anticipated about a particular source in the bibliography of my senior research paper on Henry VIII. I remember the hot discomfort of the moment when they picked a young woman from Texas for the Rhodes. What a waste, I thought, to send her to study chemistry, rather than English, at Oxford.

I finished graduate school in five years with a good scholarship and a job opened up in my specialty area at my alma mater, Southern Nazarene

University. For years I periodically wrestled with the question, "Why did God bring me that close to the Rhodes only to deny me the opportunity?"

In 1991, a phone call came out of the blue. Would I be willing to fly over to Oxford and spend a few weeks of the summer with a handful of students to start up a study program for the Council for Christian Colleges and Universities (CCCU)?

So began a series of summers spent in Oxford with CCCU students, researching in the Bodleian Library, conversing with Oxford faculty whose books I had on my shelves, getting to know Oxford intimately. The program grew rapidly, from less than twenty to more than one hundred students each year. It turned into a full-fledged fall and spring semester program. Some of the students who completed it went back to Oxford and earned their masters and doctorates and then went on to leaven the academy, public service, and the church.

Eventually it hit me—had I gone to Oxford as a Rhodes Scholar, how could my individual contribution to God's kingdom, however strategically placed, come even close to what these students were already doing? I had been called to use my preparation, in turn, to prepare all these exceptional students. In God's providence and economy, it had happened and continues to happen in ways I could never have imagined.

Commit your work to the LORD, and then your plans will succeed. Proverbs 16:3 NLT

ONE WHO TOOK A CHANCE ON ME

Robb Redman
Dean, Simpson Graduate School of Ministry
Simpson University
Redding, California

GROWING UP in the semi-arid desert of Central Washington's Yakima Valley, I knew I wanted to go to college on the wetter and greener western side of the Cascade Mountains. By my junior year in high school I had settled on Willamette University in Salem, Oregon.

There was a problem, however. I had been less than motivated as a high school student. The "C's" and "D's" I had earned in the ninth grade had driven my parents crazy. The following year wasn't much better. Though I accepted Christ the spring of my sophomore year, and He turned my life around, the academic damage had already been done. I started my junior year with my college dreams hanging by a thread.

That's when I met Geneva Renn. I had signed up for her Greek mythology class. When we dived into the world of the ancients, I was immediately hooked, finally realizing that I loved to learn. I sat spellbound in Mrs. Renn's classes. She challenged me to think for myself, encouraged me to integrate my new faith with my newly discovered love of learning, and warned against going too far. "Don't be so open-minded your brains fall out," she chided.

Mrs. Renn's investment in me started paying off. My grades started getting better. Still, when I sent my application off to Willamette the next year, my parents gently cautioned me about getting my hopes up too high. When I got the acceptance letter, I was relieved. My parents offered the deepest prayer of gratitude they could muster. And Mrs. Renn was pleased. Somehow, even though my cumulative GPA stood at an underwhelming 3.085, I had managed to get into one of the most prestigious private colleges in the Northwest. Never mind how I got in; I resolved to make the most of my academic second chance.

One day during my sophomore year at Willamette, Jim Sumner, then director of admissions, summoned me into his office. "I want to show you something," he said, rifling through a file on his desk. He pulled out a sheet of paper. It was a letter of recommendation from Geneva Renn. As I read it, tears formed in the corners of my eyes. It was more than a boilerplate letter of recommendation; it was the faith of a teacher in her pupil poured out in print. In elegantly moving prose she pleaded my case to the university, staking her professional reputation on an underachieving kid. As I handed the letter back to Jim, he smiled and said, "That is the finest letter of recommendation I have ever read. It's the reason you're here."

Somehow, God had used Geneva Renn to leverage my love of learning. And she, in turn, had willingly used her reputation to leverage me into the college she knew I had my heart set on.

Now that I'm a teacher and a dean, I know what it's like to believe in students more than they believe in themselves. I've used that leverage countless times; sometimes it works and sometimes it doesn't. But every time I'm challenged to invest myself in a student, I thank God that Geneva Renn took a chance on me.

Piam memoriam Geneva Renn.

Do everything you can to help Zenas the lawyer and Apollos on their way and see that they have everything they need. Titus 3:13 NIV

THE TENTH MEETING

"Come and hear, all ye that fear God, and I will declare what he hath done for my soul."

Psalm 66:16

Don Mason
President Emeritus, Central Christian College

Susan VanZanten Gallagher
Professor of English, Seattle Pacific University

David G. Clark
Chair, Department of Biblical Studies and Philosophy, Vanguard University

David Lawson
Professor of Psychology, Palm Beach Atlantic University

Dan G. Blazer
JP Gibbons Professor of Psychiatry and Behavioral Sciences, Duke University Medical Center

John F. Van Wicklin
Professor of Psychology, Houghton College

Richard E. Sours
President, William Penn University

Steve Timmermans
President, Trinity Christian College

Katherine Koudele
Professor of Animal Science, Andrews University

John Collins
Professor of Religion, Wake Forest University

MRS. ANDREWS, PREXY, AND THE ALTAR CALL

Don Mason
President Emeritus
Central Christian College
McPherson, Kansas

DURING MY high school days, I had come to the conclusion that the Christian life was not for me. Of course, I was still a "good guy" and didn't "drink or chew or go with girls who do." But after many trips to the altar, being "saved" repeatedly had not worked.

I had also observed that many church members seemed to me to be hypocrites. They would testify to following Christ and yet their lives didn't match their testimony. I had determined that living for Christ was fine for some people, but not for me.

I never seriously considered going to college anywhere but Central Christian College. Many of my friends were going. I had visited several times and liked the place. And my father, a Free Methodist minister, was a trustee. But I wasn't going for the Christian part. I just wanted to enjoy college life with friends and fun and whatever classes were necessary to justify my being there. I specifically made a point of not attending any optional religious services.

My casual stance toward matters of faith became known around campus—there really were very few secrets around Central in those days. I learned that students were praying for me. And Lydia Andrews, one of the saints of our McPherson Free Methodist Church community, had noticed my lack of commitment. She had a "burden" for me. By the time of the semi-annual ten-day revival series at Central during the fall of my freshman year, it became evident that I was her target for salvation.

All students were required to attend the evening services. Of course there were long altar calls, complete with the singing of many verses of "Just as I Am" designed to give the stubborn sinner every opportunity to succumb. And in the special tradition of the time and our community it was not unusual for church members to personally seek out "sinners" during these altar calls and encourage and escort them to the front. Sure enough, at one of the evening meetings early in the revival, Mrs. Andrews found me at my place in the back and pleaded with me to go to the altar. Her invitation was kind and genuine, but I refused; after a final plea, she returned to her seat.

I determined that nothing of the sort would happen again. At the final meeting of the series, I deliberately sat in the very middle of the back row, with some of my big basketball friends sitting in front and on either side. I was safely out of the sight line of Mrs. Andrews from her traditional seat near the front of the chapel. But I had forgotten about the aisle behind the back row. So during the altar call, I felt the terrible tap on my shoulder.

Even then, I didn't yield to her embarrassing invitation. But I knew that it had softened me. I was genuinely moved that a lovely Christian woman was so concerned for my soul.

One day my roommate told me that I was being summoned to the president's office. I had no idea why Prexy, as we affectionately called President Elmer Parsons, wanted to talk with me. But as I sat down with him in his office, I was not completely surprised by his very direct question. "Don, why are you not a Christian?"

He was a genuine Christian man, so I didn't feel the need to be guarded or evasive. "Well, Prexy," I replied, "I just don't really feel I can live a consistent Christian life. I have tried it and always failed."

His response was unexpected and right on target. "Don, that may be the problem. YOU don't live a Christian life–Christ lives it through you!" I cannot really remember the rest of our conversation, but those Spirit-inspired words stuck with me: "Christ lives it through you."

During the next weeks and months, all of my well-thought-out arguments disappeared. My close friends continued to pray for me. Christian faculty assured me of their prayers and interest. And Mrs. Andrews always had a kind word of greeting along with the assurance that she was praying for me. Eventually, the Spring Revival came and my heart was ready. When the invitation came during the second service, I went forward, without any pleading from Mrs. Andrews, and publicly accepted Christ as my Savior and Lord.

God had used Prexy's frank questions and Mrs. Andrews's unflagging zeal to reach my stubborn heart.

Now, some fifty years later, and after completing nine years as president of Central Christian College, I have proved Prexy's words again and again. "Don, you don't live the Christian life–Christ lives it through you."

I have been crucified with Christ and I no longer live, but Christ lives in me. Galatians 2:20 NIV

IT HAD NEVER CROSSED MY MIND

Susan VanZanten Gallagher
Professor of English
Seattle Pacific University
Seattle, Washington

WHEN I ENTERED Westmont College as an undergraduate, I wanted to be a lawyer. My mother was a politician, and I had been a prize-winning high school debater. I saw a career in law, and perhaps eventually politics, as a meaningful way that I could serve God. I wasn't interested in making a lot of money; what I wanted was to contribute to the creation of public policies and social structures that would help the poor.

To pursue these worthy aims, I began a double major in English and political science, having been advised that this would be excellent preparation for law school. I also honed my writing skills and received a crash course in academic politics by working as a reporter for the student newspaper.

In the fall of my junior year, I had one course left to complete for my political science major—a required internship. Since I wasn't interested in corporate law, I arranged a placement with a local legal aid society. Santa Barbara had strict rent control policies to keep landlords from ratcheting up the rents in this desirable housing market. Subsequently, some landlords tried to evict their tenants on trumped-up charges, leaving them free to raise the rent on their apartments for the next tenant. The legal aid society for which I worked spent most of its time helping older people on fixed incomes, single mothers, and disabled individuals fight these evictions.

I quickly learned how to research each case in the law library and to write up effective depositions. My supervising attorney was pleased with my work, complimenting me on both the thoroughness of my research and the clarity of my writing. This was the kind of law that I wanted to practice: helping people. I had the intellectual gifts to do such work well. But much to my dismay, I hated doing it.

At this point of vocational crisis, one of my English professors, Dr. Arthur Lynip, asked me to come to his office after class one day. His request didn't worry me, as I was doing well in his course in Modern American Fiction. I had even recently led a lively class session on a Faulkner short story, which I had thoroughly enjoyed.

I sat down in Dr. Lynip's book-lined office. "Susan," he slowly began, "have you ever thought about going to graduate school and becoming an English professor?" I was flabbergasted. The thought had never before crossed my mind. "You have a gift for analyzing literature," he continued. "You also did a superb job of helping other students understand and appreciate a rather complex story. You would be a good teacher."

It took only a few days of prayer and family consultations for me to realize that Dr. Lynip was absolutely right. The thought of becoming an English professor clicked in a way that being a lawyer had not. So as one door slammed right in front of my face, another was graciously opened by a perceptive teacher. I had found my vocation.

Now there are varieties of gifts, but the same Spirit; and there are varieties of services, but the same Lord; and there are varieties of activities, but it is the same God who activates all of them in everyone. 1 Corinthians 12:4-6 NRSV

THE SPIRITUAL MYSTERY OF GIVING

David G. Clark
Chair, Department of Biblical Studies and Philosophy
Vanguard University
Costa Mesa, California

THOUGH I GREW UP in a good, nominally Christian family, it wasn't until a few months after graduating from high school that I made a personal decision to follow Christ. I immediately felt led to earn a college degree. After I had attended a junior college for two years, someone in my church youth group returned "on fire" from a Bible college in south Wales. I determined to go there too.

Lacking money for transportation and tuition, I took a job working at McDonald's. During that year, I often found myself working alone, getting the store ready to open. Many Sunday mornings, when I would rather have been in church, I was emptying trash bins out in the parking lot. As I complained about the stale Cokes dripping down my arms, I could hear God asking, "Do you really want to attend Bible school?" When I finally had earned enough to get into college, I was ready to apply myself.

Since I had given my life to God, He had spoken to me about tithing, reminding me that He is the source of all I am and all I have. So even though I was a cash-poor student, I gratefully gave money back to Him from my meager resources. After returning from Wales, with three more years of college to complete, I was giving about 30 percent of my income to my local church and missions. My frugality must have been noticed by a few of my fellow students, because they took me to a local shopping center and "encouraged" me to get some new clothes!

I wasn't tithing to receive but to acknowledge the One who was guiding and blessing my life. And God did bless my college experience. He transformed me from someone who disliked most of high school into someone who enjoyed study. During my senior year, I felt that God might be calling me to the classroom, so I applied for a doctoral program at the University of Notre Dame. I'll never know just why a Catholic university accepted a "holy roller" Pentecostal like me, but I was admitted with a full scholarship. Though my studies there took six years, teaching and research assistantships covered the tuition and provided living expenses as well. Of course I tithed that income too.

God is so faithful! Tithing continues to be a "spiritual mystery" to me. God can make nine-tenths go farther than ten-tenths! Giving tithe back to God is a step of faith and an act of obedience. Writing a tithing check is one of the most spiritual things I do!

The classroom has now been my place of ministry for more than thirty years. As a professor of New Testament and Greek, I've had the privilege of investing in many lives. But first God invested in me, and I'm grateful that tithing is one of the tangible ways He has given me to acknowledge that investment.

What do you have that you did not receive? 1 Corinthians 4:7 NIV

THE TEARS OF ANOTHER GREAT AWAKENING

David Lawson
Professor of Psychology
Palm Beach Atlantic University
Orlando, Florida

MY FIRST GREAT AWAKENING occurred during my childhood and adolescence; this was when my belief and faith in Christ deepened and became integrated into my identity. My second great awakening occurred through the exhilarating experience of going to college. It was there that I cognitively explored my faith, gaining a deep appreciation for the complexity of God.

I spent my first four years of college at a public university. Many of my professors were not Christian; some were vigorously antagonistic to belief in God. This challenged me to create answers to complex social, moral, and spiritual issues. These professors must be asking universal questions, and I was sure there must be answers.

I devoured books on apologetics and theology. Lewis, Schaeffer, and Spurgeon were the beginning of my reading list. I wrestled through many philosophy books, and books on science and Christianity. This forced me to think beyond the simple boxes that I had created for God during my first great awakening.

As my cognitive skills grew, so did my courage. I no longer worried about professors' comments. Emboldened with knowledge, I began challenging many of the professors who had attacked God. I began rebutting ideas and confronting logical fallacies. Unfortunately, I also became aggressive and arrogant with them. This carried over into my personal relationships as I forced friends and family into debates, imposing my logic and theology on them. I had become supercilious and uncaring in my striving to strengthen their faith.

This pattern continued during the summer break of my junior year. At the end of a week of particularly intense family debate, when I returned home from work one day, my mother told me that my father wanted to speak with me. I knew immediately I was in for another challenge. I prepared myself, mentally checking references to theologians and philosophers and lining up Bible verses to help defend my position.

I entered the room where my father was and found him sitting in the corner, his Bible open and his head bowed. *Good*, I thought, *it's a duel of biblical interpretation*. My father had always been a quiet man, extremely intelligent and composed–a true challenge for me. I cleared my throat to announce my presence.

He kept looking at the Bible. I finally became impatient and said, "I know I have been arguing too much."

He looked up with tears in his eyes and said very gently, "You have become arrogant and hurtful. That is not what God wants for you."

Those words, along with my father's tears, resonated with my spirit. I immediately began crying and asked for forgiveness. I knew he was correct. I had become extremely vain and arrogant and had used what God had taught me to hurt others. This was not what God wanted.

Thus began my third great awakening, a deep love and deep compassion for people. Although I gained much in college intellectually, the greatest lesson I learned was from the tears of my loving father.

The eyes of the arrogant man will be humbled and the pride of men brought low. Isaiah 2:11 NIV

READING MYSELF INTO SERVANTHOOD

Dan G. Blazer
JP Gibbons Professor of Psychiatry and Behavioral Sciences
Duke University Medical Center
Durham, North Carolina

MY STORY does not begin with a dramatic conversion experience, nor does it include a spectacular mid-course correction in my spiritual pilgrimage. Rather, my story from my college days and onward is one of gradual spiritual growth through the spiritual calling of reading.

The beginning of my journey is unremarkable. I grew up in a faithful evangelical family and faith community. To this day I have not left that community. My basic beliefs have changed little over time since I entered Vanderbilt University in 1962.

Where I am now on that journey, long into my career, is as unremarkable. I am at core first a Christian, second a husband and father, and third an academic psychiatrist. I spend most of my time in research. I write about faith and psychiatry, but that is not my primary focus. An active churchman, I probably am viewed at best as a simple servant. So the bookends of my story are rather boring. Yet what lies between is my sacred journey as a reader.

We grow spiritually in whole, not in part. For a student and an academician, that means we must grow intellectually in all those areas that touch our spiritual growth if we are to become whole.

God would not let me sit still in college with my understanding of Scripture even as I was growing in my knowledge of biology and psychology. So He led me to take many courses in religion. I read voraciously, I prayed, I questioned, I even tried to write.

This continued into medical school, where I realized that I wanted to specialize in psychiatry. So I read everything I could find at the interface of psychiatry and faith, from Freud through Fromm to Allport. When I finished my residency, I established a habit of reading every night for at least an hour (I read the Great Books from age forty to age fifty). Every morning I read spiritual works, from the Bible to Thomas Merton. I talked with spiritual leaders to find what I should be reading next.

Am I just a reading addict? I don't think so. Reading doesn't tell the entire story. I pray, I teach, I question, I write, I pray some more. On it goes, day after day, year after year.

The fruits of this labor of love for me (love because I love it so much) have been manifold. First, I have never found myself doubting my basic beliefs. Through my reading and questioning I have anticipated much that could have shaken my faith during my life in a secular university.

Second, I occasionally have had an answer for questions and doubts posed by other believers in the academic world in which I live.

Third, and most important, my commitment to the basics of my faith has been strengthened. Through my spiritual journey with books, I have learned that what really counts is love of God, belief in the risen Savior, love of neighbor, hospitality, and humility. As to humility, therein lies the paradox of my journey. God has not called me to be a great Christian writer. He has simply called me to read myself into a simple servant.

Open thou mine eyes, that I may behold wondrous things out of thy law. Psalm 119:18

WHAT MY HEART INSISTS ON REMEMBERING

John F. Van Wicklin
Professor of Psychology
Houghton College
Houghton, New York

AT SOME POINT during high school, I convinced myself that my professional future would be brighter if I went to a secular college with an excellent reputation. My father, having succeeded in business with only a high school education, was mostly concerned with what college might do to my faith. With the application process looming, he announced that I had a choice to make. He would pay all of my expenses if I were to attend a Christian college. If I chose a secular college or university,

I was on my own. Wheaton College quickly became a reasonable choice for the fall of 1964.

My freshman year was a transitional point in Wheaton's history. Dr. V. Raymond Edman would complete twenty-five years as president and become chancellor. I was in awe of this man–popular college administrator, mentor to Billy Graham, and one who led Wheaton during World War II and into a time of prosperity.

One day I was walking along a sidewalk near the health center when I noticed Dr. Edman approaching from the other direction. I offered a quick hello as he neared, not expecting him to even break his stride. To my surprise, he stopped, looked right at me with a warm smile, and asked me who I was. When I identified myself, his face brightened as he informed me of the delightful coincidence that he had prayed for me by name that very morning. A brief conversation followed as Dr. Edman sought to learn more about me. I would later learn that he made a habit of rising early with rosters of students and other college personnel in hand to pray for each one by name.

I next saw him in the very last moments of his life. I was in chapel on September 22, 1967, when he walked onto the platform wearing our senior class blazer, to give his message, "In the Presence of the King." He described with great admiration a brief but memorable encounter with Emperor Haile Selassie of Ethiopia. He urged us to consider chapel as a time when we enter into the presence of our Lord and King, and for our conduct to be appropriate to that setting. I remember an ethereal look on his face as he wondered aloud what it would be like when he met his heavenly King face to face. Within minutes of expressing that sentiment, he collapsed on stage from heart failure and died.

My roommates and I learned that Billy Graham would speak at the memorial service, so we arrived well ahead of time to get seats very close to the front. Graham eulogized Dr. Edman–who arose early and prayed for the likes of me by name–as one who "touched more lives personally than any man I ever knew." I understood. And forty years later, as I look back on my undergraduate years, I am surprised to discover what my mind and heart insists on remembering.

Your attitude should be the same as that of Christ Jesus: Who, being in very nature God, did not consider equality with God something to be grasped, but made himself nothing, taking the very nature of a servant. Philippians 2:5-7 NIV

MOLDED TO MODEL

Richard E. Sours
President
William Penn University
Oskaloosa, Iowa

WHEN I BECAME a college teacher, I gradually realized the extent to which I was a role model for my students. And I also recognized that God used various events and people in my own academic experience to mold me into a better model for others.

In my junior year, a physics instructor gave a take-home examination. Soon after the assignment was given, I realized that many of my classmates were collaborating with each other, and getting help from other students, both contrary to the instructor's guidelines. I was not the strongest student in the course, and the pressure to do well on that test mounted as I learned about the cheating of my classmates. Although I did not realize it at the time, I am sure that God was using this to reinforce my desire to be honest. I did not cheat on that test, a fact that was evident to my instructor when he read my paper. At the top of it he wrote, "Even though you did not earn a top grade, I respect your honesty."

A similar thing happened when I was a master's student. There was rampant cheating on take-home tests in one of my courses. Eventually I went discreetly to the instructor to inform him. I don't know whether he believed me, but he chose to do nothing. So throughout the course, my honesty kept me behind the grade curve because others were dishonest.

I am not bragging about my honesty; rather, I'm reflecting on those situations where I now know that God was shaping me for later responsibilities. In the years since, as a faculty member and an administrator, I have come to realize the extent to which my being a role model is essential to students, faculty, and staff at my institution. My behavior, especially respect and honesty, is a very important part of setting the standards at my institution.

When I was a young student struggling to deal with those challenging circumstances, I did not realize that the Potter was shaping me to be ready to fulfill my current administrative role. Even today, He continues to use people and events to help me become a more faithful ambassador of His Kingdom, to be a model of Christian behavior that will bring glory to Him.

Like clay in the hand of the potter, so are you in my hand. Jeremiah 18:6 NIV

THE RINGS OF THE LORD

Steve Timmermans
President
Trinity Christian College
Palos Heights, Illinois

AS A YOUNG CHILD, I was fascinated by collapsible travel cups. Though I haven't seen one in years, I clearly recall the design: a series of rings, each one just slightly smaller than the next, so that when collapsed, they would all fit inside the largest, outer ring. When expanded, each ring would give way to a slightly larger one, rising up to become a complete cup.

For me, college was like that cup; each circle of new understanding provided me a wider view of God's world. Three distinct rings are etched in my memory.

I brought my first ring with me when I entered a Christian college. This ring of my faith formed a tight circle: personal devotions, church attendance, and Christian behavior all were within my ring of understanding. My faith development provided me a 360-degree view of Christianity.

During my first year of college, I found that my ring needed to be enlarged. My theology professor told us about the weight-loss results he had achieved by exercising and dieting. It is important to understand that this was well before the national secular fixation with health and exercise. With religious fervor, the professor told us that he was pursuing these healthy goals in response to his Creator. He talked earnestly of his faith, which required more than personal devotions, encompassing not only his soul but also his physical body. Through the example of my professor, my faith increased to become a second, broader ring–still 360 degrees, though now expanded to include a bigger circle of understanding. But that wasn't my last ring.

Having grown up in the suburbs, I was only vaguely aware of poverty, racial discrimination, and other urban problems. That changed during my second year of college, when I started working in the service-learning center. My job there, matching up male college students with "little brothers," was only a small part of the center's broad purpose.

The center's director, though not a professor, was very much a teacher. He explained to me how each engagement with the needs of the city should be understood as a responsibility to "reclaim" the world for Christ. And he suggested that this reclaiming business didn't only relate to overt witnessing. For when we painted an elderly couple's house, we were helping to make the world a bit more like God desired it to be. When we tutored children, we were helping them understand their God-given gifts better. When we assisted a family's move to a new apartment, we were seeking God's justice and mercy. Once again, my circle of understanding had to expand. Now the ring within which I understood the call of the Gospel was bigger yet.

Since college, my faith journey has continued to add new rings of understanding. Over the years, I have acquired a cup of ever-increasing rings, each one slightly larger than the one below it. Together, these rings form a cup of blessings that God continues to fill to overflowing.

And I pray that you, being rooted and established in love, may have power, together with all the saints, to grasp how wide and long and high and deep is the love of Christ, and to know this love that surpasses knowledge—that you may be filled to the measure of all the fullness of God. Ephesians 3:17-19 NIV

THE WITNESS AND THE WANDERING SHEEP

Katherine Koudele
Professor of Animal Science
Andrews University
Berrien Springs, Michigan

AT THE BEGINNING of the fall quarter of my senior year, I arrived on the beautiful but huge campus of Michigan State University (MSU). It's the largest contiguous university campus in the United States, with 2,000 acres of developed campus and 3,000 acres of farms. I was there to take a class I needed to complete my pre-professional program at Andrews University, where I'd done all my previous undergraduate work.

Besides being big, MSU was full of students—more than 40,000 were enrolled. I was the product of 15 years of Adventist education, eight of which were in a two-room country school. I'd never been in a class of more than 50 students. Now I was in classes four times that size. The secular "anything goes," post-Vietnam mentality swirled around me.

I lived off-campus with another girl (and her practically live-in boyfriend) and I was free to come and go and do as I pleased. No one was checking me in at night or seeing that I had attended my quota of dorm worships. I felt the undertow of the whole experience begin to pull me into its humanistic way of thinking. My desire for things spiritual began to wane.

When the weather was pleasant, the street-corner-preachers appeared—from saffron-robed Buddhists to undisguised Marxists. They espoused almost every belief system known. The group that drew the biggest crowds, however, were the black-suited Bible thumpers. These young men seemed determined to bring down judgment on the entire student body for its sinful ways. They delighted in engaging passersby in heated debates about who would be saved or lost. Their brand of Christianity left a bad taste in my mouth.

One day, late in the fall when the preachers were in full cry, an argument broke out that almost turned into a shoving match between a Bible-thumper and an avowed atheist. This kind of confrontation made me feel quite uncomfortable, so I shrank back into the crowd.

Just as the tension peaked, a slim, dark-haired student stepped up and placed herself between the combatants. In a calm, quiet voice she began to explain to the atheist the Gospel truth clearly and simply and with a depth of understanding that spoke of her personal relationship with Jesus.

The scoffing crowd settled down and listened intently as she spoke. The arguing atheist was engrossed and asked her question after question which she answered in a loving, Christ-like manner. The preacher soon realized he had lost the crowd, so he stepped over to another bench and again took up his harangue. Not a soul moved to follow him; they clustered around the girl.

Her act of bravery in speaking out for truth reached out like a shepherd's staff and hooked my heart. God used her that day not only to reach the atheist but to bring back one of His wandering lambs.

I myself will search for My sheep, and will seek them out. As a shepherd seeks out his flock when some of his sheep have been scattered abroad, so will I seek out My sheep. Ezekiel 34:11, 12 RSV

THE ATHEIST AND THE VOICE OF GOD

John Collins
Professor of Religion
Wake Forest University
Winston-Salem, North Carolina

COLLEGE WAS a liberation for me, both cognitively and socially. I grew up a conservative Southern Baptist. All my relationships had been with persons who were, from all external appearances, like those in my home. I had never met an atheist or an agnostic. Nor had I known any person of color, any "liberated" female, or anyone who wasn't "straight." I knew that there were people whose religious traditions were different from my own, but I had been taught to keep my distance from them lest they try to persuade me to abandon my Baptist convictions and practices.

But when I enrolled in a state university, my isolation was aggressively challenged. I became friends with African Americans who, in defense of their right to freedom and dignity, brilliantly dismantled my Jim Crow heritage and challenged that heritage's confusion with the gospel. I met homosexuals. I encountered atheists and agnostics who seemed better able to defend their positions than I mine. I met and became respectful of persons of other faiths. And through my interactions with these people,

God liberated me. By the time I graduated from college, I was committed to the social gospel, the ecumenical movement, and interfaith dialogue.

Most of my undergraduate professors, even those of secular or agnostic perspectives, respectfully challenged me to think more deeply about my faith and convictions. And that was helpful. My major professors in the physics department were something else. They openly criticized anyone who believed in anything supernatural; for them, all religions were generated from "neurotic illusions." Three of these professors dominated the department. They had played a significant role in the "Manhattan Project." The most celebrated of the three had developed a theory of fluid mechanics related to U235 that enabled the United States to build the bomb before Germany and Russia. He was a genuine American hero.

But this intellectual genius was a devout secularist and outspoken atheist. For him, all forms of religion and spirituality were not only dead wrong but were dangerous to modern society. Even so, since my field of specialization was theoretical physics, I chose to remain at that school for graduate studies under him. I expected him to be my dissertation supervisor.

One day near the end of my first graduate year, this celebrated professor called me into his office. He said that belief in God and an irrational commitment to religion and spirituality was incompatible with being a physicist in the twentieth century. He acknowledged that I was an excellent student and a good person, but he would not accept me as his student, nor would he even sit on my examination committee. He strongly recommended that I change areas, or leave physics altogether. The conversation was over.

I left his office devastated and went straight to the Baptist Student Union prayer room. But even as I went, I felt a sense of consolation and relief. I soon recognized that while my true calling was still to be a college teacher, I didn't particularly like teaching physics. What should I teach, then? The answer came quickly: "Teach what you know best–religion!"

I've now enjoyed more than forty years of a career in teaching religion that might have never happened except for that professor, the "orthodox atheist," who was the voice of God to me.

Let the wise listen and add to their learning, and let the discerning get guidance. Proverbs 1:5 NIV

THE ELEVENTH MEETING

"Come and hear, all ye that fear God, and I will declare what he hath done for my soul."

Psalm 66:16

David Davenport
Distinguished Professor of Public Policy, Pepperdine University

J. Thomas Whetstone
Chair, Organizational Leadership and Management, Regent University

G.E. Colpitts
Chair, Department of Art and Design, Judson College

Mary Alice Trent
Associate Professor of English, Oral Roberts University

Gary Oster
Associate Dean for Academics, School of Undergraduate Studies, Regent University

Barry M. Smith
Vice President for Student Life, Roberts Wesleyan College

Leon Smith
Professor of Communication Studies, Wingate University

Brad D. Strawn
Vice President of Spiritual Development and Dean of the Chapel, Southern Nazarene University

Ivan Filby
Professor of Management, Greenville College

Peter Lillback
President, Westminster Theological Seminary

LEARNING FRENCH A BETTER WAY

David Davenport
Distinguished Professor of Public Policy
Pepperdine University
Malibu, California

STUDYING ABROAD is much more common today than it was in my student days. Those of us who did have the opportunity mostly went to Europe, where we studied and took classes four days a week, with a three-day weekend reserved for travel. Every Thursday afternoon, it was a race to the train station to see how far one could get and still make it back by Sunday night.

That was my plan, too, until God revealed a different itinerary for me. Early in the school year, I took a shorter weekend jaunt to Paris where, among other things, I visited a small church on Sunday morning. The people were exceptionally friendly, defying the stereotype that the French only tolerate those who speak their language well. I was invited to lunch, and to come back the following Sunday, which I did.

Soon my Thursday afternoons found me headed not to Ireland or Italy, but back to this little church on Moulin Vert in Paris. The church needed an English teacher for the neighborhood kids on Thursday afternoons and, I thought, why not me? Of course, in the process the children taught me as much French as I taught them English.

Next, I found that the church needed someone to fill in as a music leader on Sunday mornings. Now I had to sing in French too. This led to my spending spring break in Belgium, not as a tourist but as a singer in the church's small chorus at a music gathering. To this day, there are many hymns that I prefer to sing in French rather than English–it reconnects me with the spirit that I felt there.

The minister and his family began to wonder why I should be spending my money in Paris hotels (though I proudly held the record for finding the cheapest pad in town). So they invited me to stay with their family on the weekends. I read their ten-year-old son the *Hardy Boys* books in English, and he shared his French comic book collection with me. We read together from the French Bible and prayed in French at dinner, enriching both my cultural and spiritual experience.

After a few months, my college buddies noticed that my French was improving faster than theirs; they starting asking about this little church where I was learning so much. Never having been much at evangelizing, I now had fun-loving college fellows wanting to come to church with me to see what they could learn. All in all, I learned far more from my weekends in the little church than I learned either in class or sprinting from the campus to European tourist attractions on the Orient Express.

That experience profoundly changed my life. For decades now, I've made it a point to worship in local churches whenever I can in my travels. Just as it was in Paris, such visits always give me an entry into the real life and culture of a community. But more than that, these visits build on the rich spiritual experience I enjoyed that year in Paris, basking in the unity and brotherhood of Christian believers.

Greet one another with a holy kiss. All the churches of Christ send greetings. Romans 16:16 NIV

WORK, REST, AND REWARD

J. Thomas Whetstone
Chair, Organizational Leadership and Management
Regent University
Virginia Beach, Virginia

FROM MY EARLY BOYHOOD I desired to be a businessman, like my father. So I earned a master's degree in business and entered corporate staff management, being promoted rapidly. God called me to faith at the age of twenty-seven, and after eight additional years in corporate life, He called me to seminary. There I met my life partner, Nancy. It was also there that I was recruited to teach business from a Christian perspective. But to do that, I needed doctoral qualifications. So we sold our house and moved to England to undertake studies in business ethics at Oxford.

After only a month, I was worn down and desperate. Though I was studying night and day, I was falling further and further behind in my assignments. Did the Lord really want me at Oxford? My wife voiced her displeasure with me when I actually went to sleep during a magnificent (she said) sermon by visiting preacher John Stott at St. Ebbe's Anglican Church. Though she repeatedly punched my side, I continued to doze.

When I prayed for a solution, it seemed that all I could think about were biblical verses on Sabbath observance. How could this be a reasonable answer? The Lord must know that I needed the rest of the day to complete my papers and other assignments. How could He expect me to give up all this time I so desperately needed?

But as in my conversion experience, I gave in. Deciding to give Sabbath observance a try, I reasoned that I was falling behind anyway. I rationalized that if the trial failed, it would be God's will. As I began to enact my new plan, I missed some parties at college, and I had to plan my use of time more carefully. To my surprise, I started to catch up and my essay grades improved. God blessed me in spite of my stubbornness.

God honored my increased obedience throughout the remainder of my studies. When Nancy was called back to the States to care for her terminally ill mother, I joined a weekly fellowship group of British Christians that further blessed me emotionally and spiritually during the long time of separation from my spouse. And while my classmates labored away on the Sabbath, I enjoyed morning worship and dinner, followed by long walks, rest, and singing along with programs featuring Christian music on British TV. The rest and change of pace left me better prepared for the coming week's work.

I still cannot fully comprehend how it all worked. But I know that my gracious Lord honored my commitment to obey Him. He made my time in Oxford fruitful. I left there with a doctorate, good friends, future research collaborators, increased knowledge, a habit of resting from job responsibilities on the Sabbath, and a heart grateful for God's mercy to stubborn sinners like me.

This is the love of God: to obey his commands. And his commands are not burdensome. 1 John 5:3 NIV

CRISIS IN THE STUDIO

G.E. Colpitts
Chair, Department of Art and Design
Judson College
Elgin, Illinois

WHEN I WAS a senior art major at Greenville College, I was dedicated to the proposition that being an art student was all about having a good time. I enjoyed hanging out in the studio with my friends, but I wasn't really working on anything. At the end of the first semester of Advanced Studio (the course leading to the one-person senior exhibition), my professor had a talk with me. He told me that my grade for the term was a "D," pointing out that I was not making any serious progress toward my senior exhibition. He also said that if I didn't get to work, I was finished. I would not graduate. End of discussion.

I went home for Christmas break in an absolute panic. I didn't know what to do; I had always counted myself a good student, lazy and unmotivated as I was. After talking to my parents, I prayed, asking the Lord to show me what He wanted me to do about the mess I had gotten myself into.

The Sunday morning after Christmas, as I sat waiting for the service to start at our church, I flipped to one of my favorite chapters in the Old Testament, Isaiah 53. But instead of reading that chapter, my eyes strayed to chapter 54. Certain lines and phrases spoke to me directly in that critical time of fear: "Do not be afraid," "Forget the shame of your youth," "I will bring you back." The passage was written to Israel in the feminine, in the metaphor of a barren woman. I was reading it as a "barren woman," that is, a non-art-making female art major, and that was what caught my eye. The instructions to "enlarge your tent, extend your cords, and strengthen your stakes," along with assurances that Israel should not fear disgrace and would not be humiliated, all spoke to me that in the midst of my confusion and fear, God had great plans for me if I would only trust Him. By the time I got to the end of the chapter, I knew without a doubt that the Lord wanted me to be an artist, and that He was calling me.

I went back to school and worked very hard through the January term and the spring semester. By the time my exhibition date rolled around, I had produced enough work for a good show. Although I didn't graduate with honors, I graduated with my self-respect and the respect of my professors. But more than that, I found that I had the motivation and the desire to keep on being an artist.

The Lord had not promised me a show at the end of that year or even that I would graduate from college. I still had my doubts about whether I could make it, but I absolutely knew He had told me very clearly that He wanted me to be an artist–He had promised me Himself.

There have been many times I have been discouraged and frustrated, when I doubted whether I ought to continue making art at all. But every time, the Lord has shown me the way through. Every time I have a doubt, He has provided assurance. So I continue in my vocation, striving to walk worthy of my calling on both fronts–faith and art–every day. The psalmist expresses well what the Lord taught me from that passage in Isaiah 54 and from my work in the art studio during that life-changing semester.

I sought the LORD, and he heard me, and delivered me from all my fears. They looked unto him, and were lightened: and their faces were not ashamed. Psalm 34:4, 5

A CRASH COURSE IN FINANCE 101

Mary Alice Trent
Associate Professor of English
Oral Roberts University
Tulsa, Oklahoma

CREDIT CARD representatives hovered over the student union like vultures, scouting their prey. It was the fall of 1983, my freshman year in college. As a full-time commuter student on an academic scholarship, which paid for my tuition, books, food, and gas for my car, I had very few expenses to worry about. I really had no need for a credit card. But the temptation was enticing all the same. A credit card would help me pay for incidentals.

A smiling company representative greeted me warmly in the student center as I approached her table. She went over the application with me, and I eagerly filled it out. But I noticed that she had not read the fine print to me. I recalled that my father had often told me to read "the small print," so I sat there and read all of it. Though I knew that the big details are usually found in the small print, I wasn't to be frightened away from this rite of passage into adulthood. I signed my name.

Getting approval was not as difficult as I had imagined it would be; I had my card within a couple of weeks. At the end of the first month, after making a few purchases, I received my first bill. I paid the minimum balance due; paying with plastic was easy. The next month, I treated a friend to lunch and bought a new pair of jeans and a sweater in the same day. Plastic was the way to go. Maybe I would open another credit card account, as many of my friends had already done.

I returned home later that afternoon to find my second credit card bill waiting for me in the mailbox. When I opened the envelope, I was alarmed to see that my original balance had now doubled. How could this be?

When my father came home from work, I had a talk with him. I could always go to Dad for godly counsel. He gave me a crash course in Finance 101 that fateful afternoon: don't live "beyond your means"; don't waste your money, because if you do, "you will have nothing to show for it"; always budget, save, and tithe your money; always pay more than your minimum balance on your credit card account until you pay it off.

Before I went to bed that night, I prayed about Dad's advice. From that time on, I saw credit cards in a different way. And I learned that just as my father wanted me to prosper, so did the heavenly Father want me to prosper: financially, physically, and spiritually.

Beloved, I pray that in all respects you may prosper and be in good health, just as your soul prospers. 3 John 2 NASB

ROPED INTO LEARNING

Gary Oster
Associate Dean for Academics
School of Undergraduate Studies
Regent University
Virginia Beach, Virginia

WHEN I RECEIVED my first college grade report, just a few short months into my freshman year, I was shocked to find that my grade point average was far lower than my recent superior high school grades.

I expressed my unhappiness to veteran religion professor Dr. Lambert Ponstein. He patiently peered at me over his glasses, a slight smile crossing his face. Without hesitation, he responded to my frustrations. "Please stop by my office this afternoon," he said in his clipped Dutch accent. "I'll provide you with an answer to your slumping grades."

"Terrific!" I thought, waiting outside Dr. Ponstein's office at the appointed time. "Somebody around here is going to discover how bright I am." Soon I was sitting in his office, scanning the titles of the hundreds of books impressively lining his walls. Perhaps one of these books contained the magical method he would suggest to pump up my disappointing grades. I was eager to find out.

"Here we go," Dr. Ponstein said as he opened a bottom desk drawer. I watched, dumbfounded, as he stretched across his ancient wooden desk to hand me a three-foot length of cord.

"What's that?" I finally exclaimed, unable to hide my incredulity.

"That's Ponstein's Rope," my host replied.

"Looks like a piece of binder twine to me," I said. "This will help improve my grades?"

"Absolutely!" he assured me. "I guarantee it. When you begin to study each day, tie one end of this cord around your ankle, and the other end around the leg of your desk. Don't untie either end until you have completely mastered your homework. Thank you for stopping by."

I returned to my dorm room and sat in the dark for a few hours, thinking about Ponstein's Rope.

I never had to tie Ponstein's Rope to my leg. Instead, I taped it to the wall above my desk as a reminder. And as soon as I changed my drive-by study habits, my grades improved noticeably. The many distractions of college life had been diverting me from the time and focus necessary for successful deep study.

But Ponstein's Rope changed more than my grades; it changed my life. Dr. Ponstein's not-so-subtle message was that there are exciting, unexplored worlds of knowledge available to all who are willing to be disciplined in their habits of study. There are many levels of knowledge of our Lord's amazing handiwork, and an unlimited variety of relationships and connections to other learning to be discovered. But this happens only through hours of concentrated reading, discussion, and thought. How wonderful that intellectual curiosity can never be completely satisfied!

In the three decades since, I have had the same conversation with students of all ages, while distributing new pieces of Ponstein's Rope. Dr. Ponstein's legacy probably has resulted in hundreds of energized, accomplished students. His simple rope "tool" opened exciting, new worlds of study to me, and I am forever grateful.

I will pray with my spirit, but I will also pray with my mind; I will sing with my spirit, but I will also sing with my mind. 1 Corinthians 14:15 NIV

GOD'S DISRUPTIVE TIMING

Barry M. Smith
Vice President for Student Life
Roberts Wesleyan College
Rochester, New York

MY SUMMER DAYS had overflowed with working full-time as a loan officer at the credit union in my hometown, completing two independent study courses, and an internship with a local pastor. But at twenty-one, I had propelled myself through this with boundless energy and confidence.

Now back at college for my senior year, I had a clear vision of the course and direction my life would take. I started the fall semester focused on life after college, moving past the "now" of papers, course requirements, and even some friendships. My attention was directed toward meeting the necessary graduation requirements, securing a good job, and proposing marriage to my girlfriend.

The semester began well and was progressing smoothly in spite of an annoying, unrelenting cold that lingered with a sore throat. But by mid-semester I was coping with constant headaches, I could barely swallow, and I kept falling asleep in class and during study sessions in the library. I was tired all the time and found no joy in any of the college activities. The academic pressure increased as my semester overload grew more difficult to carry. Finally, a blood test at the college health center revealed what had become obvious to others: I had mononucleosis.

The symptoms and illness could have been much worse, but I was upset at how "God's timing" disrupted my schedule. How could I finish all of my objectives and get on with my life? These circumstances seemed so unfair and out of alignment with my understanding of what God had in store for me. What was He thinking? What was He doing? I freely expressed these feelings–when I wasn't looking for the nearest place to lie down and sleep.

I spent the next week in a semi-conscious state of recovery at the home of my future in-laws. They were very gracious, even though I was a lousy guest who did little more than eat modestly and sleep constantly. After that week, I flew home for three more weeks of sleep and extended care from my own family.

I missed a month of my senior year, and with it many unique experiences of closure and transition that a senior year normally brings. When I returned to campus, I made every effort to pick up where I had left off, but much had changed. I was different. Having mono significantly affected how I looked at college, my classes, and my future plans.

My experience certainly was not unusual or spectacular. Events like this happen, particularly to college students who extend the margins and push their physical limits. I thought my agenda was set and the next steps established. But my timing was not God's timing. Through a case of mono, He taught me a better, richer way to see what I was and how I should live.

This is what the LORD says: "Let not the wise man boast of his wisdom or the strong man boast of his strength or the rich man boast of his riches, but let him who boasts boast about this: that he understands and knows me, that I am the LORD, who exercises kindness, justice and righteousness on earth, for in these I delight." Jeremiah 9:23, 24 NIV

FROM HELL TO HEAVEN

Leon Smith
Professor of Communication Studies
Wingate University
Wingate, North Carolina

I WAS ALWAYS a late bloomer. I walked late, talked late, gave up the baby bottle late, and went through spiritual rebellion late. However, when I was twelve, I actually experienced God's presence. During a confirmation class, I became certain that God was real, that He cared for me personally, and that He wanted me close to Him.

I came home from that class basking in the glow of His presence. Soon, however, my attention was diverted. I had to help Daddy cut down a tree, pulling my end of the two-man saw. As I pulled, the glow of His presence drained away.

"If it was really from God, it wouldn't have faded like that," said a voice. I had to admit that I agreed with the voice. It never occurred to me to ask God.

I went through with getting baptized, but without joy, because I was without God. Church membership was a very poor substitute for friendship with Him. But I did not yet walk away. Once, in great mental anguish, I begged Him for help. But He was not to be found. I was disappointed, but not surprised.

In a revival meeting during college, I felt the glory of God again. Overwhelmed by joy, sorrow, happiness, disappointment, and regret, I began to sob. I could not stop sobbing, even to talk with the counselor. I left the church as empty as I had come in.

In graduate school things got worse. I began studying for my master's degree under a popular professor who was enthralled by meaninglessness, nothingness, and futility. In light of my own experience, his views began to make sense. And the church I had chosen provided no countervailing force, for its erudite and dignified minister was more concerned with the masters of literature than the Master of the universe.

While still attending that church, I joined a jazz combo. Once, with permission, we set up in the church's education building to rehearse. We had barely begun to play when we were distracted by shouts from down the hall. The next moment, we were mortified when the pastor charged in, angrily ordering us to get out. We packed up our instruments and walked away.

For a long time after that, I kept on walking away–from the building, from the institution, from the Book, and from the Savior. As apparent justification for my walk into calculated unbelief, I enlisted the absent God, His departed glow, my unanswered prayer, my helplessness, and even my being cast from the church.

A thousand more days of hell on earth would pass before God's relentless pursuit caught me in His love, and I turned, finally, completely, to the Way of Life.

If I make my bed in hell, behold, thou art there. Psalm 139:8

THE GROUP AND THE CALLING

Brad D. Strawn
Vice President of Spiritual Development
and Dean of the Chapel
Southern Nazarene University
Bethany, Oklahoma

IN THE GROUP dynamics course that I took my junior year of college, there were no readings, no assignments, and no tests. It was an experiential course. When the professor arrived the first day of class, he instructed us to put our chairs in a circle, and then he just sat there, not saying a word. He looked at us, and we looked back at him, and then at each other, and then at the floor. I had never been so uncomfortable in my life. We eventually figured out that if we were going to learn about how groups worked, we were going to have to become a group, and to do that we were going to have to get to know one another.

Over the course of the semester we did come to know each other, primarily by sharing our stories and developing trust. I doubt I will ever forget that particular session when one of the members began sharing a struggle in his life. I acutely remember that it was very difficult for him, and none of us seemed to know what to say. An uncomfortable silence fell over the group as he finished.

Suddenly, our instructor shifted ever so slightly in his seat toward the struggling group member. The professor began to talk slowly to him like someone trying to coax a small child out from under a bed. He used empathic words, gentle tones, and cautious language. That anxious, isolated group member slowly began to unfold like a flower reaching for the sun. My professor had become a warm, accepting person that this frightened young man could warm himself beside and find refuge.

It was in that moment that I first learned the power of being understood, the impact of empathy, and the grace of acceptance. In that instant I witnessed a kind of relatedness that I had never before experienced. It felt as if God had walked into the room and said, "It is good." I didn't have words for it at the time, but I now understand that moment of connection as a glimpse of what it means to be made in the image of God. When we humans connect, we are imaging the inextricable relatedness of the triune God.

This was the moment when I knew what I wanted to do with my life. I longed to be able to connect, to bring about healing and restoration in the wounded and broken. It was then that my vocation became clear.

Now I am finishing my tenth year doing exactly what I dreamed of as an undergraduate–teaching at a Christian university and practicing clinical psychology. But deeper than that, everything I do focuses on connecting with others to bring about restoration and healing. I am thankful that God worked through my college professor to shape my vocational aspirations. I pray that He uses me as effectively to mentor my students.

Dear friends, since God so loved us, we also ought to love one another. No one has ever seen God; but if we love one another, God lives in us and his love is made complete in us. 1 John 4:11, 12 NIV

THIRTY FLIGHTS OF STAIRS

Ivan Filby
Professor of Management
Greenville College
Greenville, Illinois

HOW WAS I supposed to know the book of Job was pronounced "Jobe"? If it were meant to be "Jobe" surely there would have been an "e" on the end. As far as I was concerned, J-o-b always spells "job." J-o-b as in "odd-job man" or as in "sleeping-on-the-job." So in my Bible study group, I called the book "job." Everyone laughed, except me. I felt stupid, ashamed, and angry.

I had come to faith just before leaving home to study management at Aston University, then the premier business school in England. I was passionate for God, but to be honest, I struggled to like His people. I just didn't fit in at all. Most of the Christians on campus seemed to have been Christians forever. They knew where to find all kinds of minutiae in the Bible; I could not even pronounce the names of the books properly!

During my second term at Aston, the Christian Union planned an evangelistic outreach. Each morning we met in groups to pray for our friends who had not yet found Christ. So it was on a cool February morning that I found myself climbing up to the fifteenth floor of Lawrence Tower to pray with a group of fellow Christians.

Fifteen stories meant thirty flights of stairs. With each step I became angrier. I was angry at the elevator (we English call it a "lift") for not working. I was angry at the maintenance men for not fixing the lift. I was angry at this group of Christians for laughing at my pronunciation of Job the last time we met. I was angry with myself for being angry. I was angry with God. "If God was so big," I mused, "why aren't His people nicer? Why is it so hard to fit in with them?"

I've no idea what we prayed for that day. I just sat there fuming. As soon as the final Amen was spoken, I bolted for the door and started to run down the thirty flights of steps. I just wanted to be alone.

I had only made it down two flights when I heard Steve's voice behind me, "Ivan, hold up!" I ignored him and raced down another flight. Steve shouted, "Ivan, hold up!" I kept running. By the time I had reached the last flight of stairs, he had caught up with me. He grabbed my arm and said, "You've got to talk to somebody, Ivan. It might as well be me."

To be honest, I didn't want to talk to him. But I was also deeply touched that someone would care enough about me to chase me down thirty flights of stairs. We caught our breath, talked over a hot drink, and became friends. During the next few years Steve mentored me, prayed with me, and encouraged me. Through Steve's practical love, Christ was able to reach the deep issues in my soul. I'm forever grateful to God for sending Steve into my life.

But there is a friend who sticks closer than a brother. Proverbs 18:24 NJKV

WASHED BY THE WORD

Peter Lillback
President
Westminster Theological Seminary
Philadelphia, Pennsylvania

IN MY FIRST DAYS at Cedarville College, I had to adjust to many new circumstances. First, I was a little homesick. Second, the dorm was overcrowded, so I had to live in the "common space" of our dorm suite. Third, I missed my steady girlfriend and future wife, Debbie, who was studying nursing two hundred miles away.

In those circumstances, I had resolved to develop the daily habit of quiet reading of Scripture. One of the things that helped me in this resolve was the new leather-bound and personalized Bible Debbie had given to me. Each morning, when I finished reading the text for the day, it was my practice to leave the Bible open to the next day's reading. That reminded me, as St. Augustine wrote, to "take up and read."

Somewhere in the middle of that first semester, the hazards of living in the common space became clear. The natives were restless one evening, and a water fight broke out. I was living in ground zero of the fight and did my best to take cover.

When the war was over, I assessed the collateral damage, and discovered to my dismay that my gilded Bible, the gift of my beloved future wife, had been "baptized" by the youthful watery fun. Only in retrospect could I philosophically enjoy the humor of some institutional symbolism in the tragedy. Cedarville had been founded Presbyterian but had become Baptist. The waters that had baptized my Bible had come from above, as in Presbyterian sprinkling, but the quantity was enough to qualify as Baptist immersion.

At the moment, of course, I only knew that I was incensed, outraged. How could they do this to my beloved's gift, to God's Word?

As I looked disconsolately at the drying, wrinkled pages, I began to read. The Bible was open to 1 Corinthians 13: "Love is patient, love is kind . . . ."

As I forgave my dormmates, I also realized God had given me a sacramental Bible. It had been baptized by the love of my future wife, and then by the grace I found in Paul's inspired words to extend forgiveness to my Christian friends.

I still look at that Bible every now and again to reflect on God's grace in Christ. And in any Bible, 1 Corinthians 13 now has special meaning for me because it brings to mind the day when my heart, like my Bible, was washed by the Word of Life.

Love suffers long and is kind; love does not envy; love does not parade itself, is not puffed up; does not behave rudely, does not seek its own, is not provoked, thinks no evil; does not rejoice in iniquity, but rejoices in the truth; bears all things, believes all things, hopes all things, endures all things. 1 Corinthians 13:4-7 NKJV

THE TWELFTH MEETING

"Come and hear, all ye that fear God, and I will declare what he hath done for my soul."

Psalm 66:16

Eric D. Moore
Professor of Graduate Education, Southwest Baptist University

Melinda Gann
Associate Professor of Mathematics, Mississippi College

Janet Borisevich Mezenov
Professor of English, Pacific Union College

John Derry
President, Hope International University

Robert Chasnov
Professor of Engineering, Cedarville University

Jill Branyon
Associate Professor of Education, North Greenville University

Robert W. Nienhuis
Executive Vice President and Chief Academic Officer, Cornerstone University

Mark A. Hogan
Associate Professor of Education, Bridgewater College

Vinson Synan
Dean of the School of Divinity, Regent University

Susan Fenton Willoughby
Professor of Sociology and Social Work, Atlantic Union College

FENCED IN BY FREEDOM

Eric D. Moore
Professor of Graduate Education
Southwest Baptist University
Bolivar, Missouri

MY LAST SUMMER before college, I was offered a full-time job at a summer camp, teaching swimming and lifeguarding. No more hay-hauling, pulling weeds out of soybean fields, and caring for cantankerous cattle. When I told my parents that I was going to work at camp all summer, my father balked. "Son, you can't go," he insisted. "I need you here this summer, building fence." I begged. He was steadfast. I was devastated.

I sulked all weekend, letting my father know by my silence how much I disliked his interfering with my freedom to live my own life. I was never going to be a farmer or a truck driver, so what could he teach me about anything?

Monday morning, with silence that would shatter glass, I gathered all the tools together. My father and I headed out to begin our summer of fence building and repair, supplemented with generous sessions of hay-hauling and other usual farm chores.

We detached and rolled up rusted barbwire. We pulled out rotting fence posts. We set railroad ties three feet into the ground for new corner posts, all lined up perfectly and squarely with the fields. We built and hung gates with such precision that they swung open and shut with barely a touch. We set steel fence posts every ten feet with a post driver. Then we strung new barbwire, stretched taut and gleaming in the sun.

Once we brought the cattle back to this field, the new fence kept them out of the corn and soybeans. I realized how important it was for the successful operation of our farm. I began to understand that swimming and lifeguarding would have been just a summer job; fencing was family.

Not far into the summer, conversation made its way back into my relationship with Dad. We talked about the beauty of a sunrise, the joy of turning over fresh earth, or the wonder of a newborn calf. We laughed over cuts and bruises. Occasionally, the harsh, steamy day would end with a wrestling contest or a dip in the pond. But every day would climax with gazing proudly at the beauty of a new line of fence. I learned much about the joy of a job done well, and about the character of a man who never quit doing the right thing. As the sun set on each day's work, I found myself gathering tools and walking back to the house in Dad's footsteps.

What is freedom? Some say I might have experienced the greatest level of freedom had I been given the choice to do what I wanted to do that summer. But I believe I was given greater freedom in the discipline I learned from my father. Great theologians have noted the dichotomy in our faith, the allegiance to God's holy and unchanging Word while claiming absolute freedom in the love of Christ. Once we love God's law, we are truly free to love, free to contribute to the world around us, free to bring about God's plan for our lives. Or maybe simply free to build a fence.

But the man who looks intently into the perfect law that gives freedom, and continues to do this, not forgetting what he has heard, but doing it—he will be blessed in what he does. James 1:25 NIV

BECAUSE HE WANTS ME TO

Melinda Gann
Associate Professor of Mathematics
Mississippi College
Clinton, Mississippi

I DON'T REMEMBER the first time that I talked to God. When I was a child, He was simply the One with whom I shared my most private thoughts, fears, and dreams. I talked with Him the same way I talked with family and friends. No "Thee" or "Thou" existed in my vocabulary. He and I simply "hung out" together each day, a habit that continues to this day.

But one afternoon during my sophomore year at Mississippi State University, God chose to change my world during that regular prayer time with Him. I was sitting at my desk telling Him about my day, as if this information was new for Him. And suddenly, without warning, God gave me a tiny glimpse of His glory.

As I sat there chattering away, I was abruptly hit with the realization of Who this was that I was speaking to. I still cannot adequately describe the powerful feeling that overcame me. At that moment, I understood the phrase "fear of the Lord." It was not a trembling of dread or terror. It was, instead, an overwhelming sense of awe and understanding. I was sitting in my dorm room rattling away to the Creator of the universe. Everything that I had known and had seen in my life was spoken into existence by Him, and could at any moment be wiped away with a single word from Him.

I went down on my knees, and my mind began to race. How dare I go barreling into the presence of the Creator? What gave me the audacity to chatter away about my day to the Sustainer of life? What made me think He wanted to hear about the mundane details of my day? He had important work to do. Why did I think I had the right to come to the foot of His throne?

Then, in the midst of my jumbled thoughts, came a clear, almost audible answer from God. "Why do you have the right to enter My presence?

Because I want you to!"

What joy and amazement flooded my soul! The Creator and Sustainer of life, the Savior of the world, the Master of the universe, desired *my* company. He was and is the One who gives me that unbelievable right, the permission to enter His presence whenever I choose. The daughter is always welcomed into the presence of her loving Father.

Today, as I enter into the presence of my heavenly Father, I smile and remember why I have that privilege–because He wants me to!

This resurrection life you received from God is not a timid, grave-tending life. It's adventurously expectant, greeting God with a childlike "What's next, Papa?" God's Spirit touches our spirits and confirms who we really are. We know who he is, and we know who we are: Father and children. Romans 8:15, 16 *The Message*

ARABIC, ALLAH, AND A CAN OF BEER

Janet Borisevich Mezenov
Professor of English
Pacific Union College
Angwin, California

AS I WALKED into the vast cafeteria for the first time, I suddenly realized more than ever that I was a stranger in a strange territory. This was my first day at the University of Washington as a linguistics graduate student. It was also the first time in my life to be a student on a secular campus.

After choosing some items from the meal line, I looked for a seat. My heart thumping, I spotted an empty chair at a table with five others who graciously allowed me to sit with them. I heard them speaking Arabic as I approached, but they stopped as I sat down.

"Please continue your conversation," I said. "I enjoy listening to other languages."

They smiled, thanking me. "You are very kind. Would you like a beer?" One can remained of their six-pack.

"No, but thank you very much," I replied.

"Please, take the last one," they encouraged me.

"Thank you very much for your generosity. I don't drink," I responded."

"You don't drink? Really?" They were very surprised.

"Yes, really," I smiled. "I honestly do not drink."

"But we thought that all Americans drink." They were still amazed. "Are you a Muslim?"

"No, I'm not. I'm a Christian."

"Then why don't you drink? Other Christians we have met drink alcohol. It's okay for them. What kind of Christian are you?" They seemed determined.

"Well," I started, "I'm a Seventh-day Adventist Christian. Drinking alcohol is discouraged by my faith because we believe that our bodies are the temples of God and that we should take the best care of them that we can. Drinking destroys brain cells and makes it difficult to make wise decisions."

"Actually, we are ashamed," one of them confessed. "We are not supposed to be drinking either. We are Muslims."

"Yes, I know," I said. "Don't you think that Allah has eyes outside of the Middle East?"

"How did you know that we were Muslims?" they asked in surprise.

"You were speaking the same Nadji dialect of Arabic that my other Arab friends speak," I continued. "I figured that you were probably followers of Islam."

One of them got up from the table and gathered all the half-filled cans of beer and placed them in the garbage can. He then sat down again. "From our hearts, we thank you for sitting with us. We know that Allah has sent you, a Christian, to our table to guide us back to the straight path. What did you say the name of your religion was? Seven days . . .?"

"Seventh-day Adventist."

"What does this name mean?" they asked. "Tell us more about your religion. We want to know more about it."

Several hours later, my new friends and I had discussed the beauty of the Sabbath invented by our Creator, the difference and the continuity between the Old and New Testaments, health issues, the earth's last days, and Jesus' Second Coming.

From that day on, I realized the magnitude of every word that we say. I could have simply declined their offer of the beer. But I had also said, "I don't drink." That simple statement gave my Muslim friends an opportunity to hear aspects of the gospel they had never heard before.

Be wise in the way you act toward outsiders; make the most of every opportunity. Let your conversation be always full of grace, seasoned with salt, so that you may know how to answer everyone. Colossians 4:5, 6 NIV

A PUZZLE INSTEAD OF A MAP

John Derry
President
Hope International University
Fullerton, California

ALL I KNEW when I started my freshman year as a ministry major at Lincoln Christian College was that I wanted to further my education. That in itself was significant in my world because I would be the first member of my extended family to attend college. I enrolled with mixed emotions and with little idea of what to expect.

Furthermore, I had some doubts about whether ministry was the right career for me. I didn't think I should have such doubts. I know now that being undecided on a major is quite common and acceptable for a college freshman, but at the time I felt as if I should have this all worked out. I wanted to follow God's will for my life but had never had a "defining moment," as some did, that gave me a clear sense of direction about my professional path. It was very frustrating to wonder, "What does God want me to do?" If only He would give me a map so I could know I was on the right road. Was I missing the signs along the way? I went about my routine of classes, studying, working, all the while waiting for an answer, but it never came.

One of the requirements of all students was to complete two Christian service projects each month. For one project I taught the fourth- and fifth-grade boys' Sunday school class at my home church. For my second project, I signed up for the "Kerusso Club," unsure of exactly what that was. Later I found out that it was the Greek word for "preaching." Every club member was assigned an area church each month at which he was to preach for a Sunday evening service. As a freshman I hadn't taken any homiletics classes yet, so I made the best of it and prepared a sermon on the "Parable of the Lost Sheep."

Shortly after I turned eighteen years old, and having just started my sophomore year, I was contacted by the minister of a small country church near my hometown. He was eighty-six years old and ready to retire. He asked if I would be interested in preaching for the congregation. The church was less than an hour away from the college, so I soon found myself writing a sermon every week. I have fond memories of that experience and of the people who shared it with me.

A couple years later I was preaching for a larger church in a nearby community and continued to do so during my senior year and through seminary. That was followed by a campus ministry at a state university, two more advanced degrees, serving as a college vice president, and then president of two other colleges. Never in my wildest dreams would I have envisioned the places God has taken me. I didn't set out to follow this path. I simply took things one step at a time and continued to ask, "What do you want me to do with my life?" Through the years I've had many opportunities to serve as an elder in a church, be on the board of a community organization, pursue another college degree, or make a career move. Each time, I evaluated the opportunity to determine whether the needs presented were those God could best use me to meet. If so, then I took the next step.

I am convinced that God uses our past experiences to prepare us for our next place of service. I can see now how every ministry, degree, and lesson learned was preparation for what I am doing today. At the time it wasn't always crystal clear. God's will unfolds slowly and can best be seen in retrospect. I can see now how it all is starting to fit like the pieces of a jigsaw puzzle coming together to form a picture. When I was seventeen years old, I wanted a map, an outline of the entire path. Fortunately, God is much wiser and led me on a journey of faith.

In his heart a man plans his course, but the LORD determines his steps. Proverbs 16:9 NIV

THE NEW CREATION THAT GOT A "C"

Robert Chasnov
Professor of Engineering
Cedarville University
Cedarville, Ohio

I GAVE MY LIFE to Jesus Christ while I was a junior at Rensselaer Polytechnic Institute (RPI). This happened while I was taking an advanced course in the philosophy of science, called Scientific Revolutions. The course addressed topics such as abortion, the origin of humanity, and space exploration. The writing assignments for the course consisted of three- to five-page responses to questions that required the students to expose their personal worldview. Throughout the semester, my inward crisis of belief must have been obvious to the professor.

At the beginning of the semester I was a seeker. I had been raised in a traditional Jewish home and started reading the Old Testament to determine God's plan for His people, Israel. By spring break I had come to understand that God sent the Messiah, Jesus Christ, to become the required sacrifice for my sins.

The final project for the semester involved a debate with another student: Evolution vs. Creation. Being a new believer, I wanted to support my newly found theistic worldview. However, being a babe in Christ, I clearly was ill prepared to support my positions adequately.

When I received my grades for the semester and saw the "C" posted next to this course, I visited the professor and asked for an explanation. He said, "Chasnov, you wavered from side to side all semester long. First you came down on one side of an issue, then you agreed with the opposing view. That's why you received a below average grade."

After thinking briefly about how I *had* "changed sides" during that semester, I simply smiled and said, "You're right. Thank you very much!" I think he was stunned by my response, expecting rather to receive a barrage of complaints from me.

Though my professor was clearly a nonbeliever, his insights confirmed what had happened in my life. He had actually noticed the outward manifestations of my inward spiritual struggle. The apostle Paul tells us in 2 Corinthians 5:17 that those who have been born again are a "new creation" of God. What a blessing it was for me to receive such a positive confirmation that I am one of His beloved!

Therefore, if anyone is in Christ, he is a new creation; the old has gone, the new has come! 2 Corinthians 5:17 NIV

INVESTMENT IN A FRIEND, DIVIDENDS FROM THE LORD

Jill Branyon
Associate Professor of Education
North Greenville University
Tigerville, South Carolina

WHEN I WAS a college student, money management was the furtherest thing from my mind. I did not have all that much money to manage. But with two electives to complete during my junior year, I chose a course entitled, "Housing and Home Planning." During the course, we had to keep records of our spending habits in order to construct a workable budget. I carefully recorded each amount into predetermined categories. I made sure to include charitable contributions as one of those categories. The pragmatic professor wrote in bold letters, "You obviously give too much to charity for your income." She had no inkling of my upcoming test of faith in the area of giving.

The inner struggle began when a sister in Christ desperately needed twenty-five dollars to attend a volleyball tournament. I knew I could meet her need, but it would take all the money I had for the whole month. After wrestling in prayer about what to do, I came to believe that God wanted me to give her the money. I told Him that I would rather please Him than myself, that I would rather demonstrate love extravagantly than be sensible about money.

The following month, as I recorded my income and expenses for the month, it became clear that the twenty-five dollars given as an act of obedience had now become fifty dollars. I had received the return of the original twenty-five and had unexpectedly received a tax refund and a gift from my aunt.

I pointed out to the professor that because of my faithfulness in giving at God's leading, I had a 100 percent return on my investment in a single month. While I am confident she did not believe that the overflow of cash came from God, I knew in my heart that God had rewarded me and met all of my needs.

When I responded to the need of my friend, God paid me back in full, "pressed down" and "running over." I believe I could never out-give God. He has proved His faithfulness over and over again.

Give, and it will be given to you: good measure, pressed down, shaken together, and running over will be put into your bosom. For with the same measure that you use, it will be measured back to you. Luke 6:38 NKJV

MY PLANS OR HIS PLANS?

Robert W. Nienhuis
Executive Vice President
and Chief Academic Officer
Cornerstone University
Grand Rapids, Michigan

AS I HEADED to the university to begin my doctoral studies, I knew exactly how the coming years of my life were going to unfold. I had carefully plotted my course and was convinced that God had given me his unqualified "Seal of Approval." My plan *had* to be God's will, I reasoned. Everything made so much sense.

Two years of coursework. Pass the comprehensive exams. Get approval for a dissertation topic. Head to a seminary (I even knew which seminary!) to begin my academic career. Finish the dissertation while teaching. Enjoy a long and fulfilling career as a faculty member in graduate theological education.

It was so clear–and so right! Imagine how surprised I was, then, while approaching the end of my two years of coursework, to receive a telephone call from the dean of the seminary at which I was planning to teach. Due to internal adjustments, there was no longer a position open for me.

In a moment's time, my plans were shattered. As I prayed and sought God's encouragement and direction, I realized that what I had decided was God's will for me may not have been His will at all. I had plotted a course and asked God to bless it rather than seek His course for me. With a humble heart and expectant faith, I confessed my arrogance and presumption and asked God to direct my steps.

Within weeks, God began to open doors of opportunity at the university that would expand my horizons of both learning and future work. For the next several years, while completing my dissertation and beyond, I was given extraordinary opportunities to learn about and work in university administration. It was during that time that God enabled me to understand my gifts and abilities and directed my course into Christian higher education administration.

Throughout that time, God's word provided a solid foundation as I prayed and waited and trusted. As I surrendered my plans and purposes to a loving, sovereign God, I began to realize that His plans for me were greater, more fulfilling, and far more worthwhile than anything I could have imagined. Rather than seeking His approval of my plans, I learned to surrender my plans and to embrace His plan as my plan.

"For I know the plans that I have for you," declares the LORD, "plans for welfare and not for calamity to give you a future and a hope." Jeremiah 29:11 NASB

FIRED, CONNECTED, AND LIVING THE SCRIPTURES

Mark A. Hogan
Associate Professor of Education
Bridgewater College
Bridgewater, Virginia

AS A COLLEGE STUDENT four hundred miles from home, I longed for connectedness. It had been a difficult transition from student to resident assistant. In the first few weeks of my sophomore year, my summer assuredness about God's call to ministry to twenty-five first-year college men began to wane as crisis and discipline issues ate away at my enthusiasm. Long hours of counseling took their toll on me, as I was challenged to show the men in their various problems that God is a God of caring.

But this crisp, cool Friday evening was my night off from the dorm, and four blocks away the town had gathered to celebrate autumn around the town square. My agrarian ancestry beckoned me to join the community and celebrate the glory of God at harvest time.

The square was filled with dunking booths, down-home carnival games, and thick spreads of baked goods, caramel apples, and popcorn. I closed my eyes and breathed in the memories of my past. For that moment I was no longer a "gown" but part of the "town," a real community. The music of the harvest dance drew me to one corner of the square. In front of me were college and community joining together, dancing in celebration. I stood and observed, thinking that this was how this college should fit into the community; not as a separatist colony, but integrated with the community.

The next Tuesday evening, as I went into a resident assistant meeting specially called by the dean of student life, I was still excited about what I had seen. But the dean expressed a different emotion. The college had been embarrassed by so many members of its community dancing on the town square. Reminding us that the college had a behavioral lifestyle contract that forbade the "three D's"– drugs, drinking, and dancing–the dean laid out the guidelines for probation and expulsion for anyone who had danced last Friday evening.

And then he said, "I know some of you RA's were there, and I want you to confess." I knew there had been seven of us there, and I felt no concern as I raised my hand in confession. But when I looked around, I saw that only three of us had confessed.

We three were called immediately to a meeting with an administrative council and asked if any of us had danced. None of us had. They gave us two days to compile a list of all the students we had seen dancing. The three of us spent many hours praying together. At the end of two days, we produced no list. We were immediately put on probation and relieved of our duties as RA's.

My human voice would have railed about what I perceived as the injustice. But a faculty mentor came alongside me with the question, "Mark, do you see how this is part of God's plan to mold you for the future?" As he and I prayed and counseled over the next few days, he encouraged me to read and live out 1 Peter 3:8-11. He promised that in these times of doubt God would reward "living the Scriptures," though I would struggle with "living the world."

Today, my response to adversity reflects what I learned at that Christian college, not so much from the classroom as from going to watch a community come together and celebrate in dance. And I celebrate the mentor who challenged me to live the Scriptures.

Finally, all of you, live in harmony with one another; be sympathetic, love as brothers, be compassionate and humble. Do not repay evil with evil or insult with insult, but with blessing, because to this you were called so that you may inherit a blessing. 1 Peter 3:8, 9 NIV

LIVING FOR THE UNDERDOGS

Vinson Synan
Dean of the School of Divinity
Regent University
Virginia Beach, Virginia

IT WAS AN AWESOME responsibility. In 1955, my sophomore year at Emmanuel Junior College in Franklin Springs, Georgia, I was elected to the student government. This gave me the fearful responsibility of sitting on a committee that handled student disciplinary cases. Decisions that we made could result in a student's suspension or dismissal from the school.

I remember well one case involving a fourteen-year-old boy in the high school academy that was then a part of the institution. He had racked up forty-nine demerits for minor infractions. The limit was fifty demerits, after which the student was to be shipped home. During the year, this boy had antagonized administrators and faculty members to the point that they were ready to kick him out. The president of the college, the president of the student council, and the faculty advisor to the council were adamant that he should leave the school.

As the proceedings went on, I began to feel sorry for the boy because he was so young and so far away from home. In a sudden rush of compassion, I begged the council to let me take personal responsibility for his behavior for the rest of the year. I would mentor him and try to save his place among us. The council grudgingly agreed.

To make a long story short, the boy made a remarkable turnaround and finished the year without another single demerit.

He went on to another college, where he graduated without any marks against his record. Years later, I visited him in Richmond, Virginia, where he had become the manager of a retirement home. He was a leading citizen of the city and was making a wonderful record for himself and his family.

But it was another part of that story that was to change my life. After graduating from the University of Richmond in 1959 with a B.A. in American history, I began working as a youth director in my denomination. But soon I received a call from the president of Emmanuel College. One of the history professors there had utterly failed in the classroom and had to be released in the middle of the uncompleted term. They desperately needed someone to complete his courses. Although I had not taught a single academic class in my life, they were calling on me. "One reason we are calling you is the way you helped save that young boy from being kicked out of school," the president told me on the phone. "I was impressed."

My acceptance of this invitation brought me into the world of academia, leading me eventually to complete my M.A. and Ph.D. degrees at the University of Georgia. Eventually, I went on to serve as Dean of the School of Divinity at Regent University, where I earned a reputation of often siding with the underdogs among both the students and faculty. That incident in junior college did more than I could have ever known to redirect my life and give me faith that even the most hopeless of people can be redeemed with a little love and care.

I tell you the truth, whatever you did for one of the least of these brothers of mine, you did for me. Matthew 25:40 NIV

A BREEZE FOR A BELIEVER

Susan Fenton Willoughby
Professor of Sociology and Social Work
Atlantic Union College
South Lancaster, Massachusetts

THE SCHOOL YEAR had ended and summer had just begun. My husband and I, with our one-year-old son, were living in married student housing. We were both students; so when our semester grades arrived in one envelope addressed to both of us, I opened it, although he was not at home.

We'd had the same teacher for one course, so we had often reviewed for examinations together and compared grades, which were usually about the same. For two working people with a young child, "B's" were good grades. This time, however, the final grade for the course showed his as a "B-" and mine as a "C+." A "C+" for me meant no Dean's List, and probably no graduate-school admissions. I knew it had to be a mistake.

I quickly met with the teacher and pointed out the mistake. He was very understanding of my concern, but showed me that there was a zero entered in his grade book for a particular test on which I was sure I had made 100 percent. I remembered my grade very well, I told him, because my husband had gotten 94 percent (still an "A") on that same test.

"If you can produce the examination with that grade on it," he told me, "I will change the grade. However," he continued, "I've never had to do that in all my years of teaching."

The ball was now in my court. And believe it or not, I found every exam for that course except the one I needed to find. Our apartment was so small that everything had to be well organized and kept in its place, so finding that test shouldn't have been a problem. After looking everywhere, I called on my babysitter for help. We prayed as we searched but found no missing exam.

Now I was desperate. The grade was no longer important. My reputation for honesty was at stake. We stopped searching, knelt and prayed earnestly for help. Then we went through all my class papers again very carefully, and still found nothing.

As we knelt to pray a second time, a breeze rushed through an open window, scattering my loose papers all over the room. In a moment I'll never forget, I saw that the papers had separated just enough to reveal that my missing exam and my husband's exam had adhered so closely together that they seemed as one.

In my distress I called upon the LORD; . . . from His temple He heard my voice, and my cry to Him reached His ears. Psalm 18:6 RSV

THE THIRTEENTH MEETING

"Come and hear, all ye that fear God, and I will declare what he hath done for my soul."

Psalm 66:16

Eric Pratt
Vice President for Christian Development, Mississippi College

Phil Lestmann
Professor of Mathematics, Bryan College

James R. Vanderwoerd
Associate Professor of Social Work, Redeemer University College

John D. Yordy
Provost and Executive Vice President, Goshen College

Penny Long Marler
Professor of Religion, Samford University

Don Meyer
President, Valley Forge Christian College

Chris Willerton
Professor of English, Abilene Christian University

John P. Cragin
Cargill Professor of Business, Paul Dickinson School of Business, Oklahoma Baptist University

Myrla Seibold
Professor of Psychology, Bethel University

Sandra A. Holmes
Associate Professor of Education and Biological Sciences, Messiah College

FAILING WHAT MATTERS

Eric Pratt
Vice President
for Christian Development
Mississippi College
Clinton, Mississippi

MY FIRST WEEK in college I thought I had entered academic heaven. When I was given reading assignments and homework that no one but me would ever see, I thought, *Man, this is going to be easy!* So I went to class, took notes, and got involved in a ton of student stuff. But I rarely did the problem sets or read the assigned chapters.

The night before my first test, I picked up the textbook and attempted to cram six chapters of chemistry and eighteen problem sets into a single six-hour study session. Obviously, there was no way. Stressed out and sleep deprived, I scored 34 percent on my first exam.

I should have taken this as some sort of sign that I needed to learn how to study. The office of academic services assured me that I could do this by spending three hours on Saturday morning in Garland Hall. Instead, I resorted to a much easier approach. I changed my seating.

This change in seating resulted in a much better score on the next exam. I got a 96. I thought I had it made. The third exam seemed to go well, too, but about three days after the test, I received a phone call from the Honor Council. There seemed to be some problem with my chemistry test. The professor had guessed that some sort of improper behavior was going on and had made three slightly different exams. I was "busted."

So what does a guilty person do when his hand is caught in the cookie jar? Deny, deny, deny! And deny I did. But after being confronted, I finally admitted to cheating on the tests. I received a failing grade and was placed on probation.

A more intelligent person would have realized that maybe some time in Garland Hall learning how to study would be a good thing. But not this boy. I still thought that I could beat the system, so I found many other shortcuts. I was still making it my way.

One day a friend came to me and asked me to go with her to the student center. When we arrived there, she pointed out a quote inscribed on a plaque on the wall: "You are taking two tests today, one in physics and one in integrity. If you must fail one, fail physics." My friend looked at me and said, "Eric, you may be passing your classes, but you're failing what matters."

This was a hard truth to believe, but I knew she was right. Now I didn't rush off and spend the next Saturday in Garland Hall, but over the next few months I did become well acquainted with academic services. And I changed seats again. I moved to the front in all of my classes so I could avoid failing what matters.

What good will it be for a man if he gains the whole world, yet forfeits his soul? Matthew 16:26 NIV

NIGHTMARE SEMESTER

Phil Lestmann
Professor of Mathematics
Bryan College
Dayton, Tennessee

DURING MY SECOND SEMESTER of my sophomore year at Biola College (now Biola University), I was carrying nineteen semester hours, two more than I had carried my previous three semesters. The courses included Old Testament Survey, German, Physical Science, Number Theory, U.S. History, Tennis 1, and Chorale. In addition to all this, I was working fifteen hours per week in a medical office, and I lived about twenty minutes from the campus.

After meeting all my classes for the first time, I was completely overwhelmed. I thought, "There is no way that I am going to have the time to get everything done this semester." Besides the ordinary weekly workload, there was a major project for the U.S. History course. The Chorale was going on a two-week tour in the spring that would cause me to miss one week of classes, so I had to be efficient enough to compensate for that missed week. And then I was paired with a lab partner in Physical Science who drove me nuts. His personality really grated on me. I was not sure that I could bear up under all this pressure.

As I was stewing in worry, the Lord put two well-known Scriptures into my mind simultaneously: "I can do all things through Christ which strengtheneth me" (Philippians 4:13), and "If any of you lack wisdom, let him ask of God" (James 1:5). These verses had never come together in a meaningful way for me prior to that time. Suddenly I saw a way to meet the crisis. I simply asked God to give me the *strength* and the *wisdom* to make it through the semester.

The result was remarkable. I was able to handle the day-to-day, week-by-week workload without a problem. I was busy, yes, but not overwhelmed. Two back-to-back evening courses were fatiguing but not impossible. By the fourth week of the semester, I voluntarily chose to present my history project in the first round. And I recognized that the problem that I'd had with my science lab partner was my problem rather than his. So I asked God to work on me to change my attitude regarding him. The rest of the semester in science class went very smoothly, the two of us actually enjoying one another as well as the work.

The upshot was that I had all the major work done by the seventh week of the semester; the rest was a downhill roll. The chorale tour went wonderfully—a highlight of my college career. And ultimately, what had started out to be a nightmare semester turned into a genuine spiritual breakthrough, one of the most memorable times of my college experience—all because I took God at His word and asked for strength and wisdom.

If any of you lack wisdom, let him ask of God, that giveth to all men liberally, and upbraideth not; and it shall be given him. James 1:5

PUSHED OFF THE FENCE

James R. Vanderwoerd
Associate Professor of Social Work
Redeemer University College
Ancaster, Ontario

I SOMETIMES jokingly tell my students "you're going to get sore if you spend too much time sitting on the fence." Choosing a career in social work means being willing to take a stand on behalf of those who are vulnerable or marginalized. I couldn't teach this, of course, if I wasn't willing to take a stand myself.

I used to be a soother, avoiding conflict and rarely sticking my neck out. I was a fence-sitter. But all that changed in my first year as a graduate student in social work in the fall of 1989. I took three introductory courses that semester, but it was events outside the classroom that really pushed me off the fence.

One morning before class, I was somewhat startled to see the spoils of a "panty raid" displayed in the dining hall. I didn't think much about it at the time. Later that morning, however, one of my professors stalked into class in a smoldering rage. She tried to begin, sputtered, tried again, and finally gave up. Then she declared, "I can't just sit here as if everything is normal. Did you see that stuff? We shouldn't have to tolerate this kind of degradation and humiliation against women!" The next thing I knew, our class was marching across campus toward the dining hall.

Our enraged professor, followed by some of my classmates, climbed up on tables and began tearing down the panty raid posters. Some undergraduate students began to protest. I became increasingly uncomfortable with the situation and started mumbling jokes with three or four other men, trying to distance myself from my "radical" classmates. Later, I was furious at being manipulated by our professor. But eventually I began to realize that actually I was angry because I had chickened out when confronted with a chance to act on what I believed.

The next morning the dining hall was festooned with the retaliatory trophies of the women who had raided the men's residences. The women had managed to exceed the men's level of degradation, using explicit symbols and slogans to belittle men and their sexuality. This time I couldn't just sit by. Three or four classmates joined me in tearing down the posters and stuffing them into trash cans. Once several beefy male undergraduate students began to bully us, demanding that we mind our own business and leave the posters alone. They even called in security guards, who threatened to arrest us for vandalizing university property.

Our actions set off a widening circle of events, including protests on campus, heated exchanges between student groups, and even national media coverage. Eventually, under the pressure of embarrassing revelations that the university had informally sanctioned the panty raids, administrators accepted responsibility and also established a women's center on campus.

Though I was only one small part of these larger developments, I now recognize that these events nudged me off the fence. I am still somewhat hesitant to be confrontational. And of course some may credibly argue that during that campus crisis there may have been other, better ways to achieve the same result than by open confrontation. But I also believe that God used those events in my life as a catalyst to disciple me into a person who would take initiative to work for respect and justice and decency. He taught me to be willing to get off the fence.

Defend the cause of the weak and fatherless; maintain the rights of the poor and oppressed. Rescue the weak and needy; deliver them from the hand of the wicked. Psalm 82:3, 4 NIV

HOLDING THE CHRIST LIGHT

John D. Yordy
Provost and Executive Vice President
Goshen College
Goshen, Indiana

LATE ONE AFTERNOON during my sophomore year in college, I knocked on my academic advisor's door. Though he was very busy, I knew he would take the time to talk with me. He always willingly answered my questions, not just about academics and college policies, but also about life and the meaning of Christian faith. I was there to tell him that I was considering leaving Goshen College for a service learning experience in Mexico.

What I did not tell him was that I had a restlessness in my soul, an uncertainty of how life and faith came together. But he seemed to know that anyway. He told me of his relief work in Europe after World War II, of what he had learned and even what he had given up to go there. He described his decision in the context of what it had meant for him at that point in time to be faithful to the light and love of Jesus.

Almost a year after that conversation, I traveled from Mexico City to a small town on the Pacific Coast of Mexico, and then walked eight hours to an Indian village nestled in the foothills of the Sierra Madres. I was there to evaluate a possible Heifer Project initiative.

The next day, Good Friday, I joined the Christians from that village for a worship service. We gathered in a simple, white-washed adobe structure marked by a cross. This church had slowly emerged over a twenty-year period while a Wycliffe Bible translator worked in that village.

As we knelt on the dirt floor, I wondered what stories of love and acceptance lay behind the decision of these people to follow the light of Christ. Kneeling there, I found that I too was being transformed, and the restlessness of uncertainty and doubt was being replaced by the grace of God.

In that moment, kneeling on the dirt floor of a simple church built by the devotion of these Christians, I remembered others throughout my life who had held out the Christ light to me as they thought and lived like Jesus. There were my parents who loved me unconditionally, a teacher who would not accept mediocrity, my advisor who cared for me as a person, and finally these indigenous Christians who demonstrated such devotion and commitment. To paraphrase the words of a hymn:

They held the Christ light for me,
    In the nighttime of my fear.
They held their hands out to me,
    And spoke the peace I longed to hear.

Because of those who held the Christ light for me, as did those Christians in the Mexican village, I was open to the call of the Spirit to join the Christian community, where forgiveness and reconciliation with God can be a reality. This community has helped me through the years to "learn to think like [Jesus]," to love, and to really connect my Christian faith to my life.

Since Jesus went through everything you're going through and more, learn to think like him. . . . Most of all, love each other. . . . Love makes up for practically anything. 1 Peter 4:1-8 *The Message*

GOD'S GONNA TROUBLE THE WATER

Penny Long Marler
Professor of Religion
Samford University
Birmingham, Alabama

IT WAS A CRYSTAL BLUE July morning on Daufuskie Island. The thunderstorm that had punctuated the climax of the mainland preacher's enthusiastic sermon the night before had also washed away the stifling midsummer dust and haze. The same storm had left both the preacher and our student missionary group stranded: we were filthy and sore after a long day of Vacation Bible School and a night on the floor of a small schoolhouse.

"It will be nice to get back to the condo in Hilton Head," I said to my summer missionary partner, "and take a bath and change into some clean clothes." The preacher who was traveling with us, however, was commandeered for an early morning baptism at the island's boat landing. My bathwater would have to wait.

I joined a growing procession of islanders walking to the landing. When we reached the dock, it was filled with young people. Their legs dangled rhythmically above the opalescent waters. My fellow summer missionaries and I sat together near the top of the riverbank. Extended family clusters of adults were scattered nearer the shoreline. Then someone started humming a vaguely familiar tune, and the sound slowly rippled through the crowd. As the music swelled, the preacher and baptismal candidate appeared on the crest of the embankment. Sheets so white they nearly glowed were draped artfully and modestly around them. As the preacher approached the water, he took the candidate's arm, moved with him into the swirling stream, and began to sing:

If you don't believe I've been redeemed,
   God's gonna trouble the water.
I want you to follow him on down to Jordan stream,
   My God's gonna trouble the water.
You know chilly water is dark and cold,
   My God's gonna trouble the water.
You know it chills my body but not my soul,
   My God's gonna trouble the water.

After a few moments and as if on cue, the whole community joined in singing: "Wade in the water, children, wade in the water. Wade in the water, God's gonna trouble the water." Swept up in this musical current, I joined the riverbank chorus as the preacher declared, "I baptize you in the name of the Father, the Son, and the Holy Spirit."

I had never witnessed a river baptism. And I had never experienced the kind of full-bodied corporate piety that surrounded the baptismal candidate on that day. I was surprised, moved, troubled, embarrassed, and humbled. After more than a little honest ruminating on the boat ride back to the mainland, I was also newly convicted. A good Southern Baptist, I had been raised to believe that a Christian's duty was to "help the less fortunate." Yet I had never considered that those we labeled as less fortunate were in many ways more fortunate than I was.

God certainly had troubled my water. He stirred up my self-righteous missionary zeal, my taken-for-granted attachment to middle class comforts, and my naïve ethnocentrism. By the end of my junior year at Auburn University, a spiritual and ethical bath just would not wait.

For as many of you as were baptized into Christ have put on Christ. There is neither Jew nor Greek, there is neither slave nor free, there is neither male nor female; for you are all one in Christ Jesus. And if you are Christ's, then you are Abraham's seed, and heirs according to the promise. Galatians 3:27-29 NKJV

GOD'S ADVISORS

Don Meyer
President
Valley Forge Christian College
Phoenixville, Pennsylvania

WE GET A LOT of advice during higher education. The best advice I ever got came in three pivotal conversations–one before, one during, and one after college.

Right after I graduated from high school in 1963, I sensed a call to ministry. Many people around me encouraged me to get involved in church work immediately, because "the Second Coming was about to take place at any time." They said things like "don't plant trees," "don't take out life insurance," and above all "don't go to college." I didn't know what to do with all this advice, so I worked on our family farm for a year, saving some money and sorting out my own thinking.

The first crucial conversation occurred during that year. I went to hear an evangelist. After the meeting, I sought his advice. His words changed my whole life: "The time you take to sharpen your tools is never wasted." I knew immediately that I had to go to college. And I did.

The second conversation came in my first year of college. As a new student trying to get my feet under me, I was talking with an upperclassman about establishing high goals and good habits. "College will be what you make of it," he told me. "You can do the minimum as you earn your degree, and when you graduate you will be about the same person as when you started. Or, you can apply yourself well and your entire experience will be life changing. It's all up to you."

Later I discovered that this upperclassman was not the only one with such advice. Long ago, artist Robert Henri said, "All education is self-education." I accepted that challenge and it truly changed my life.

After finishing a bachelor's degree, I went on to the Wheaton Graduate School, where I had the privilege of studying under Dr. Merrill C. Tenney. It would be impossible to describe how much influence Dr. Tenney had on me. He was partially retired, yet his class lectures had the tone of a fresh, new professor. Though he had a Ph.D. in Classics from Harvard University, his spirituality had the fervency of a brand-new Christian. Every day in class he made those graduate courses practical and relevant.

As my program ended at Wheaton, I was invited to join the faculty of North Central Bible College (now North Central University) in Minneapolis. Before leaving Wheaton I met with Dr. Tenney to try to express my gratitude to him for his enormous influence on my life. This was my third critical conversation.

"Dr. Tenney," I said, after stumbling around a bit to express myself, "if I can be half the teacher you are when I get to North Central, I will feel as though I will have had an effective ministry."

He could have truthfully replied, "Yes, you are right." Instead, with genuine humility, he graciously advised me, "Don't be a second Tenney; be a first Meyer." The fragrance of those words is still with me to this day.

Prepare well. You are responsible for your own education. Be yourself.

An evangelist, a student, and a professor–their simple counsel, as God's advisors, gave me the best pieces of advice I ever got.

A word fitly spoken is like apples of gold in settings of silver. Proverbs 25:11 NKJV

STEEP STAIRS IN THE IVORY TOWER

Chris Willerton
Professor of English
Abilene Christian University
Abilene, Texas

SOME COURSE READINGS make you shrug. Some leave you shaking.

For me, the great undergraduate mind-expander was a set of honors colloquia I took as a junior and senior: "The Nature of Man," "The Nature of Society," "The Nature of the Universe," and "The Nature of Values." These two-hour seminars were where I first read Nietzsche, Kierkegaard, Skinner, Maslow, and a dozen other supercharged minds. But we did far more than just read them. We went to the mat with them. We argued back at them. We rejoiced over them. Most days, it was hard to get a word into the clamor my friends and I made.

In the sixties, people were arguing about the "ivory tower" and the irrelevance of university studies. But the colloquia helped confirm for me that the life of the mind is really real. What's at stake is not life and death, but the meaning of life and the meaning of death. I remember the class's dismay at Dean Wooldridge's *Mechanical Man: The Physical Basis of Intelligent Life*, which did its best to dismiss the soul and eternal life as smoke and dreams. "Could it be true?" someone asked the professor, a chemist. "I hope not," he said quietly, and we understood that he saw the abyss as clearly as we did. It was no mere academic exercise.

Another thing I learned in those classes was to tolerate unanswered questions. I'd come as a kid off the prairie with a great respect for academic authority. When authorities disagreed with each other, I figured that each must be partly right and it was my job to reconcile the claims. Or squint until I saw the truth that lay between them.

I remember making that assertion one day in a colloquium and getting shot down for it. "There has to be a way to connect these things," I had said. "You have to figure out how they fit."

A girl swung toward me with a raised eyebrow and a half-smile and said, "No, you don't." Her tone said, "No, you don't, you twit. Get over it." Intellectually, she was a decade ahead of her time, postmodern before any of us even knew the word. Those three syllables, "No, you don't," were decisive. I was stunned. It was a lonely day after that.

During this time, my girlfriend came for a visit one weekend, and we walked in a park. She was excited and chatty; I was in a brown funk from reading Schopenhauer. I stretched along a park bench and rested my head in her lap for solace while I tried to explain the angst. Sensible Christian girl that she was, she told me that I should just stop reading.

All I could do was sigh and admit that she might have a point. Even so, I knew I couldn't *not* wrestle with the issues. God calls us to try to understand.

Now we see but a poor reflection as in a mirror; then we shall see face to face. Now I know in part; then I shall know fully, even as I am fully known. 1 Corinthians 13:12 NIV

THE THIRTEENTH MEETING

A REAL COST-BENEFIT ANALYSIS

John P. Cragin
Cargill Professor of Business
Paul Dickinson School of Business
Oklahoma Baptist University
Shawnee, Oklahoma

IN JUST A FEW MINUTES the room will begin to fill with eager undergrads, and I will step to the front and write my name and the course title on the white board–*John P. Cragin, Ph.D., International Business 485*. I am a college professor, business owner, international consultant, and associate staff of Campus Crusade for Christ. Forty years ago I sat in this very chair in this very classroom, a scared college freshman with an undeclared major.

It was not the rigors of academia that frightened me, but the cost. I knew my education would be by far the biggest investment of my life. Though I had a number of scholarships and fellowships, my mother went to work to help pay part of the tuition for my sister and me. Each summer, I worked hard and saved every dollar I could. I painted houses, moved furniture, and sold books. I worked at a hardware store, and even at Disneyland.

I knew that the real cost of my six years of higher education would be many times greater than the university bills. Forty years ago, tuition, fees, books, room, board, and essentials for six years of undergraduate and graduate school cost about $80,000. Had I been working instead of studying, my income would have totaled roughly $100,000. Amortized over 30+ years at 5 percent, that made the financial cost of my education worth approximately $750,000 in 2006 dollars. I was keenly aware that someday I would have to make an accounting.

But of even more concern to me than the money was the almost incalculable value of six years of my life. Even as I entered college, I knew that in just 2,700 weeks I would be sixty-five years old. Was this really the best way to maximize my lifetime impact for Christ and His Kingdom? Frankly, college just didn't seem to add up. But then, neither did Joshua's marching seven times around Jericho.

Forty years and forty countries later, I can see a little more of what I could not see then. My college years were not unlike the few years the disciples had with Jesus. Jesus taught me many things–how to master Scripture and to allow it to master me, how to walk by faith in the power of the Holy Spirit, how to pray, how to confess my sin, how to share my faith effectively. He revealed my strengths and exposed my weaknesses. He taught me to believe and obey Him. He taught me how to lead.

As I sit here in the same chair in the same classroom, I now have about 3,700 days left to serve Him on this earth. Forgive me if I laugh at myself and bow to worship Him. It's just that I see so clearly how the next 3,700 days will yield an exponential return for the Kingdom because of the time and money I was so worried would be wasted in college.

Please excuse me. Class is about to begin, and I have something important to say.

Trust in the LORD with all your heart, And lean not on your own understanding; In all your ways acknowledge Him, And He shall direct your paths. Proverbs 3:5, 6 NKJV

REJECTION AND SURRENDER

Myrla Seibold
Professor of Psychology
Bethel University
St. Paul, Minnesota

FROM MY EARLIEST CHILDHOOD I remember my father, a Baptist pastor, counseling church members about their personal problems. He often lamented that many church members were reluctant to seek professional mental health treatment, even if they really needed it, because they believed God, without any human involvement or interactions, should be the answer to all their problems. Thus, from an early age, and through the influence of my father's work, I could see the need for trained Christian psychologists.

By the time I was in high school, I felt a distinct call in my life to become a clinical psychologist. From the school career counselor, I learned that to be a psychologist I would need a Ph.D. From that moment on, my life goal was a Ph.D. in clinical psychology.

As a psychology major in college, I refined my goal: I wanted to have my Ph.D. by the age of twenty-five. I heard about a Christian Ph.D. program in clinical psychology at Fuller Theological Seminary, but when I learned that it took six full years of post-baccalaureate study, I decided I would apply to secular schools where I could keep to my plan of blitzing through school.

I applied to clinical psychology doctoral programs at three of the top secular universities at a time when admission to such programs was as competitative as medical school. I simply knew that God would get me into one of those programs. It never occurred to me that I might be one of the 790 people not accepted into a program that had 800 applicants and only ten openings. So I was devastated when all three programs rejected me. Confused and bewildered, I wondered if this door slammed in my face meant I should be doing something else with my life.

My undergraduate advisor didn't allow me to wallow in a pool of self-pity for long. He called colleagues around the country and found several master's programs in psychology that were still accepting applications. My bruised ego was somewhat soothed when I was accepted into an M.A. program and did well.

After graduation I took a position as a psychologist in the juvenile court. I loved my work, but my heart and mind were restless; I knew I wanted more skills that only a doctorate in my field would offer. This time I was not a Jonah; I believed God wanted me to train to be a Christian psychologist and that Fuller was the place for me. I worked hard on my application and sent it off, having no doubts that God wanted me to go there.

I was stunned to receive a rejection letter from Fuller. I didn't know how to make sense of this; I had been so sure that God was leading me to go to Fuller. I prayed earnestly, trying to be open to what God wanted me to do with my life. I finally offered up my dream of a doctorate to God, asking Him to use me in Kingdom service according to His plan, rather than mine.

A few weeks later, another letter from Fuller appeared in my mailbox, announcing that I was accepted into the Ph.D. program. I had learned an important lesson in surrendering and trusting my heavenly Father.

. . . being confident of this, that he who began a good work in you will carry it on to completion until the day of Christ Jesus. Philippians 1:6 NIV

A LESSON FROM A BUTTERFLY

Sandra A. Holmes
Associate Professor of Education and Biological Sciences
Messiah College
Grantham, Pennsylvania

ELATION OVERWHELMED ME as I scanned the return address. This envelope would reveal my financial aid award. My clamoring children greeted me at the door. "Is it here, Mom? Is that it?" I smiled. With my grades, surely I, a single mother of four children, would be awarded funds to reduce the awful financial strain of paying college tuition.

Around the table in the squalid kitchen, we shared chairs, the only chairs we owned. I unfolded the first flap of the letter and noted an original signature in blue ink. My anticipation soared as I realized that this was not a form letter. I opened the second fold and began to read: "Unmet need of $43,000–no funding available." I felt sick to my stomach. I examined the words again. They didn't change.

My face must have darkened. The girls stopped grabbing at the letter; they stopped imploring me to read it aloud. They waited in absolute stillness until finally I whispered, "There is no money to help us."

My oldest was in her first year of high school; the middle two, in junior high; the youngest, fourth grade. Although their bodies were of varying sizes, we pooled all our clothes so everyone had something to wear each day. We lived in a 900-square-foot apartment, sharing beds and dreams of a bright future. I wondered how much more I could bear, and how much more the girls could endure.

Dispirited, I went outside. My daughters already knew the stigma of not being able to afford the necessities their peers enjoyed. My desolation about our financial situation would not soothe their fears.

I sat down on the grass and prayed to know why our much-needed help had not arrived. Then I just sat there for a while. My eyes wandered to a cocoon hanging beneath a low tree branch.

Looking closer, I saw a butterfly struggling to escape through the small opening at the top of its cocoon. As I watched, the creature seemed to give up, overwhelmed by the task. Certain that it wouldn't make it without help, I reached up and I enlarged the hole.

The graceful butterfly wriggled out. Unfortunately, its wings were shriveled and useless. I hadn't realized that my well-intentioned intervention would interrupt a natural process, that the difficult squeeze through a small opening was essential for pushing the butterfly's blood into its wings. Instead, though the butterfly had escaped the cocoon easily, its deformed wings would never enable it to fly.

It was then I realized my heavenly Father had answered my prayer. Without this current struggle, I would be hindered, prevented from growing the strong wings I would need to shoulder the continued responsibilities of raising four children alone.

While the letter that day promised no financial aid, that day my heavenly Father promised me that He would walk with us through life, meeting our needs while we were discovering skills, talents, and strengths we did not know we possessed.

I want you to be free from anxieties. 1 Corinthians 7:32 NRSV

THE FOURTEENTH MEETING

"Come and hear, all ye that fear God, and I will declare what he hath done for my soul."

Psalm 66:16

Wayne Joosse
Professor of Psychology, Calvin College

Larry V. Turner
Professor of Education, University of Mobile

Donald Good
Vice President for Academic Affairs, University of the Cumberlands

Karin Heller
Associate Professor of Theology, Whitworth College

Wesley K. Willmer
Vice President, University Advancement, Biola University

Philip W. Eaton
President, Seattle Pacific University

Sheri Adams
Professor of Church History, Gardner-Webb University

Sigrid Luther
Professor of Music, Bryan College

Lourdes Morales-Gudmundsson
Professor of Spanish, La Sierra University

Renata Nero
Chair, Department of Behavioral Studies, Houston Baptist University

TOUGH LOVE

Wayne Joosse
Professor of Psychology
Calvin College
Grand Rapids, Michigan

THE MOST MEMORABLE moment of my college career occurred in the early weeks of my freshman year. I was taking English 100, taught by a young part-time instructor. She asked us to write a brief essay based on the word *pedantic*. I'm embarrassed to say that I wrote a cocky piece lamenting that a gifted creative writer like me was being constricted by such pedantic assignments.

A few days later, the instructor approached me and said it was hard to grade such a paper objectively. Rather innocently, or so it seemed to me, she asked, "Would you mind if I give it to Professor T to grade?" The name meant nothing to me, so I probably said the equivalent of today's "whatever." Later I learned that Professor T was notorious for being the most demanding teacher and hardest grader on campus.

When the two-page essay was eventually returned to me, all eight margins were filled with red ink. It appeared that the essay had no merit, and that I had violated every rule of grammar and syntax. I was stunned. At the end of the essay he'd written a blistering paragraph. Forty-five years later, I have never forgotten his last line: "Meanwhile, your grade is "D-," and that more in recognition of potential than actual accomplishment." "D-," and that's a gift. I suspect I made my way back to the residence hall with tearful eyes. His comments had punctured my bravado and convinced me that I had a lot to learn in college, and in life.

Given the tenor of contemporary higher education, I suspect few professors today would dare to put someone in his place in that manner, and would probably get in trouble if they did. And not without some reason. Such professorial behavior could be very destructive. But that was exactly the kind of tough love I needed. It smashed my veneer of cockiness, humbled me, and led to constructive, growth-producing motivation. I now believe that God directed that I should have this shake-up.

I went on to become an English major. In subsequent years, Professor T and others were supportive and nurturing; I never got zapped again. But I'm truly thankful that it happened once.

Admonishing and teaching everyone with all wisdom . . . . Colossians 1:28 NIV

I ONLY HAD TO TRUST

Larry V. Turner
Professor of Education
University of Mobile
Mobile, Alabama

IN MY FIRST SEMESTER at the Harvard Graduate School of Education (HGSE), I took a core course called Organization: Theory and Behavior. This course had the reputation of being a very difficult study. My first assignment was to compose an essay based on course materials. When the papers were returned a few days later, I was disappointed to see that my grade was a "B-." This is not usually considered to be a bad grade, but at HGSE, anything below a "B+" was considered unacceptable.

I left the classroom as quickly as I could and ran back to the graduate center where I lived. That "B-" devastated me. It was enough to make a grown man cry. And I did. After several minutes of tears and agony and prayer, I felt as if a voice spoke to me: "Larry, have you forgotten Isaiah? I did not bring you here to be a failure. So get up and go attend to your business."

Before I had left my Alabama hometown for graduate school "up north," a dear friend had said to me, "The Lord gave me the 43rd chapter of Isaiah to share with you as you depart to work on your doctoral degree. I hope it has special meaning for you."

In this moment of crisis, I remembered Isaiah 43. I immediately returned to campus to visit with my professor in his office. I pulled the essay from my book bag and expressed to him my deep concern with the grade. He explained to me where my analysis had gone astray, and agreed to reconsider my grade if I was willing to rewrite the essay. I was thrilled at the opportunity.

By the end of the semester, my grade had completely recovered; I made an "A" in the course. Furthermore, I went on to be the first person in my class to complete my doctorate, only two and a half years after I began.

There is no doubt in my mind that God gave me Isaiah 43 to comfort and encourage me during my graduate study. There were many trials and tribulations during my time there, including the death of my mother back in Alabama. But God was with me. I just had to learn that He would do what He said He would do. He is true to His promises; I only had to trust Him.

When you pass through the waters, I will be with you; and when you pass through the rivers, they will not sweep over you. When you walk through the fire, you will not be burned; the flames will not set you ablaze. For I am the LORD, your God, the Holy One of Israel, your Savior. Isaiah 43:2, 3 NIV

WHEN GOOD ISN'T GOOD ENOUGH

Donald Good
Vice President for Academic Affairs
University of the Cumberlands
Williamsburg, Kentucky

SOMETIMES WHAT APPEARS to be the most mundane is actually the most miraculous. When I went away to college, I attended a mid-sized state university. Though I grew up in church, and I had always been "religious," no one would have described me as a person of real faith. But what happened during my time in college was critical to my spiritual development.

I do not have what most people would consider a dramatic testimony. I had no drug or alcohol problems. I never lived a life of crime. I didn't even have an inclination to rebel. While I certainly was not an angel, and never gave much thought to whether I was a Christian, I had always been a "good" boy. And I don't say that just because my name is Donald Good. I was literally, and metaphorically, a Boy Scout.

How could such an upstanding young man ever see his own sinful nature and the need for more of a relationship with God? Furthermore, how could that same man become a person of faith at a secular university, the very type of institution that is so frequently portrayed as being anti-God? Therein lies the miracle.

Through Danny, my randomly assigned roommate who happened to be a Christian and the son of a minister, I soon discovered a group of dedicated Christian students affiliated with a para-church organization on campus. I gravitated toward this group, and grew close to Danny's family and church. As I did so, I began to realize that though I was a good person, I was not a true Christian. It wasn't enough to be just a good person. I could never be good enough to save myself.

When I finally comprehended this void in my life, I asked God to fill it. I made a deliberate choice to accept God's gift of salvation and commit myself to Him. In the joy of my new relationship with God, I became very involved in the campus Christian group. Eventually, as gifts of teaching and administration became apparent in me, I assumed a leadership position in the group.

These events, while outwardly nondramatic, set the direction of my life. Not long after graduating from college, I felt a call to help students experience the same type of spiritual change and growth. Eventually it occurred to me that, since God had given me those gifts of teaching and administration, I might actually become a faculty member of a college community where I could guide students through their own development in ways similar to what I had experienced.

Now, after earning subsequent graduate degrees and working in higher education for more than twenty years, my motivation has not changed. I do what I do because I want to help make a positive and profound difference in the lives of students. Whether teaching a class or facilitating the weekly student Bible study my spouse and I host in our home, I am frequently taken back to those similar settings from which I benefited as an undergraduate student. I hope and pray that the Lord will use my experiences to help these students grow in Him. Especially the ones who, like me, aren't "good" enough.

They took him aside and explained to him the way of God more accurately. Acts 18:26 NASB

SINGLE FOR THE SAKE OF CHRIST

Karin Heller
Associate Professor of Theology
Whitworth College
Spokane, Washington

THE QUESTION OF MARRIAGE became very prominent during my first two years of college. I had already struggled to convince my parents to let me study theology. It was only a foretaste of a greater struggle. My parents dreamed about the day when I would be married to an influential and handsome young man, capable of ensuring a wealthy and comfortable life for his beloved and brilliant wife. And I was quite open to that, except that I was determined to find this charming prince on my own.

I was living and studying in the beautiful city of Salzburg, Austria, known for Mozart, "The Sound of Music," delightful mountains and lakes, and a bubbling social, cultural, and intellectual life. Opportunities abounded to meet charming princes from all over the world. I was grateful to my parents for setting high standards for me. My own standards were high too. But those high standards also made it difficult for me to come to a decision. Whenever I found myself seriously considering someone, there was always something about him that did not fit.

There was a fundamental difference between my parents' values and mine. While I never doubted that they really wanted what was best for me, my parents were caught up in worldly considerations. I, on the other hand, had come to a knowledge of Jesus Christ in my childhood. As a young adult, I was becoming mysteriously and increasingly passionate about this "Son of Man," and about studying theology to learn more about Him. So quite naturally, Jesus Christ set the standard in my mind and heart for whatever image I had of a charming prince.

In the Catholic tradition, since the beginning of Christianity, women had been allowed to devote their lives to Christ in a contemplative or apostolic society or order. But this was not the kind of lifestyle I felt called to. One day I was studying Dietrich Bonhoeffer's *Cost of Discipleship* for one of my seminars. I read a passage that confirmed what my heart was starting to faintly perceive: "What is said about discipleship? Follow me, walk behind me! That is all. Going after him is something without specific content . . . . There is no other content besides Jesus. He himself is it" (Chapter 2).

I felt myself being called to a relationship with Christ, like that of a woman in love with her husband, going with Him through thick and thin. This decision not to marry for the sake of Christ created one of the toughest struggles of my life. My parents were not pleased with my choice to remain single, and it caused a break with my family. But Christ has proved to be better than a husband, in a relationship I could never have imagined, even in my boldest dreams.

Listen, O daughter, consider and give ear: Forget your people and your father's house. The king is enthralled by your beauty; honor him, for he is your lord. Psalm 45:10, 11 NIV

THE HOME TEAM WEARS WHITE

Wesley K. Willmer
Vice President, University Advancement
Biola University
La Mirada, California

"LET IT NEVER be forgotten that glamour is not greatness; applause is not fame; prominence is not eminence. The man of the hour is not apt to be the man of the ages. A stone may sparkle, but that does not make it a diamond; a man may have money, but that does not make him a success." –*Joseph R. Sizoo*

Athletics was my life and my identity when I was in high school. While I was heavily involved with student leadership activities, sports dominated my world. I trained year round, competing in football, basketball, and track. I enjoyed success in all three, but most of all in football, so it was not a surprise when offers arrived from most of the Division I universities. It looked as if football would be my life in college too.

But God had something else in mind. During my senior year in high school, at the apex of this recognition, I became increasingly unsettled in my spirit. Despite the awards and opportunities, I wondered, "Is running and lifting weights how I should spend the next few years?"

During this time, I was working as a medical orderly for Brian Sternberg, a former world-record-holding pole-vaulter who was paralyzed in a trampoline accident. We traveled to speaking engagements, where he gave his testimony of faith in Christ. I was Brian's arms and legs, responsible for getting him places, dressing him, and lifting him into his wheelchair. If I played college football, I would have to end this relationship.

As my unsettledness grew at the thought of moving forward with football in college, I took a year off to sort through priorities and to reflect on how to best use my faith and giftedness. The next year I enrolled at Seattle Pacific College, which sat just a few blocks from home. All the while I continued trying to sort out my struggle with faith and football, but the unsettledness did not leave.

I became involved in student government and was elected sophomore class president; this seemed to be a sign that I was meant to stay at Seattle Pacific. Eventually I held just about every student leadership role possible. When I became student body president in my senior year, I attended leadership team meetings on a weekly basis. God used these leadership meetings to create in me an interest in college administration.

Two weeks after graduating, I started working in Christian higher education leadership. Now, thirty-five years later, I look back and see God's hand at work. He turned my attention to faith and Christian service and away from football and fame, a turn I have never regretted. I now feel the peace and joy of using my God-given gifts in a great vocational fit. God affirms to me that I am where He wants me, and that He uses me as an instrument of His Holy Spirit.

Ironically, my elder son Brian did play college football, becoming a decorated linebacker at UCLA. God used football to launch his life of faith and witness to Christ. But as for me, though I didn't keep playing football, I have no doubt that I've been a player on the home team.

They shall walk with me in white: for they are worthy. Revelation 3:4

BIG QUESTIONS DURING CHRISTMAS

Philip W. Eaton
President
Seattle Pacific University
Seattle, Washington

I CAME HOME for Christmas vacation after my sophomore year in college thinking I was very smart. I was a budding intellectual, after all, my mind racing to comprehend exciting new territories of ideas, language, and culture. As I look back, I acted, well, sophomoric, a bit arrogant, on my return home. I thought I was some kind of new person, and I needed to spread it around some.

The new discoveries for me came through literature, rich language, edgy stories, new horizons of thought, and image and metaphor that both frightened and powerfully drew me in. I had grown up somewhat protected from these kinds of encounters. My folks were not college educated. My father, while a godly man, was practical and concrete, a man of business and no nonsense. His reading ranged from the King James Bible to the newspapers, with little in between, but he devoured both with curiosity.

And so this literature thing I was toying with was new territory. I knew, somewhere deep down, this was just the ticket to stretch the boundaries of my identity, just out of the comfort zone of my family and church. That was a good feeling for a sophomore.

I had carried home with me my Shakespeare text, huge and impressive, I thought. I remember the scene vividly: my father came into my room and picked up this massive work, thumbed through it a bit, and then asked me a question that may have changed the course of my life—"Was Shakespeare a Christian?" I suddenly felt slightly guilty, and I guessed that he wasn't, or at least he didn't talk like any Christian I knew. "What practical good is this stuff?" my father persisted. "Why should Christians read Shakespeare?"

Here I was, split, a chasm opening between my childhood, with all of its safety and caution and protection, and this new-found passion, this new, exhilarating exploration. And what towering models my professors became for me, all of them winsome and articulate Christians and yet people compelled by this same literature I found so fascinating. This, I'm sure, was a very typical reaction for a sophomore, but nevertheless thrilling and a little frightening all at once.

I look back now and know, with great certainty and clarity, that God was powerfully present in that vivid moment of my journey. I also know that God was nurturing this exciting, newly discovered encounter with culture. Why should a Christian read Shakespeare? Indeed, I have spent the rest of my life answering that question. The direction for all of my studies, the shape of my chosen career, in some ways moved forward from that moment, and from my father's thoughtful question.

God's call on my life was somehow ultimately to interrogate the culture in light of the transforming gospel of Jesus. Open it up, without fear, with curiosity and joy. Engaging the culture must be our posture as Christians—exuberant engagement, never closed to what's going on in the world. This must be our posture if we hope to be effective voices in a culture that desperately needs the good news with which we have been so wonderfully blessed.

Always be prepared to give an answer to everyone who asks you to give the reason for the hope that you have. But do this with gentleness and respect. 1 Peter 3:15 NIV

WHAT I LEARNED FROM LINDA

Sheri Adams
Professor of Church History
Gardner-Webb University
Boiling Springs, North Carolina

MY CLASSMATE LINDA and I spent many happy hours together in our childhood. But we drifted apart as we progressed through school. I went to college; she married and followed her husband through several military moves. I kept up with her through my mother, so I was aware that she had had a child, had been diagnosed with a fast-growing cancer, and had moved back to our hometown to be near her mother.

One weekend when I was home, my mother urged me to go see Linda. "You are going to regret it if she dies before you see her," she said. The very idea was terrifying to me, and I made excuse after excuse. When I finally went, Linda made things easy for me. As soon as the "long time, no sees" were over, she said, "I guess your mother told you that I have cancer."

As I visited Linda often over the next two years, I could see that she was growing spiritually. She talked openly about the struggle to reconcile her almost-certain death with her desire to stay alive and raise her child. I was in seminary during those years, learning big-time stuff, but I was afraid of God. I always had been and was certain I always would be. Linda, however, was talking more and more about God as though there was nothing to fear, even in the face of death.

During those seminary years, I was trying to sort out what I felt God wanted me to do with my life. Should I go on to get a doctorate? If so, in what field? And for what purpose?

The last time I saw Linda she was resting on her mother's bed. I went into the bedroom and lay down beside her. We both knew there would not be many more visits. As we lay there chatting, she abruptly shifted the conversation. "Sheri, I would give anything if I could tell you what I have learned about God!"

That conversation was a defining moment in my life. Three days later, at the funeral, the grief I felt was not so much that an exceptional life had been cut short, or that a young husband was heartbroken, or even that a very young child would not know her mother. Rather, it was a grief that I was so stunted spiritually and still so afraid of God and of dying. I knew there was no way on earth that I could have faced my own death with so much courage and in such acceptance of God's will.

At that point, I wanted more than anything to know God as Linda did. I prayed that God would lead me in making that a reality in my life.

I decided to stay in seminary, and eventually got my doctorate in theology. Studying theology helped in my quest, as did a decade on the mission field and many years of teaching. Raising my own child helped more. And a midlife crisis helped me see I had not come as far as I thought I had. Fear has not been easy to overcome, and trust has been hard for me. But I shudder to think where I would be spiritually more than three decades later had Linda not shared her incredible journey with me.

I tell you the truth, whoever hears my word and believes him who sent me has eternal life and will not be condemned; he has crossed over from death to life. John 5:24 NIV

LESSONS IN MORE THAN MUSIC

Sigrid Luther
Professor of Music
Bryan College
Dayton, Tennessee

ARRIVING at the voice-teaching studio of Grace Levinson, I heard a soprano voice on the other side of the door, repeating and refining a single phrase of an operatic aria. I was a freshman piano major, feeling fortunate for an opportunity to earn pocket money by accompanying some of Dr. Levinson's voice lessons.

The singing ceased and the door opened. I was greeted by a short spry old lady. Wavy white hair framed her wrinkled skin and sparkling eyes. This was Dr. Levinson.

After ushering out the singer and her pianist, "Dr. Lev" focused her attention on me as I crossed the room to the piano. Bluntly she corrected my posture, encouraged me to take smaller steps, and advised me to brush my bangs back off my forehead.

Even after the tenor I was to accompany arrived and his lesson had begun, I was still very much under her scrutiny. It was now musical suggestions. She pressed on my back to demonstrate the touch I should use on the piano. Moving her bony fingers onto the piano keys, she showed me how to subordinate my playing while still supporting the vocal line, how to feel a phrase and "breathe" with the singer, and how to carry the mood through interludes.

Although Dr. Lev could be intimidating, I soon learned that this strong personality was totally dedicated to God and to the ministry He had called her to. Perhaps her most memorable lessons were those that centered on sacred texts. From gospel song to oratorio aria, Dr. Lev brought both singer and accompanist deep into the meaning of each phrase, teaching us to express God's truth in song with conviction. It was impossible for me to be a part of this process and not be uplifted spiritually. Though we students were in her studio training to be a future blessing through music, we were blessed by the training process.

And so I sat at her piano and played for countless voice lessons throughout my undergraduate years, my fear turning to wonder and appreciation. The singers were undergraduates, graduate students, and even members of the faculty and administration. No matter the age or advancement, Dr. Lev poured her energy into every lesson, intensely involved and unrelenting in her quest for excellence. When the time came for public performance, I remember her bringing small cards backstage, each with a pertinent scripture passage. She never let us forget the source of our talent and our purpose in glorifying God.

As I approach my own old age, I am as inspired today by the memories of this vibrant voice teacher as I was by her teaching over three decades ago. Her body was hunched and frail, but her spirit was youthful, energetic, and absorbed in investing in the lives of others. Dr. Levinson served the Lord with whole-hearted passion, gave unselfishly of her time and talents to help others, and never "retired" from being useful for Him.

Serve the LORD your God with all your heart and with all your soul. Deuteronomy 10:12 NIV

THE TRUNK

Lourdes Morales-Gudmundsson
Professor of Spanish
La Sierra University
Riverside, California

"DO YOU MEAN it's okay for me to go?" I asked incredulously of my mother.

She couldn't help chuckling at my delight. "Yes, you must go." Her voice trailed off absent-mindedly, but I was too young and too restless to grasp the enormous pain that choked off my mother's words.

Mom understood well why I *had* to go. We were a poor family, recently moved from the inner city into a comfortably upper-middle-class Seventh-day Adventist neighborhood in Southern California where both our ethnicity and our economic status made us stick out like sore thumbs. I often looked at the girls who attended my school and wished that I could have the clothes they wore. I knew I couldn't ask Mom for more clothes because she was already doing heroic deeds to see us through Christian schools. But none of that kept me from eyeing greedily the possessions of my classmates.

To make matters worse for my already seriously compromised self-esteem, my brothers, Ralph and Raul, and I were grappling with the tentacled implications of our older brother Tito's recent diagnosis of schizophrenia. Our life had suddenly taken on a surreal quality with regular visits to the mental hospital carrying large jars of carrot and celery juice and other imaginative provisions for miraculous healing. Now, in my irrational and self-preserving adolescent form of thinking, going away to college seemed wrenchingly necessary—going far away from my house.

A radio evangelist had just returned to our church community from studying in Argentina. Now there was a solution, I thought. I'll go to college in Argentina.

Ever the thorough and sacrificial provider, Mom packed my trunk to the brim with huge quantities of clothes and shoes. After all, I'd be gone a whole year, she reasoned. I was ecstatic about having so many new things to wear. I wasn't as thrilled about my grandmother's old fur coat and the ubiquitous vegetable juicer.

Providence would have it that I got to the school in Argentina before my trunk arrived. I looked around and noticed the spare wardrobes of my Argentine counterparts: two skirts, three blouses, two pairs of shoes, one or two church outfits, and that was it. For the whole school year. Then I remembered that overgrown footlocker floating inexorably south and began praying with all my heart for it to sink into the ocean somewhere, anywhere between California and Argentina.

But the embarrassing evidence of my comparative wealth inevitably arrived. And what a ruckus it produced. All the girls in the dormitory (or so it seemed) came down to inspect the contents of the "americana's" trunk. They gawked and oohed and aahed at everything they saw—all of this interspersed with questions asking my assurance that all of that stuff REALLY was all mine. I had never imagined I would ever in my life be wishing to have less rather than more than I actually had.

Necessity eventually relieved my discomfort. My parents didn't have enough money to pay my way back to the United States, so I sold that old trunk and all its contents to buy my ticket home.

Therefore do not worry, saying, "What shall we eat?" or "What shall we drink?" or "What shall we wear?" . . . But seek first the kingdom of God and His righteousness, and all these things shall be added to you. Matthew 6:31-33 NKJV

GOD'S ACTION PLAN AND A GIFT FROM DADDY

Renata Nero
Chair, Department of
Behavioral Studies
Houston Baptist University
Houston, Texas

EVER SINCE I was twelve years old, I knew I wanted to become a clinical psychologist. My ninth grade English teacher reinforced this desire by commenting on a creative writing assignment that I had great insight into the human psyche. That was all I needed to hear. When many high school students were still exploring career possibilities, not only did I know what I wanted to be, but I had an action plan: 1) attend college, 2) complete doctoral study, and 3) become a clinical psychologist.

While I accomplished the first step toward becoming a clinical psychologist without a hitch, the second step proved to be more elusive. I was not accepted into a clinical psychology doctoral program immediately after college. Well-meaning graduate admissions departments encouraged me to apply to doctoral programs in related areas, but that was not part of my plan. Instead, I entered a master's program and, two years later, reapplied. This time I met with success and was on my way to completing the second step in my action plan. Or so I thought.

Doctoral study proved to be more challenging than I had anticipated. I found that I was not prepared to tackle the graduate-level statistics course. But the plans I had made many years ago hinged on passing this class. In graduate school, grades below "B" are unacceptable, so when it became clear that I would make a "C" in the course, I withdrew. My department did not look favorably on this; it was made clear to me that I had to pass this course. The fear of failure overwhelmed me to the point that I considered taking a year-long sabbatical from the program to prepare for the statistics course.

While visiting my parents during the summer break, I discussed with them this new wrinkle in my plan. My mother stared at me sympathetically, but my father's immediate response was, "Where do you plan to live during your sabbatical?"

"You mean I can't stay here?"

At this point, Daddy said something that has been etched in my memory ever since: "If you start running from problems now, you'll be running for the rest of your life."

I was disappointed about the prospect of facing possible failure, but I readied myself to go back to school. As I finished packing, I could hear the pecking of typewriter keys, but I thought nothing of it. Then, just as I was leaving, Daddy handed me something he had taken the time to type for me.

It was a copy of Helen Steiner Rice's poem "Storms Bring Out the Eagles."

As I look at this framed poem that now sits on my office desk, I realize that a lot has happened since that fateful day on August 14, 1983. Not only have I completed the third step of my action plan, but also I am chair of the behavioral sciences department at a Christian university. Ironically, I have even sometimes taught a statistics course. Clearly, there's a plan bigger than my own: God's action plan for my life.

And we know that in all things God works for the good of those who love him, who have been called according to his purpose. Romans 8:28 NIV

THE FIFTEENTH MEETING

"Come and hear, all ye that fear God, and I will declare what he hath done for my soul."

Psalm 66:16

Mike Rowley
Associate Professor of Communication, Huntington University

Pete C. Menjares
Associate Provost for Diversity Leadership, Biola University

Robin Gallaher Branch
Associate Professor, Biblical Studies, Sterling College

Thomas Buford
Louis G. Forgione University Professor, Professor of Philosophy, Furman University

Dennis R. Lindsay
Vice President for Academic Affairs and Dean of the Faculty, Northwest Christian College

Roger McKenzie
Chair, Division of Religion, Southern Wesleyan University

Dan G. Lunsford
President, Mars Hill College

Gail Perry Rittenbach
Professor of Education and Psychology, Walla Walla College

Brenda Ayres
Professor of English, Liberty University

Bill Wohlers
Vice President for Student Services, Southern Adventist University

THE DISSERTATION AND THE DIVINE DELAY

Mike Rowley
Associate Professor of Communication
Huntington University
Huntington, Indiana

MY FLORIDA STATE University doctorate was finished, except for my dissertation. I had flown through my coursework and my comprehensive exams, passing everything with flying colors, and now I was eager to begin my dissertation. I knew what I wanted in life and I knew how to get it.

Once I received the okay from my major professor, I aggressively began my research. It wasn't long before I had completed my prospectus, gotten approval, and begun collecting data. It didn't take me long to collect the data, and then I was in the home stretch. All that was left to do was run the analysis and write the results and discussion sections. These sections typically take only a fraction of the time and effort that go into a prospectus. With graduation a few months away, it would be easy sailing from here on out.

Or so I thought. I'm not sure exactly what happened, but once I had all the data collected and entered into the statistics program, I could not make myself do the next step. It was the most frustrating feeling. I knew exactly what to do and how to do it. I knew that I had all the information I needed. But I just couldn't bring myself to do it.

I'd like to say this little dry spell lasted only two or three days, but it lasted a year. I missed my graduation date. I argued and fussed with God and myself. Why couldn't I simply sit down and do the next step? Something would not allow me to run the analysis. It wasn't an issue of apathy; I cared very much. I just could not make myself do it.

I stayed at FSU an extra year, taking a bunch of statistics courses, believing that if I was going to be there, I should be doing something productive, even if wasn't my dissertation.

Toward the end of that frustrating year, a former classmate, who had graduated when I was supposed to, came back for a visit. She invited me to a state park for a get-together with old friends. One of the old friends who showed up was Terra, a girl I had dated briefly but hadn't seen for a long time. That day at the park, Terra and I rekindled an interest in one another.

Curiously, when I returned to my apartment that day, I was able to sit down and work on my dissertation. After doing nothing with it for an entire year, I was able to complete the results and discussion sections in only six hours. What was God trying to do to me? What was He teaching me?

Today, Terra and I are married and have two beautiful children. Had I graduated when I was supposed to, I would have found a job somewhere and Terra and I would never have found each other again. God wanted me to stay and wait, so that I might receive a blessing far richer than any Ph.D. can ever provide.

God had planned something better for us so that only together with us would they be made perfect. Hebrews 11:40 NIV

THE GREAT COMEBACK

Pete C. Menjares
Associate Provost for
Diversity Leadership
Biola University
La Mirada, California

I HAD NEVER before walked away from a challenge. After all, I had faced immense challenges throughout my growing up years, prior to my coming to faith one year after high school. My father died tragically at an early age. I was raised by a single mother who would lose her battle to cancer at age forty. I lived in neighborhoods where gangs and drugs were the rule rather than the exception. These challenges were far greater than any I could possibly face in my first year of college. Or so I thought.

My conversion to Christ at the age of eighteen had been dramatic, and my newfound love for God's Word soon led to a desire to study formally. Encouraged by this, I enrolled at the local community college to work on my general education requirements before entering a four-year Christian college. However, within weeks I fell behind in my studies because I was having trouble following lectures, completing assignments, and getting to class. In no time at all, I began to give in to the belief that I just did not have what it took to do well in school. My commitment to formal schooling waned. I eventually surrendered to the poor study habits, lack of discipline, and loss of confidence that I had developed through my years of failure in elementary and secondary school.

These disappointments took their toll on me. Before the midterm of that first semester in 1974, I decided to walk away from school. I did not officially withdraw or even attempt classes and fail; I simply walked away. But not without consequences. To this day my official transcript reads in block letters the designation SCHOLASTIC PROBATION, the result of my earning five "F's" and one "withdrawal." That was the beginning of my career in higher education.

Eventually, I began to wonder if this initial college experience was a test of my faith designed to produce perseverance and greater dependency on God. Clearly, this semester had tested my intellectual and personal abilities. But I had to admit that, in spite of my bruised ego, my faith in God never wavered and my love for Him remained as strong as ever. I concluded that my heavenly Father was graciously providing me an opportunity, through this initial failure, to face my human weaknesses so that I might trust Him more fully and recommit myself to a regimen more conducive to success in school.

I decided to take time out from school to work on developing the proper study skills and discipline I would need to be a successful student. I began by recommitting myself to daily prayer and Bible study. I took copious notes and began to systematically memorize large passages of Scripture. In time, I took a number of correspondence courses. When I went back to school in 1980, I was more adequately equipped with the skills and discipline I had previously lacked, and I began to experience success in the classroom. For me, it was a remarkable comeback. By the grace of God, that next semester I earned nearly all "A's." Not bad for starting out on SCHOLASTIC PROBATION!

You know that the testing of your faith develops perseverance. Perseverance must finish its work so that you may be mature and complete, not lacking anything. James 1:3, 4 NIV

DEBT-FREE SLEEPER

Robin Gallaher Branch
Associate Professor, Biblical Studies
Sterling College
Sterling, Kansas

WHEN I FELT called back to school in mid-life, I made a one-sided bargain with the Lord: "Yes, I'll obey you and go to graduate school, but I want to get out debt free." Because of my age and the fact that I was beginning a second career, I was wary of the possibility of astronomical debt. So by teaching English and writing for local newspapers, I put myself through graduate school in Oklahoma and then a doctoral program at the University of Texas at Austin.

The Lord honored my ultimatum in wonderful ways. I frequently came to Him saying, "Lord, it's Robin again. I need money. Please provide." He always did. Usually it was something like an extra freelance story, help from my family, maybe a landslide like an extra class at a community college, or a bonus scholarship. But my heart's desire was a full fellowship, something I called a "free ride." I spent most of every January applying for scholarships for the following year. Some came through–and I was grateful for the two hundred dollar, five hundred dollar, or full tuition. But I still had to live, pay the rent, and get my hair cut!

So the Lord and I talked a lot about finances. One semester I held seven part-time jobs in addition to going to classes full time and maintaining a 3.94 GPA at UT.

Exhaustion slowly crept in. Close to breaking, I remember coming to Him and saying, "Lord, I need money again. I'm tired, and I guess I'm mad! You know that what I'd really like is a free ride! Oh, Lord, with a full fellowship, I could finish the dissertation and write for you! Lord, I'm so tired. Could you get me a job I could sleep through? But I guess that's too hard, even for you!"

With that, I stomped out of His presence. Very soon, probably the next Sunday, the answer came. As I was leaving St. Matthew's Episcopal Church in Austin, a woman I didn't know called out, "Do you house-sit?" Surprised, I affirmed that I did. "Do you like dogs?" she added. "Oh, yes," I smiled.

She contacted me that week and asked me to house-sit for her. She and her husband had a dog, Gambler, a black dachshund that wore a rhinestone collar. Gambler and I hit it off just fine. The woman and her husband and I became good friends, too.

House-sitting for Gambler led to other house-sittings in the church; these in turn led to house-sitting at UT sororities when the regular house-mothers were away. I loved staying in the sororities' guest bedrooms. The food was great, and I had the run of the house.

House-sitting work was easy, the fellowship fun, and the various homes and sororities a nice change from my student apartment. I apologized to the Lord for my earlier rudeness. I'm sure I heard a divine chuckle. Truly He answered my prayer. He gave extra jobs that I indeed could sleep through! And He gave me even more: free laundry and food, beautiful surroundings, new friendships, and happy memories. And yes, I am debt free.

He giveth his beloved sleep. Psalm 127:2

THE WATCH FOB AND THE REVELATION

Thomas Buford
Louis G. Forgione University Professor
Professor of Philosophy
Furman University
Greenville, South Carolina

WHAT SHOULD I DO with my life? That question had persisted in my mind all through high school. Though I had found God through Christ as a young man, I didn't understand how He wanted to work in my life. Behaving in a Christlike manner became clearer as I grew in faith. My calling did not.

From the third grade through high school I played the trombone. Sidelined from athletics by rheumatic fever and a heart murmur, I devoted every available moment to music, dreaming of playing in a major symphony.

I spent the summer after graduating from high school at National Music Camp. I played first stand in the National High School Band and Orchestra. It seemed that I was a gifted musician, and I was planning to enter Eastman School of Music that fall. Yet somehow I was not fully convinced that I should do so.

During the short period between attending National Music Camp and the beginning of school in the fall, I decided instead to study to be an attorney. But why? Did I really want to be an attorney? My parents had encouraged that goal because their uncles had been successful attorneys. Though I prayed about it often and long, no answer came, but being an attorney just seemed the right direction for my life.

A few months into my first year of college, I joined the debate club and found another first-year student to be my colleague. One of the most brilliant persons I have ever met, he seemed to know where he was going and why. He knew God's will for his life. I thought I did, but I was not convinced. He had direction; I was floundering.

One day my friend and I were talking with our Bible instructor at the Student Union. The instructor took out his pocket watch with a long watch fob. Holding the watch in his hand and swinging the fob around a finger, he asked us what one question each of us would ask about what he was doing. Immediately, my friend asked, "How are you doing that?" I wondered, "Why are you doing that?" At that moment I realized something very important. That instructor's simple exercise revealed something of how both of our minds worked. It confirmed my friend's practical gifts, which led him eventually to become a distinguished seminary president and church leader. My answer to the pocket watch question, however, demonstrated my theoretical gifts, leading me into the study of philosophy and college teaching.

Later on, I began to understand the way God had worked with me. On the one hand, He had created me with gifts that I had to discover, develop, and act on. That was my side of finding God's calling for my life. On the other hand, to develop my gifts and provide opportunities, God had worked through prayer and Bible reading, my family, my church, my Bible instructor, my friends, and my philosophy teachers in seminary and graduate school. I've since learned to describe the way I discovered how to live my calling as creative finding. I must continually find the gifts God gave me, and I must act creatively to fulfill those gifts in service to Him and His Kingdom.

We have different gifts, according to the grace given us. If a man's gift is prophesying, let him use it in proportion to his faith. If it is serving, let him serve; if it is teaching, let him teach. Romans 12:6, 7 NIV

THE WORST AND BEST ADVICE

Dennis R. Lindsay
Vice President for Academic Affairs
and Dean of the Faculty
Northwest Christian College
Eugene, Oregon

IT WAS THE WORST advice I ever received from a college professor. I was a senior Christian ministry major at a Christian college in Illinois. I had excelled academically. I was sensing the "call" to a ministry of teaching, and I was exploring ways to take that next step, perhaps at one of the "big name" seminaries like Princeton, Harvard, or Yale.

"Dennis, if you go there, you will lose your faith," one of my professors warned. "You need to stay here for your seminary education." Regardless of my green-from-the-farm inexperience, regardless of my over-confident naïveté, regardless of the acknowledged fact that I did stay at that particular seminary and that I did deepen my faith there–regardless of all these things–I believe this was the worst advice I ever received from a professor.

I have never experienced an academic endeavor that has diminished my faith. This is not to say that my faith has remained unchallenged as I have attempted to follow God's call. God's calling is, by its very nature, faith-challenging. I firmly maintain that a faith that is neither open to nor capable of being challenged is a faith that is not worth keeping. Moreover, I have found to be fundamentally flawed the notion that exposure to new, radical, or otherwise "wrong" ideas causes people to lose their Christian faith. This is far too trite. The greatest faith challenges of my academic career have had less to do with challenging new ideas, and more to do with challenging, practical circumstances–challenges that caused me to grow faint-hearted in my resolve to follow the call of God in my life.

One such challenge confronted me shortly after I began my doctoral program in theology at the University of Tübingen, Germany. My wife and I were certain that God had opened the doors for us to study abroad. But there was great uncertainty as well. How would we finance this program when the two-year scholarship ended? How would we navigate the intimidating bureaucracy of the German university? How would we hold up under the ongoing critique of family members who were certain that this was a vain pursuit? So I decided to scrap the Tübingen studies and return to the more "certain" setting of an American seminary–somewhere like Princeton, Harvard, or Yale.

Then I received a letter from a former professor–not the undergraduate professor who had given me such bad advice, but another, highly-esteemed former teacher. His words sobered me: "Dennis, you are in danger of losing your faith! There's nothing wrong with those American seminaries, but there's something wrong with you. God has given you a tremendous opportunity. Stay put and let your German professors make a scholar out of you!" This was the best advice I ever received from a college professor, and it led to a most profound deepening of my faith.

Abraham stood firm in his relationship with God, and it was credited to him as righteousness. Genesis 15:6 author's translation

FROM HURDLES TO PASSION

Roger McKenzie
Chair, Division of Religion
Southern Wesleyan University
Central, South Carolina

I ENTERED Anderson College (now Anderson University) in 1978 as a somewhat reluctant freshman. Coming from a large extended family that is primarily agricultural or blue-collar, I was among the first of my scores of cousins to go to college. Though my high school had prepared me well academically, I still felt rather intimidated about higher education. I was going to college only because I sensed a call of God on my life to enter the ministry, and I was resigned to the fact that I needed a college degree to gain opportunities to serve as a clergyperson in my denomination.

While my family knew and respected many college-educated persons, there remained an aura of suspicion about higher education, particularly when it came to those in the ministry. The underlying attitude by much of my extended family was that if you were called to ministry, you found a place and preached. College was viewed by many as unnecessary, and by others as a place where you risked losing your spiritual fervor. So my approach was quite pragmatic. I was anxious to finish the requirements, get the degree, and move on. Higher education was a series of hurdles to be cleared, not an opportunity to grow and be spiritually shaped for my anticipated career in ministry. With these kinds of opinions shaping my perspectives on education, it is clearly an act of God's grace that I benefited much from college.

However, my attitudes changed as I began building relationships with other students and with members of the faculty. As I started to trust my teachers, I began to see how rich this educational experience could be. I also began to recognize just how much I did not know about Scripture, life, and ministry. Early on in my college years, I had tended to keep both people and ideas at arm's length. But as a result of those growing trust relationships, I became increasingly able to take the risk of carefully considering ideas that originally had seemed unimportant or that had challenged my somewhat uninformed belief system.

Much to my surprise, as I neared the end of my undergraduate years, something inside was drawing me toward graduate seminary education. The transformation of my view of education only started while I was an undergraduate; it accelerated during my seminary years. I no longer saw my education as a hurdle to jump on the way to my ministry career. As my passion for education developed, I began to understand that my educational experience was my appropriate response to God's call on my life.

The fear of the Lord is the beginning of knowledge, but fools despise wisdom and discipline. Proverbs 1:7 NIV

SNACK BAR MENTORS

Dan G. Lunsford
President
Mars Hill College
Mars Hill, North Carolina

AS I BEGAN my junior year at Mars Hill College, I got a job in the Student Center as a short-order cook in the snack bar during the last shift of the day. As a boy, I had learned some basics about cooking, with a special emphasis on clean-up.

Most days in the snack bar were routine: hamburgers, french fries, hot dogs, grilled cheese sandwiches, soft drinks, and a lot of clean-up. But when some ladies from the bookkeeping department who were taking staff development classes started to come by for dinner prior to their class, the routine changed for me. At first it was the standard fare for them, but one evening one of them asked if I could fix omelets. Omelets were not in my basic food preparation skills, but I expressed a willingness to learn. Over a period of three weeks, the bookkeeping staff gave me lessons in omelet preparation. They were patient, precise in directions, forgiving of mistakes, and ultimately declared my omelet good. I always thought they were too kind in pronouncing that I made good omelets.

While I am quite sure that those ladies quickly forgot that experience, I often thought of it as a highlight of a rather ordinary work experience. I witnessed teaching, humor, and kindness, and learned a lesson that has remained with me for more than thirty-five years. It taught me that the simplest of acts can make lasting impressions—that what some may see as insignificant, others see as significant. How is it that in everyday life it is more often the simple things that can establish or destroy relationships?

Much of the message of Jesus is found in simple words and simple actions. Those ladies, through their simple words and actions, taught me how to cook omelets. But far more important, they also taught me that people are people regardless of their "station in life." Or, put another way, "We are all God's children."

"Be merciful, just as your Father is merciful. Do not judge, and you will not be judged. Do not condemn, and you will not be condemned. Forgive, and you will be forgiven. Give, and it will be given to you. A good measure, pressed down, shaken together and running over, will be poured into your lap. For with the measure you use, it will be measured to you." Luke 6:36-38 NIV

FENCED IN AND NOT THROWN OUT

Gail Perry Rittenbach
Professor of Education and Psychology
Walla Walla College
College Place, Washington

I DON'T KNOW why I did it. It was a stupid thing to do.

After being in the dorm four years at two boarding academies, the second year in a dorm in the late 1960s at Walla Walla College seemed a bit stifling. In at 10:00 p.m. with a sign-in-sign-out after-dark policy made me want to stay out.

I *had* to get out of the dorm, if just for a weekend. My roommate joined me and we worked out a simple scheme. She called her home in Portland, Oregon, and had her housekeeper call the dean to say that both of us would be home that weekend. The weekend-leave slip was signed and we were on our own.

We bought groceries–spaghetti, sauce, and breakfast cereal; put the groceries on the counter in a sparsely furnished relative's apartment; and wondered what to do for the weekend. We were three blocks from the dorm, so we couldn't go very far from the apartment. Certainly, we couldn't go to church–the deans would see us. We had to stay away from the town of Walla Walla; it was so small, we'd probably be spotted. We spent the weekend in hiding.

By the time Sunday morning dawned, responsibility kicked in. I was the secretary for the dean of men, Mike Loewen, and was responsible for recording the worship attendance. I guess I figured that Sunday was a quiet enough day that I could work all day in his office with nobody noticing. So I did. Then I checked into my dorm, supposedly having returned from my trip to Portland. An hour later, the women's dean called me into her office.

On Monday, when word came back from Dean's Council that I was on probation instead of being expelled from the college, I knew that Dean Loewen had interceded for me. It wasn't a long speech he greeted me with that afternoon, and it contained some gentle irony: "I can always count on you to be at work. Thank you." He believed in me.

Therefore submit yourselves to every ordinance of man for the Lord's sake, whether to the king as supreme, or to governors, as to those who are sent by him for the punishment of evildoers and for the praise of those who do good. For this is the will of God, that by doing good you may put to silence the ignorance of foolish men–as free, yet not using your liberty as a cloak for vice, but as bondservants of God. Honor all people. Love the brotherhood. Fear God. Honor the king. 1 Peter 2:13-17 NKJV

THE REAL EDUCATION OF A HIPPIE

Brenda Ayres
Professor of English
Liberty University
Lynchburg, Virginia

BY THE TIME I began college, I had already earned a degree in nihilism. Although I had attended church nearly every Sunday since age four, by age sixteen I was a diehard atheist.

Once in college, I took every course in philosophy that I could. Existentialism was my thought of choice, but the *Bhagavad-Gita*, *Siddhartha*, and *The Prophet* became indelibly etched into my psyche. I tried every drug. I adhered to a macrobiotic diet, eating only peaceable animals like fish and poultry. I practiced yoga, trying to be in tune with the animal world.

Along with hundreds of other students, I protested the war in Vietnam, marched for civil rights, demanded equal rights for women, refused to eat grapes from California, demonstrated in sit-ins against capitalism, helped collect recycled glass (before it became one's civic duty), wrote articles about ecology and global warming (before they became soundbites), burned a lot of incense, and meditated around candles into the waking hours of morning. A group of us, called the Celebration Troupe, traveled to other campuses throughout Pennsylvania, playing our guitars and singing "You Got to Make Your Own Kind of Music."

By the time I finished my sophomore year, I had exhausted my life. I simply wanted to die. In fact, I knew that I was going to die on that darkest of dark nights, that twenty-fifth of August.

I was living by myself in a trailer then. Thirty out of the thirty-three people who lived in the commune where I had been living had turned into intolerable Jesus Freaks. It was 1972, and the Holy Spirit was moving on campuses along Interstate 80, from one end of the country to the other.

And here was one of those expatriates, sitting on my sofa, reading from the Bible: "I am the way, the truth, and the life: no man cometh unto the

Father, but by me" (John 14:6). At another time, I would have attacked him for what I perceived as sheer arrogance and narrow-mindedness in insisting that there can be only one spiritual truth. This time, however, Jesus was standing right there in my tiny living room, and I knew that the words were true, whether I wanted to become a Christian or not. The Jesus Freak read another verse: "Behold, I stand at the door, and knock: if any man hear my voice, and open the door, I will come in to him, and will sup with him, and he with me" (Revelation 3:20). I knew nothing then but that Jesus had His arms wide open. There wasn't much left of me, but what there was–all that there was–ran straight into Jesus' arms. And I know that those arms snatched me out of the very jaws of hell.

Thus began my real education.

But God hath chosen the foolish things of the world to confound the wise; and God hath chosen the weak things of the world to confound the things which are mighty. 1 Corinthians 1:27

WINNING BY LOSING

Bill Wohlers
Vice President for Student Services
Southern Adventist University
Collegedale, Tennessee

LEARNING TO ACCEPT the benefits of unrealized ambition was a lesson God taught me more than once.

My instruction actually began a couple of years before college while I was still attending the neighboring parochial high school. When I lost my first student association election, the event allowed God to show me He always has better ideas for us than we do for ourselves.

Not to be denied, however, I didn't wait long before planning further political adventures. I was convinced that my high school disappointment had to presage collegiate success. In my college sophomore year I again decided to become a campus politician. This effort looked like it would be easy since there appeared to be no opposition. But the student association election commission took care of that by nominating a good friend of mine. He won by four votes.

One year later I was back, seeking votes again from my fellow students. By this time hubris was certainly clouding my judgment, since I, a village student, decided to challenge the exceedingly successful and popular dorm club president. My temerity lasted long enough to withstand the extended ovation for my opponent's speech from the overflow audience in the college chapel. I went ahead and spoke anyway; I also went ahead and lost–by a landslide.

Whether God wanted me to lose all those elections, I really can't be sure. I'm positive, however, that He helped me to grow because of them. One simple lesson was to accept that some defeats can be expected as a part of life. More immediate, if not more gratifying, were those unsought after opportunities to contribute to my college community even without occupying some lofty elected position. Many of those post-election responsibilities prepared me much more for my current vocation (which in college I could only imagine *not doing*) than any victory ever could have.

Because of my own experience, I'm able to tell students today that losing can build more character than winning. And that's not simply a cliché.

O Lord, my heart is not lifted up, my eyes are not raised too high; I do not occupy myself with things too great and too marvelous for me. Psalm 131:1 RSV

INDEX OF AUTHORS

INDEX OF INSTITUTIONS